Life with the SAT

Life with the SAT®

Assessing Our Young People and Our Times

George H. Hanford

With a Foreword by David Riesman, Harvard University

COLLEGE ENTRANCE EXAMINATION BOARD, NEW YORK

The College Board is a nonprofit membership organization committed to maintaining academic standards and broadening access to higher education. Its more than 2,700 members include colleges and universities, secondary schools, university and school systems, and education associations and agencies. Representatives of the members elect the Board of Trustees and serve on committees and councils that advise the College Board on the guidance and placement, testing and assessment, and financial aid services it provides to students and educational institutions.

Copies of this book may be ordered from: College Board Publications, Box 886, New York, New York 10101. The price is $27.95 for the hardbound edition, and $17.95 for the paperbound edition.

Editorial enquiries concerning this book should be directed to Editorial Office, The College Board, 45 Columbus Avenue, New York, New York 10023-6992.

TO ALL THOSE WHO HAVE TAKEN, OR ARE YET TO TAKE, THE *SAT*

Contents

Foreword by David Riesman

Life with the SAT engaged this reader because of its topic and the portrait it provides of George Hanford's working life during the increasingly tumultuous 30-plus years he spent with the College Entrance Examination Board. The Board is an association where higher education and precollegiate education encounter one another—hence where professors, schoolteachers, counselors, admissions officers, and students and their parents converge. Through subcontracting the preparation of its tests to Educational Testing Service (ETS), the Board is also a broker in the advancing science of psychometrics and confronts antagonism from the romantics among us who oppose everything seen as mechanical, bureaucratic, or organized. (Perhaps because of their "wholesome" origin in the Middle West in Iowa City, the tests of the American College Testing Program (ACT), used for college admissions by less selective colleges particularly in the Middle West and South, have been less besieged.) People such as Hanford, often derogatorily termed bureaucrats because of their affiliation with associations, were not the creators of the College Entrance Examination Board. That was in 1900 the initiative of academicians from private institutions in the Northeast, led by President Charles W. Eliot of Harvard and Nicholas Murray Butler of Columbia, in an effort to widen the orbit of recruitment to these institutions through a program of common entrance examinations that would allow

David Riesman is Henry Ford II Professor of the Social Sciences *Emeritus* at Harvard University.

nonelite private schools and, more remarkably for the time, even public schools to participate. School principals and headmasters took part in the initial enterprise, and eventually the new breed of college guidance counselors was also brought within the increasing scope of the College Board.

Sixteen years ago, Gene Maeroff, an education reporter for *The New York Times*, called attention to the decline in SAT scores of high school graduates that had begun in 1963. This recognition gave the SAT a new salience as a rough-and-ready measure of how well or how badly our high school students are doing in developing fundamental cognitive skills and, correspondingly, as a rough-and-ready measure—some would think all too rough—of how well particular high schools or regions or whole states are doing in terms of precollegiate education. Hanford resisted such use of the SATs, out of fear of unfair disparagement of some school systems and states and perhaps unwarranted approbation of others. At a meeting of the Governors' Higher Education Council on October 11, 1990, which I had the good fortune to watch on C-Span, Hanford's successor, Donald Stewart, former president of Spelman College, similarly resisted attempts by the governors to use the tests as a means of judging the failures and successes of school reforms and as an index of school miasmas. He feared that "teaching to the test" could get in the way of broader educational objectives. Lauren Resnick, director of the Learning Research and Development Center and professor of psychology at the University of Pittsburgh, argued that examinations geared to specific curricula, when combined with feedback, were useful to teachers and students alike; moreover, a program of national examinations could be used as leverage to propel students, teachers, parents, and other members of society toward greater seriousness and expanded academic achievement. Schools and their students, of course, do not always have compatible interests. I was reminded of my own experience when I took the College Boards, as they came to be called, in 1926, when they were written exams in particular subjects rather than the pair of verbal and mathematical SATs. My antiquated preparatory school, William Penn Charter School in Philadelphia, required its students to take two years of ancient history to ensure that even its most laggard students could get into Princeton, then the favored choice of my classmates. Our ancient-history master, Mortimer Graves (later president of the American Council of Learned Societies), defied the school by telling me it did not make sense to spend two years when one year sufficed, and in the last weeks of the spring term he coached me in Roman history. To justify his belief, I knew I had to do well in the exam, and fortunately, I did.

Today, the College Board Achievement Tests in history and other subjects can be used to supplement the SAT, and the Advanced Placement (AP) Examinations assess students' knowledge of college-level subject matter studied in high school.[1] There is an advanced Achievement Test in English involving a writing sample, which is still handled in the old-fashioned way, and most of the Advanced Placement Examinations have substantial portions in the written, free-response mode as well. But now, as Hanford makes plain, the volume of applicants to colleges—including the many nonselective institutions that use the SAT or Achievement Tests not for admissions but for placement once a student arrives—cannot be handled by the cohort of readers at ETS in Princeton who evaluate written work. It would have been impossible at the time the veterans streamed back to college under the GI Bill after World War II to find enough graders, or enough places to put them, if testing had not by that time become far more standardized. Thanks to the psychometricians, one could have reasonable confidence in the multiple-choice, mechanically scored examinations. The confidence is not in the pertinacity of the applicant—indeed, Hanford reports a case, and there must be others, where someone on purpose did badly on the SAT in order not to be consigned to the Ivy League—but rather in the predictive power of the tests for the not so dissimilar examinations of students once they land in college. At the very top (800 on both tests) and for those scoring over 600 on the verbal SAT and over 700 on the mathematical SAT, the prediction is less reliable than it is at lower levels—in part, Hanford suggests, because for outstanding students the middling level of the tests is rather boring, even while for those at the lowest level the tests may be intimidating.[2]

Hanford describes the remarkably noncantankerous rivalry between Educational Testing Service and its competitor, the American College Testing Program, which is used by the majority of nonselective institutions in the Midwest and South. The College Board itself has long since gone national. Hanford recounts the high drama of desegregating testing locations in the South at a time when the schools were still segregated. Today the College Board has integrated test centers all over the country and field offices in six regions. In the Puerto Rico Office in San Juan, there were developed Spanish versions of the Achievement Tests and also of the SAT.[3] Some of the most interesting pages in *Life with the SAT* are devoted to the Spanish language program and more generally to the international reach of testing programs which allow access to an American university from almost anywhere on the planet.

The College Board under Hanford's leadership created the Student

Search Service, which permitted colleges to find students with particular talents and especially, when that became the norm for the more selective institutions, to discover black and other minority students who were willing to be identified as such. *Life with the SAT* describes the effectiveness of the Student Search Service in providing greater access to higher education and widening opportunities for black and Hispanic students who had taken the tests, no matter where they had attended high school. Such efforts, however, availed nothing in rebutting the relentless barrage against the SAT for its supposed exclusionary biases vis-à-vis blacks and, at a latter point, vis-à-vis women. In this debate, as in so much discussion of higher education, the focus is primarily on the minority of highly visible "brand name" institutions, 150 or thereabouts out of 3,000, which are heavily over-applied.[4] Most students attend what may be termed "available" colleges, 80 percent of them in the public sector. If these institutions use SAT or ACT scores at all, they do so for placement, such as recommending remedial programs, for these colleges are open to virtually all high school graduates, including many who have not taken a college-track program. But it is the highly visible colleges—the Ivy League and Stanford and a wider league that includes Wesleyan and Georgetown, Rice and Carleton, Pomona and Swarthmore—that use the SATs as part of the admission process and are familiar to the educated, including the men and women of the media.[5] It is in this sector that the set of tests originally developed to make selective colleges available to more people than those in the Northeast Corridor prep schools has come to be assailed when seen as a barrier. Hanford's pages reminded me that several years ago the Berkeley sociologist Troy Duster spoke on college admissions to our departmental colloquium. He began by saying that the SAT was developed in order to exclude Jews from the Ivy League and similar selective locales. I commented that I did not see how this could be true, particularly since the SAT antedated the "Jewish problem" by many years. But what Hanford reports is that at an earlier time, when SAT results were not reported to the candidate or to the latter's high school, some Ivy League colleges were alleged to have pretended that a Jewish applicant's SATs were below the threshold, and thus falsely exploited the tests to maintain a ceiling on Jewish students.

For a significant minority of prospective undergraduates, for their parents, and for those who advise them, it is important to know their SAT or ACT scores. Secondary school guidance counselors are particularly hard-pressed, and as I repeatedly discover in my yearly meetings with some of them at the Harvard Institute on College Admissions, they are remarkably dedicated. For them, as for me at Penn Charter, the school may have objectives that are not in the best interests of the student—for example, pressing a student to attend Harvard College or one of its competitors because the student is a legacy, a daughter or son of an alumnus, who may stand a good chance for admission,[6] but might be overmatched by a more academically capable peer group. Counselors can also protect students from parental, teacher, or other disparagement of someone with high test scores. I have had the good fortune to teach some bright working-class students at Harvard, a number of them women, for whom Harvard would not have been an option had their high scores not defended them against a formerly more common parental practice to pay more attention to the education of sons than of daughters. These students were often discouraged from even exploring an out-of-state option. To put my position differently: students' and counselors' knowledge of SAT scores can be as much invitation as deterrent, encouraging students to explore beyond the available college nearby or, indeed, to make the decision to attend college at all, whether a community college or a four-year institution.[7]

I do not think Hanford will be happy with what I have just written. Knowing the predictive limits of the tests, he wants both students and colleges to use them sparingly. He refers sympathetically to my friend and colleague Howard Gardner, who has written compellingly about all the different kinds of talent and forms of intelligence. Gardner would like to see portfolios used, which would permit a wider assessment and might protect those whose gamesmanship on multiple-choice tests is not at the level of their multiple gifts. Actually, many within the small circle of highly selective colleges do take a fine-grained look at talents. Sarah Lawrence College is one of a number that have used student portfolios in their admissions procedures. The difficulties with that approach lie in its unreliability in terms of who prepares the portfolios when the stakes are high and, more significant, in the unmanageability of such an arrangement when one is dealing with many tens of thousands of applicants and a total population of 1.7 million taking the SAT. Moreover, there is one factor working in favor of the SATs in that they measure potential, in some sense, rather than achievement, that is, general verbal and quantitative reasoning as opposed to subject mastery, thus facilitating the college chances of potentially capable, alert students (not including dyslexics) in a less than challenging secondary school. In a topflight secondary school, a student will be prepared for the Achievement Tests in specific subjects and also may be helped in developing a promising portfolio. There is understandably a high correlation between the SATs and the Achievement Tests, but I am talking about margins of difference that would matter at the most highly over-applied institutions.

In 1969 Bowdoin College announced that it would no longer require the SAT and thus positioned itself as enlightened, modern, and nonconformist, on the hunt for students whose talents could not be reduced to the answers, often guesswork, on multiple-choice tests; Bowdoin gave each applicant the sense, as one of them recently put it, that she was not a mere number but a person. Bates College later followed the same policy, but both institutions ask students, once admitted, to take the test (most will already have done so) and to report their scores in order to help the college place the students in their courses. Lewis and Clark College in Oregon is planning to follow the portfolio road, seeking to assure the veracity of what it receives by asking school principals to certify that the work submitted is actually the student's own.[8]

As recently as 1952, Harvard and Radcliffe Colleges combined had about 4,000 applicants, with Harvard admitting 63 percent and Radcliffe 42 percent—Radcliffe, one-quarter Harvard's size, had SAT verbal scores 48 points higher. For the integrated colleges today, for the class admitted in fall 1990, there were 12,000 applicants, of whom 18 percent were admitted. In this climate of heightened competitive stress at the top, it is not surprising that the SATs have been among the targets of widespread suspicions concerning higher education, shared in different variants by the educated and the general population. In the visions of some critics, the SATs are seen as part of an overmechanical, overorganized society, but they are also regarded as a conspiracy that permits unfair discrimination to occur behind an "aura of secrecy." The phrase is from an article by two psychologists at Harvard Medical School, Warner V. Slack and Douglas Porter, titled "The Scholastic Aptitude Test: A Critical Appraisal," published in *Harvard Educational Review* 1980, vol. 50. Ralph Nader has brought to this cause the moral weight he continues to carry.[9] The truth-in-testing law he helped push through the New York State legislature forced Educational Testing Service to reveal questions after they had been used (instead of keeping them secret so that they could be used again), thus increasing costs and decreasing the number of tests, not only for colleges but for graduate and professional schools as well, that could be administered in New York State.[10] Hanford describes his experiences, commonly batterings, in defending the tests, not only against sophisticated critics, but also in the face of nagging from talk-show hosts. He was always handicapped by his refusal to simplify, even while graced by his own decency and lack of bitterness in the face of either elite or counterelite critics.

Since I wrote a draft of this Foreword, a committee chaired by David Gardner, president of the University of California system, and Derek Bok, now retiring as president of Harvard, has encouraged a revision of the SAT providing for a written essay and for problem sets (for which calculators can be used) on the mathematical side. The test revised could roughly be described as a mix of aptitudes and achievements. The usual array of critics has called the changes cosmetic, but they indicate the willingness of the College Board to help promote student learning in precollegiate education through somewhat more substantive tests. The fundamental conflicts addressed in George Hanford's book will surely not go away!

Even so, letters have lost reliability, marginally increasing the importance of the tests. More generally, one of the great advantages of the SATs is that they help to buffer teachers against parents who have influence in the community and vis-à-vis the school to write glowing recommendations to the selective colleges, in some cases perhaps to the prejudice of their more capable students.

Salient in *Life with the SAT* are the conflicts Gunnar Myrdal thought to be a single "American dilemma," but which have turned out to be an ever-widening set of dilemmas. In Chapter 5, "Minorities and the SAT," Hanford discusses his experience that blacks involved with the College Board did not want scores published by race because it would confirm stereotypes, showing the 100-point gap between whites and blacks, whereas Hanford insisted that the data be published to point to the educational deficits that it was up to blacks and whites to confront. Such attacks did not come only from blacks. Hanford writes: "It always seemed ironic to me that the liberal white establishment (of which, doubly ironically, I was assumed otherwise to be a part), in its call for equality of educational opportunity, denied the likelihood that there are bright, academically able black and Hispanic students who can take advantage of the Advanced Placement Program." It is in this broader context that Hanford describes the attack on Proposition 48 of the National Collegiate Athletic Association, which was intended to hamper the recruitment of athletes, primarily black basketball and football players, with combined SATs under 700 (the range begins at 400 and the top is 1600), a measure John Thompson, the forensic coach of the Georgetown University basketball team, denounced as racist in intent and in effect. (Hanford does not mention that Arthur Ashe, also black, former tennis star and dedicated reformer against athletic abuses, defended the rule as protective vis-à-vis blacks who might otherwise be recruited to college to play games without much hope of ever learning anything or graduating.) Hanford reports the ways in which ETS routinely tests for bias, and of course both the College Board and ETS include blacks in their supervisory and technical staffs, to ensure that blacks are not discriminated against. (If there is any tilt vis-à-vis blacks, it is the possibility that the SATs marginally overpredict black performance in college; that is, grades and graduation rates of black students are lower than would have been anticipated from their SATs. If this is so, it may perhaps reflect the degree to which black, especially male, leadership in predominantly white institutions, reacting to what for some is felt as an alien and intimidating environment, has mobilized to define what is "authentic," disparaging those blacks who appear overstudious or insufficiently involved in black affairs.) Hanford, however, agrees with John Thompson: he never wants the SAT used in isolation to keep anybody out of an institution, even when the scores are so low as to render problematic even the likelihood of remedial help at the college level.

When Hanford's life with the SAT began, gender bias did not appear to be a problem; although women had consistently lower scores on the quantitative or mathematical section of the SAT, they had higher verbal scores—congruous with our image of girls as the cohort that listens more, generally talks more, and almost invariably reads more than do restless, roving boys. But in 1972, for the first time women began to score marginally lower than men on the SAT verbal section. Rebutting the charge of bias, Hanford explains a considerable part of the decline of women's SAT scores as the result of the far greater number of women, including those of lower socioeconomic background, who are today entering college (in the case of blacks, almost twice as many women as men). Hanford does not discuss at any length the drop of SAT scores for both sexes beyond what one might attribute to the greater number and diversity of high school students taking the tests.

The period of decline—that is, the last two decades—is a period in which all but a very small proportion of boys' schools have become coeducational and the great majority of Catholic girls' schools, like girls' schools generally, have become coed. In *Girls and Boys in School: Together or Separate?*, published by Teachers College Press in 1990, in the chapter "Reconsidering Single-Sex Education," Cornelius Riordan comments that ". . . coeducational schools are really boys' schools; that is, they mainly serve the interests of boys." (148). He adds that "Males in mixed-sex schools succeed at the expense of females" (149). I do not know whether or not there is a breakdown of SAT scores for girls who have attended the remaining single-sex schools, with comparisons adjusted for parental education and socioeconomic background. Riordan's main theme, echoing earlier work by James S. Coleman, is that the adolescent subculture is a boys' subculture with girls as cheerleaders. The differential decline in scores for males and females seems to reflect this interpretation of coeducation. Riordan notes that black and Hispanic males also profit from the discipline of single-sex schools, as do minority and white females (white boys do also, but to a lesser degree). I have long advocated experimentation with boys' boarding schools for blacks, to see what the educational consequences might be. At the college level there is considerable evidence, reported in a number of works by M. Elizabeth Tidball, professor of physiology at George Washington University, that graduates of the remaining women's colleges, if other variables are held constant, are more likely to continue in careers in academe, notably so in the sciences.

In addition to these considerations, on which there are some, although only partially substantiating data, I am inclined to believe that changes in the family and in society since the sixties have had a disproportionate impact on girls. It seems likely that the general score decline of both boys and girls reflects in some measure the influence of the visual media and the declining resort to print media, whether in school assignments or away from school. Mothers are less often at home. Girls who need never make a break from their mothers in the way that boys in our culture, and in some measure in most cultures, are required to do may suffer stress from their mothers' absence more than boys are likely to do, for boys are out of the home, into sports or hanging out, rather more than girls are. Physiological puberty happens earlier now, and psychological sexuality—and all that goes with it in terms of same-sex as well as cross-sex relations—also happens earlier, so there is almost no childhood, and certainly little innocence is left. Even so, for most boys, girls remain generally a sometime thing, but the reverse is not true. More sensitive in any case to personal relations, more aware of stress in the home, whether from two-career parents or from divorcing parents or from a mother who wishes she could afford a divorce—all these shifts in home and family may have greater impact on girls. Also, the counter-culture has remained part of the adolescent subcultures. Girls often smoke because they think it "cool" and that it will attract boys; in contrast, sports and coaches provide an element of discipline for boys more than for girls. Indeed, I have sometimes suspected that boys may read a bit more because many of them read the sports pages, and of course the preoccupation with statistics, notably in baseball but in other sports also, cues boys more than girls to the quantitative sections of the

SAT. Hanford judiciously avoids speculations of this kind, but if a sociologist can be defined as someone who, if given a fact—whether the fact be the case or not—can give an interpretation, then I am someone who cannot resist interpretation!

Most of us who live the life of a college or university professor have little sense for the infrastructure on which we depend, namely, those who staff our colleges and those who staff the education associations such as the College Board, which in turn support the colleges. Correspondingly, not many persons enter the kind of career George Hanford pursued in order to rise in the academy. He mentions Neal Berte, who began his career, after receiving his Ph.D. in educational psychology from the University of Cincinnati, in the Western Regional Office of the College Board and has for many years been the entrepreneurial and highly visible president of Birmingham-Southern College. But in general, admissions and financial aid, though important parts of the work of that small fragment of private colleges that are heavily over-applied, are rarely a route to the top. Like the librarians and the registrars, all fairly invisible to many faculty members, those people concerned with college admissions serve faculty and students in an altogether unshowy way. George Hanford, as the head of the College Board, has been more visible than most and correspondingly more besieged. He took on the task of presiding over the College Board during the era when American higher education expanded enormously in what has been termed the shift from elite to mass higher education. Along with the shift came the "nationalization" of the most selective private institutions, moving away from their regional attachment areas to court, and hence also to have to reject, a national student constituency. Correspondingly came suspicion of admissions tests that were seen as gatekeepers, notably the SAT. The attacks on the College Board deflected hostility away from the bad news about what was happening in America's schools and focused instead on the tests that brought the news. George Hanford always tried to focus the debate onto the patient and away from the thermometer. It makes me feel sanguine about the human capacity to endure that he can write a book so generous and so lacking in rancor.

Notes

1. Achievement Tests and Advanced Placement (AP) Examinations can be used by eager, ambitious, and/or penurious students to gain Advanced Standing in cooperating colleges, sometimes entering as sophomores. In colleges such as Harvard, it took consid-

erable persuasion before prideful faculty members would agree to let a high school student's history or French or mathematics course count for as much as one taught by the eminent professors—and indeed sometimes, among Harvard College undergraduates proud of having gotten out of "mere" introductory courses, I thought that they might have missed, for example, the opportunity of experiencing John Finley's magnetic General Education course in the Greek classics. But in general, and depending on context, I favor not so much skipping freshman year as encouraging more students to skip their senior and perhaps less commonly their junior high school years, moving directly to the college milieu, particularly today, when high schools rarely provide shelter against peer pressures for a kind of instant, unstudious adulthood. A book published by the College Board in 1978 titled *Don't Hold Them Back: A Critique and Guide to New School-College Articulation Models,* by Baird W. Whitlock, makes this point.

2. When I was teaching in the College of the University of Chicago in the late 1940s, the External Examiner tested students by multiple-choice examinations. I was puzzled by the non-stellar showing of some of the most evidently gifted students in my sections. I went through with a number of them how they had reasoned on the tests. Often, they had gotten it wrong by not being able to believe that the examiner would ask so simple-minded a question and was not out to trip them, leading them to far-fetched alternatives. I considered the possibility of allowing a line in which students could explain their answers, but concluded that in terms of students' time constraints, even apart from the logistics of the grading process itself, this was not a good alternative. Thereafter, in effect I coached students to assume that the Examiner was an "*homme moyen sensuel,*" an unconspiratorial, rather mundane person.

3. Hanford mentions the efforts to develop a test in black English in response to the charges of racial bias in the tests, but the black English test proved to create no more access for black students than did the regular English version already screened for possible biases. The Spanish SAT does not help Hispanics in the United States, being appropriate for those educated in a Spanish milieu.

4. Approximately 25 colleges and universities, most of them nationally visible (though tuition-free Pratt Institute in New York City is not widely known) accept fewer than 36 percent of applicants. Since at this level of eminence the applicants are likely to make multiple applications, even these colleges must sometimes resort to a waiting list to fill their ranks.

5. In "Financial Aid, College Entry, and Affirmative Action," published in the *American Journal of Education,* August 1990, Gregory Jackson writes: "College admission decisions play a remarkably small role in college choice, except for a small group of talented, affluent students. Most students seriously consider only colleges located relatively near their homes and presenting no extraordinary financial or academic obstacles" (530).

6. See David Karen, *Who Gets into Harvard?* (Yale University Press, forthcoming). The Harvard admissions office gave Karen, then a Ph.D. candidate in sociology at Harvard,

a great deal of data on its proceedings, and his book should help dispel some common misconceptions. With similar demystifying intent, Williams College in the spring of 1986 allowed the *MacNeil/Lehrer Newshour* to film a discussion among members of the admissions staff about a group of applicants to this heavily over-applied "Little Ivy," showing the great care taken to recognize idiosyncratic talents but also, to this viewer's uneasiness, willingness to take a chance particularly on black students, seen as a risk for the college, but perhaps not always quite sufficiently as a risk for the eager applicant.

7. I found a vivid sense of counselors' difficulties and opportunities explored in David R. Holmes, Herbert F. Dalton, Jr., et al., eds., *Frontiers of Possibility*, published by the National College Counseling Project in 1986.

8. The small liberal arts colleges place considerable reliance on interviews with prospective students, in part as a counterweight or supplement to the SAT, in part to establish a personal tie, often with an alumnus or older student, and in part, as Harvard does, to distinguish among applicants with 800's on their Achievement Tests, and the many hundreds of students with combined SAT scores over 1400. However, the Harvard Business School, concluding that interviews predicted students' first-year performance less well than did scores on the admissions test, has until just now dispensed with interviews, regarding them as more likely to be biased; currently, it is starting to interview again on a limited, exploratory basis.

9. However, I believe Nader harmed government when he played a salient role in forcing Congress into the immediate repeal of the pay raise it granted not only to itself but to seriously underpaid federal judges and high federal officials. For a sympathetic portrait of Ralph Nader, see Jason DeParle, "Eclipsed in the Reagan Decade, Ralph Nader Again Feels the Public Glare," published in *The New York Times*, September 21, 1990, A14.

10. The law requires only the disclosure of scored questions, thus allowing ETS to try out questions to see whether or not they are biased or confusing even to the notably adept. In 1990 the law was successfully challenged in court by the Association of American Medical Colleges on copyright grounds as an area preempted by the federal government, and while the case is on appeal, the SAT has returned to using some undisclosed items in New York State. Some testing companies have concluded that the law makes the testing process less unfair by allowing everyone to study the scored questions, not just those who can afford the coaching services.

The Left does not hold a monopoly on suspicion of the college admissions process. When he was a senator from New York, James Buckley, a man of the political Right, fathered what has come to be known as the Buckley Amendment, which permits students to see the recommendations written on their behalf by their teachers and others. Buckley suspected that leftist New York City schoolteachers were giving negative recommendations to students of conservative temper, and he believed that the availability of their recommendations would inhibit these prejudices. The result has been to lead knowledgeable students to waive their Buckley Amendment rights to give added credibility to recommendations written on their behalf, while fear of suits for defamation or at least embittered complaints leads many recommenders of whatever persuasion toward "letter inflation," or to resort to the presumably unmonitored telephone.

Acknowledgments

In recounting my years with the College Board and the SAT, it follows that many people were involved during those years, and a few are mentioned in the text. Many more could and should have been, but there wasn't room. I regret the omissions. Also not identified are some people I want to thank for helping me in the production of this book: Elaine, my wife, for not only putting up with me while in the throes of creation but also for her encouragement; Don Stewart, my successor as president of the College Board, for his interest and support; Bob Seaver, vice president for communications, for his gentle questioning, which helped move the idea from conception to completion; Jack Mullins, the Board's former vice president and treasurer, and Gretchen Rigol, its overseer of the SAT, for their careful reviews of the manuscript; and Carolyn Trager and Pat Wyatt in particular among the members of the Board's communications staff who shepherded the creation from typed draft, to edited manuscript, to galleys, to page proofs, to finished books. Thanks are also due to Don Writer, production manager, who exercises his special skills in overseeing production of all the Board's publications. I am indebted to David Riesman, Harvard's sociologist extraordinary, for his thoughtful Foreword; that he considered my effort worthy of his insightful commentary was especially rewarding. Finally, I have to acknowledge that perhaps the next greatest satisfaction I derived from the entire effort was the realization that I had typed (and retyped) the original manuscript myself. My admiration for the secretaries who helped me over the years was further enhanced by that exercise.

CHAPTER 1

Introduction: Glimpses of Life with the SAT

My association with the Scholastic Aptitude Test (SAT) has been different from that of most people. They, if exposed directly to it at all, have spent a couple of Saturday or Sunday mornings taking the test, preceded by perhaps several more getting ready for it. I spent nearly a third of a century living closely with it. For them, it was a necessary and impersonal rite of educational passage. For me, it provided a special window on the world in the years since World War II, a unique vantage point from which to observe the changes taking place in national and international affairs, in business and technology, and in education and even intercollegiate athletics.

Early on in my life with the SAT I learned about its history, about its roots in the closing days of the industrial revolution, and I later observed its part in the technological revolution. I learned about its origins in tests developed during World War I to help mobilize and classify the nation's military manpower and witnessed firsthand its use of technology to replace the traditional written "College Boards." And I saw the role it played after World War II in the deployment of the vast numbers of students aspiring to college as a result of the GI Bill, the so-called baby boom, and the civil rights movement. Conceptually, I came to appreciate that much of the misunderstanding that attends the SAT derives from the test's application of scientific principles to a process that is essentially judgmental—the assessment of academic performance. Scores on the SAT are assigned to individuals according to precise, statistically determined rules; school and college grades are assigned by human beings according to their own best judgments. Operationally, I saw the scoring of the SAT transformed from a labor-intensive to a machine-intensive process as hundreds of graders, who used templates to "read" the answer sheets, and keypunch operators, who transferred those readings to IBM cards, were succeeded successively by high-speed mark-sense and then even higher-speed optical scoring machines.

In more than 31 years with the SAT, I saw the number administered annually grow from just over 155 thousand in 1954–55 to over 1.8 million in 1985–86. As a result, I was privileged to take part in the growth of a bureaucracy from a five-person professional staff (one woman and four men) to one more than 30 times that size, to witness the growth of the nonprofit enterprise that sponsors the SAT (the College Board) from a $1.7 million operation to a $120 million one, and to observe the controversies that continue to swirl around the world's best-known and most highly regarded test. And I witnessed the results of the effort by respected educators to establish a testing enterprise that would become the world's leading center of expertise in assessment—Educational Testing Service (ETS)—an effort that in the mounting failed to take account of the fact that businesses and educational institutions finance expansion differently. Along the way, I spent countless hours trying to explain the difference between the College Board and Educational Testing Service.

As a graduate of the Harvard Business School, I was intrigued to witness competition at play in the nonprofit sector—competition among colleges for able scholars as well as able athletes, among unions for the hearts of teachers, and among associations for the loyalty of individuals and institutions. Although the College Board as sponsor of the SAT was touched by all these tensions, its fate was most directly affected by the latter-day establishment of the American College Testing Program (ACT). The competition that emerged from this development in the nonprofit testing arena was for the most part genteel, in all parts spirited, and in every way beneficial. I believe in the free enterprise system and am convinced that the existence of competition in the college admissions testing field has benefited the young people of the United States. Along the way I learned what a monopsony is and that ACT stopped the College Board from being one (see Chapter 2).

In 1975 I saw a front-page story in *The New York Times* transform the average annual SAT scores into what I call the gross education product (GEP), education's counterpart to the economy's gross national product (GNP). It was a transformation that moved the test squarely into the political arena. There I met legislators, both state and federal, who contrastingly at both levels were seeking either to destroy tests like the SAT or to extend their use as instruments of accountability. And I met governors, mostly from the South, who were seeking to overcome the deficiencies in their states' education systems to which SAT scores had helped call attention. Testifying before both houses of Congress, I came away with something less than enthusiastic regard for the hearing process. The hearings I took part in weren't anything like the televised versions; the public wasn't watching or listening and neither were most of the few subcommittee members present. I also appeared before a committee of the National Governors Association and before the governing bodies of the American Federation of Teachers and the Education Commission of the States. At these appearances my hearers were on the same level as I was and paid polite, if not always rapt, attention to what I had to say.

In addition I was interviewed on radio and television as a panel member and as a talk-show guest. I came away from these sessions, too, with mixed feelings—in this instance, of course, about the media. The moderators and hosts ran the gamut from television personalities who are polite, are genteel, and do their homework to self-centered individuals who are biting as well as opinionated and have their minds made up and axes to grind. I was interviewed by newspaper reporters of the same ilk and everything in between. By and large they were a responsible lot, some more responsible than others, but I couldn't help being reminded from time to time of my father's experience with the press as a college dean. In later years he would observe that, in 20 years of deaning, he was usually either misquoted or quoted out of context.

With distressing frequency I saw the SAT mistakenly identified in the press and elsewhere as the most important factor in college admissions and falsely accused of depriving talent, particularly minority talent, of educational opportunity. Those charges always bothered me because I know firsthand the part the SAT had played in helping to generate the early success of the civil rights movement by identifying untapped college potential among the nation's black young men and women and attracting that newfound pool of talent to the nation's colleges and universities. Unfortunately, I was also on hand to witness the later falloff in those numbers—a decline that must have had something to do with shortcomings in the schools that prepare culturally different students for college and in the higher institutions that accommodate the new populations. And yet the schools must have been doing something right, because the gap between SAT scores earned by majority and minority youngsters has grown smaller in recent years.

Not surprisingly, I suppose, in light of the SAT's public prominence, I observed that its scores were misused in a variety of ways. There were parents who misused them to prove that their offspring were brighter than those of other parents. Some high school principals misused them to judge the quality of their teachers, and others misused them to demonstrate the superiority of their schools. And there was the secretary of education who misused the scores in ways that led to misleading comparisons of the quality of education among the 50 states. I saw the SAT, in a bizarre twist of fate, caught up as a target of the consumers' movement when the test became the scapegoat for able majority students who considered themselves the victims of reverse discrimination; they took it out on tests like the SAT in the belief that those tests had something to do with minority students getting places in higher education that the majority students thought they themselves deserved.

After spending a six-month sabbatical leave studying intercollegiate athletics for the prestigious American Council on Education (ACE) and suggesting that college sports were in a sorry state and needed reform (and then being virtually ignored by university presidents, the sports fraternity, and the press), I found myself embroiled a few years later in the controversy over the eligibility of freshman athletes to compete in college sports—embroiled because the National Collegiate Athletic Association (NCAA) foolishly decided to misuse the SAT as one means of determining whether those first-year students could play. With more than a passing knowledge of the scene, I applauded what the NCAA was trying to do but not the way the association did it.

In my prelife with the SAT, I heard the Marshall Plan proposed by its author, Secretary of State George C. Marshall, at the Harvard commencement in 1947. Later, in my professional life with the SAT, I saw the test play a part in generating the brain drain as our nation's schools and colleges sought to provide education to young men and women from developing countries then unable to provide it. Association with the SAT also allowed me to become acquainted with the international testing community (see Chapter 8) and to visit or meet with its members in all parts of the globe. Those experiences made possible my firsthand observation of many political, social, and environmental problems facing the world today—problems of famine and poverty, of nationalism and transnational migration, as well as those resulting from the advent of the atomic and space ages. I saw the nation and the world grow smaller in the era of jet travel and modern communications. And I concluded that because the problems I had observed aren't going to be solved through ignorance, education is man's best rational hope for peace and progress in the world. That, not so incidentally, is why I chose to spend my working years in education.

During the 1980s I saw the business community's disregard for national manpower considerations replaced by a recognition of the changing demographics of the nation's young people and a further recognition of its stake in the educational enterprise. With its scores serving as surrogate for the gross educational product, the SAT played a prominent role in getting the attention of the country's corporate leaders and demonstrating for them the size of the educational deficit the nation must overcome if it is to continue to have a dominant position in the international marketplace.

The decline in the national average SAT scores during the 1960s and 1970s involved me in my most interesting single assignment at the College Board. As staff coordinator for the blue-ribbon panel invited to explore the reasons for the phenomenon, I was able to watch that fascinating mix of panelists make sense out of one of the most intricately complex developments of the twentieth century. Most observers date the beginning of the school reform movement from the publication by the National Commission on Excellence in Education of *A Nation at Risk* in 1983. My landmark has always been *On Further Examination: Report of the Advisory Panel on the Scholastic Aptitude Test Score Decline*, published by the College Board in 1977. The SAT scores began to recover in the early 1980s and could have done so only as the result of changes initiated before 1983.

Lower academic standards in schools and colleges around the point of transition from secondary to higher education constituted but one of many reasons identified by the Advisory Panel as responsible for the decline. Because those lower standards were directly related to the mission of the College Board, however, the panel specifically challenged the Board to "do something" about that condition. Responding to that challenge resulted in the mounting of two of the most significant activities at the College Board during my presidency: the Educational EQuality Project, designed to define college admissions standards for the closing years of the century, and the Commission on Precollege Guidance and Counseling, appointed to find ways to keep the higher education options more effectively open for all the nation's young people.

At an earlier stage in my life with the SAT, I was party to the growth of two new professions during their formative years. Frank H. Bowles, the Board's first chief executive officer after the founding of ETS in 1947–48, helped college admissions officers create an identity for themselves as a profession apart—that is, from the all-encompassing American Association of Collegiate Registrars and Admissions Officers (AACRAO). A few years later I witnessed the emergence of the student financial aid profession to implement the concept of aid awarded on the basis of need. This concept, promulgated by the College Board's College Scholarship Service (CSS)—which began to function in the academic year 1954–55—became not only the national institutional norm but also the basis for distributing an ever-increasing amount of state and federal dollars. The College Board provided the first associational home for the men and women administering those dollars on campus, a home later transferred to the newly created National Association of Student Financial Aid Administrators (NASFAA). The on-campus tensions between these two professional constituencies spilled over into the affairs at the College Board and added spice to life with the SAT.

Constituencies and staff! The individuals who constitute them make the College Board run. I was privileged to work closely with them and observe them for more than 31 years. They care about young people and about education. Because they do, they were a joy to work with. The young men and women of the United States are fortunate to have so many dedicated persons working on their behalf to ease the transition from high school to college.

These glimpses of life with the SAT suggest what the remaining chapters of the book are all about—about national manpower problems and international affairs, about civil rights and intercollegiate athletics, about television and the press, about politics and bureaucracies, about demographics and individuals, about the science of psychometrics and the technology of testing, about education and going to college in the United States—as seen from my SAT window on the world.

CHAPTER 2

The SAT's Origin and Place in the Testing World

The Scholastic Aptitude Test, familiarly if not fondly known as the SAT, probably entered my life briefly around 1935, when it was 10 years old and I was 15, in prep school and preparing to take the college entrance examinations of the College Entrance Examination Board. The examinations, then familiarly if not fondly known as the College Boards, evolved in the following way.

The Original College Boards

Until this century, each college that chose to use entrance examinations had its own. Because the subjects examined varied from college to college, secondary schools with students aspiring to a lot of different colleges had to have almost as many preparatory programs as the number of colleges their students were considering. This circumstance bothered a number of outspoken secondary school headmasters, and they complained. Their protest was heard, and in 1900 a small but influential group of colleges in the Northeast responded. They agreed on common subject-matter requirements and then on the need for common entrance examinations in those subjects. For the administration of those examinations they established the College Entrance Examination Board on the Columbia University campus in New York City. For unclear reasons the examinations were called the College Boards, which is what I was being prepared for.

They were made up of essay questions, which students answered by writing in a blue book. My schoolmates and I took them for real in the subjects we were studying, but we also took a number of experimental tests of the then new multiple-choice variety. The SAT must have been one of them. I say that because at my retirement party the master of ceremonies confessed that he had tried to get my SAT scores, but Educational Testing Service (ETS) wouldn't release them. This implies that they may exist, and I'm glad ETS wouldn't reveal them; I was an average student and suspect that my SAT scores wouldn't do much to enhance my academic image. By the end of World War II the blue book examinations had been replaced, and in the years since then the SAT has become the centerpiece of the modern College Boards. What happened?

The original College Boards were based on precise and detailed descriptions of what a student should have studied in secondary school. In the beginning such precision was necessary to advise schoolteachers what to teach and to assure college faculty members that entering students had been exposed to the "real thing"—the essential subject matter of the essential courses. As time went on, however, those narrowly prescribed requirements began to get in the way of colleges' attempts to look beyond their natural feeder schools for potential students. The College Entrance Examination Board, which in its early years was in effect an elite membership association composed of colleges that used its examinations, responded by developing a set of instruments based on more comprehensive and less prescriptive course descriptions. This approach worked but still not as well as the colleges would have liked. Lots of schools around the country still weren't teaching lots of able students what the new College Board "comprehensives" were examining.

Multiple-Choice Model

In its search for ways to deal with this problem, the CEEB (as the organization came to be known) engaged the interest of a professor of psychology at Princeton University, Carl Brigham, later called the father of the SAT. He theorized that a new approach to testing, which had proved helpful to the military in sorting recruits into appropriate assignments during World War I, might do the trick; thus it was that the Army Alpha Test provided the multiple-choice, general abilities model on which the SAT was based.

Because tests made up of multiple-choice questions could include so many questions and could sample a candidate's developed abilities and acquired knowledge so broadly, they could be less curriculum-specific than were the old essay examinations. As a result, what a student had studied in high school wouldn't make as much difference. This possibility appeared attractive, and Brigham was encouraged to pursue his theory. He did so, and in 1925 the CEEB voted to administer the first SAT in June 1926. Thereafter, experimental use of the test continued for some time because many faculty members remained skeptical of this strange new assessment instrument.

Meanwhile, colleges moved slowly to expand their recruiting horizons. I witnessed one of those moves firsthand. My father, dean of Harvard College during the 1930s, served on the Committee on Admissions when the decision was made to broaden the college's outreach. In opting to become a truly national university, Harvard needed to attract students from all parts of the country; yet it found itself stymied by its own entrance examinations requirement. To deal with that barrier, the committee devised alternative routes to admission. In one plan, any student in the top seventh of his (only "his" then) high school class automatically qualified for admission to Harvard College. The plan worked, at least to the extent that the student body became more geographically diverse. But the college soon discovered that "top sevenths" were not always alike and continued to explore other mechanisms for achieving its goal. It tried the SAT. Like so many other institutions that took a chance on this newfangled instrument, Harvard discovered that the test, when used as a scholarship selection device in its then new National Scholarship Program, did an effective job in helping the college diversify its student body.

By 1941 the SAT had proved its worth, and when the United States entered World War II, the test—together with some multiple-choice subject-matter achievement examinations that had been developed at the same time—was ready to take the place of the comprehensive essay examinations. It had to. Wartime meant travel restrictions, and the written essay examinations required bringing college professors and schoolteachers from around the country together in New York City to grade them. And so it was that without any debate over whether the move was wise, the multiple-choice SAT and the objective subject-matter Achievement Tests replaced the traditional free-response essay examinations. By the time the war was over, colleges had become used to the new instruments, and as far as I have been able to discover, no serious thought was ever given to returning to the prewar College Boards.

It wasn't just the new familiarity with the SAT that resulted in its continuation as part of the new College Boards. Numbers also played a significant role. The nation's decision to reward its World War II veterans through the GI Bill created such a sudden and sizable demand for a college education that it would have been impossible, practically speaking, to rev up the old essay grading process. As the numbers continued to grow, I often observed in later years, the College Board would have had to hire Madison Square Garden to accommodate all the graders necessary to handle the volume of entrance examinations being generated.

This brief recital of the origins of the SAT explains how it came to be and why its multiple-choice answer sheets replaced blue books. It tells little, however, about the circumstances in which it came to prominence or about the broader world of testing in which it exists. This background is essential for understanding the role the SAT plays today and the perspective it provides on the educational scene.

Other College Board Tests

As noted above, the SAT was not alone in replacing the essay examinations; subject-matter Achievement Tests were an integral part of the original package. The SAT is a test of verbal and mathematical reasoning. It is not necessary for students to have studied any particular subject or mix of subjects, but simply to have had the opportunity in and out of school to learn about and to use words and numbers. Brigham and his colleagues were sharp enough to realize that those general academic abilities alone, however, would not satisfy college faculty members used to entrance examinations of knowledge gained in specific subjects. Accordingly, they had adapted the new multiple-choice format to the development of subject-specific Achievement Tests. Because the Achievement Tests, like the SAT, could ask many questions in a short period of time and thus sample broadly across a variety of courses of study, they went a long way toward satisfying the colleges' need for entrance examinations that would permit them to recruit from a wider spectrum of schools. But even so, colleges discovered that the SAT gave them still more latitude in this regard.

Along the way, a number of colleges found that the SAT alone was sufficient for their admissions testing needs. One reason was that the Achievement Tests were intended for use by the more demanding colleges in making difficult choices among the academically ablest students, and the SAT-only users didn't have that need to discriminate. To do their job, the Achievement Tests were pitched at a somewhat higher level of difficulty than was the SAT, a characteristic that remains in effect today;

both the SAT and the Achievement Tests are usually required by selective colleges, and only the SAT is required by less selective colleges. Today the two are administered as part of what has come to be called the Admissions Testing Program (ATP), the latter-day counterpart to the original College Boards.

The College Board's success in multiple-choice, objective testing wasn't confined to these two instruments. Brigham's work attracted other interests, and before long the CEEB was administering tests for graduate and professional schools: the Law School Admission Test (LSAT), the Graduate Management Admission Test (GMAT), the Medical College Admission Test (MCAT), and the Graduate Record Examinations (GRE). Tests were also administered for the State Department and the Selective Service System, among others. All this testing activity was going on in Princeton, New Jersey, not New York City; Brigham obviously preferred the more reflective environment of a college town to the hustle of a big city. By the end of World War II, only the secretariat needed to serve the membership association remained in New York City.

Founding of Educational Testing Service

This separation did not go unnoticed by the leaders of the education establishment, who had a couple of other matters in the field of assessment that they wanted to take care of. The College Entrance Examination Board wasn't the only nonprofit enterprise in the testing business. The American Council on Education (ACE) had its Cooperative Test Service, and the Carnegie Foundation for the Advancement of Teaching had its National Teacher Examinations. Both sponsors were losing money. The CEEB wasn't. Also, all three organizations were doing research in psychometrics. Led by President James B. Conant of Harvard, the leaders of the academic community concluded that American education would be best served if the testing activities of ACE and Carnegie could be folded into the CEEB operation at Princeton to take advantage of economies of scale and, if the research activities of all three could be combined, to avoid duplication. They proposed to accomplish these goals by separating the testing operations of the three organizations from the sponsors and forming a new enterprise to be called Educational Testing Service (ETS).

At the College Board there were those in the constituency who saw the proliferation of its testing activities beyond the SAT and the Achievement Tests as reason to support the move. Others opposed giving away the store, but the consolidators prevailed. Granted a charter by the New York State Board of Regents on December 19, 1947, Educational Testing Service started operations on January 1, 1948.

In the process of consolidation, the CEEB turned virtually all its assets over to the new organization and then turned around and contracted with ETS for the testing services the CEEB had up to that time provided on its own. At that point the CEEB SAT and Achievement Test activity accounted for roughly 25 percent of ETS business.

While ETS was getting off the ground, the question of what to do with the CEEB secretariat remained up for grabs. After considerable discussion, which included consideration of disbanding the organization, the decision was made to give the CEEB a chance to revitalize the associational aspects of its activities. In 1948 a director in the person of Frank H. Bowles, then director of admissions at Columbia University, was chosen to lead the effort. The title of Bowles's book *The Refounding of the College Board, 1948–1963*, an annotated compilation of papers written during his term as chief executive officer and published by the College Board in 1967, suggests the nature of that effort. The contents attest to his success in undertaking it.

The differences of opinion within the CEEB constituency over the founding of ETS, together with the tensions that naturally developed between the two organizations as the membership association sought to establish its independence from the testing enterprise it had helped create, influenced the life of the SAT in important ways. Under the contractual arrangements drawn up in 1947, ETS gained exclusive title to the individual test items used in the SAT (and in the Achievement Tests) except for those in the most recent operational forms of the tests, which in their entirety were the property of the CEEB. It is important to note that from the outset of the new arrangement, neither the CEEB nor its SAT was irrevocably tied to ETS. If the contract between the two organizations were to be terminated, the CEEB would be entitled to use those recent forms while it sought another supplier, and ETS would own all other items developed for use in the SAT and be free to use them in any way it might choose—but not under the SAT title. Similar provisions remain in effect today.

Another feature of the original contract that has remained in force is the vesting of policy control over the SAT in the hands of the sponsor (CEEB), not the test maker (ETS). This provision represented a significant change from the earlier circumstances in which the test maker (CEEB) was also the sponsor and therefore had total control. In 1948, however, with the refounding of the College Board, the test maker (ETS) became accountable to a second party (CEEB). Casual critics of the SAT scene tend indiscriminately to lump ETS and CEEB together as a single entity. And uninformed commentators still sometimes refer to ETS as a subsidiary of the College Board or to the College Board as an arm of ETS. In doing so, these critics and commentators are overlooking the creative and occasionally uncomfortable tension that has existed between the two organizations since the establishment of ETS in 1947–48. In my judgment it has been a healthy tension for the evolution of the SAT.

This tension was perhaps most apparent in the late 1950s, when ETS found itself the victim of its own success and was literally bursting at the seams. As more young people sought to pursue education beyond high school under the impetus of the GI Bill, the demand for services from ETS grew rapidly. In the process, the CEEB's portion of ETS business increased from a quarter to nearly two-thirds. Outgrowing the space it had taken over from the CEEB in downtown Princeton, ETS was operating in a number of widely dispersed locations around town. The time had come to move out and consolidate. The problem was money.

The founders of ETS were educators, not businessmen. As school but primarily college administrators, they were used to having physical facilities underwritten by taxes or gifts, and therefore no provision was built into the initial ETS financial planning for the accumulation of capital with which to expand. Under the original contractual agreement between the CEEB and ETS, for instance, the CEEB was to pay ETS operating costs plus a modest research fee, period. Having no alumni or other benefactors, and in the absence of tax support as a nonprofit enterprise, ETS asked the CEEB and its other clients to increase the research fee to provide funds for the necessary consolidation and expansion of its facilities. The CEEB demurred initially in response to concerns expressed by its constituency and asked that the matter be studied by a joint committee. It was.

To help the committee work through that particular tension, the accounting firm of Arthur Andersen and Company was engaged to provide consulting assistance. In the course of the committee's meetings I learned a new word from one of the accounting representatives, *monopsony*. He used it to characterize the relationship between the two enterprises as one involving a *monopoly* (a single supplier, ETS), and a *monopsony* (a single buyer, CEEB). He also characterized it as "the damnedest relationship I've ever seen, where the producer [ETS] has no control over the price charged for the product [the College Board still determines how much candidates will be charged], and the party that sets the prices has no control over the costs of production."

In the event, that particular negotiation was successfully concluded and served to set a precedent for the ongoing triennial renegotiation of the financial terms of the contract between the two organizations. Over the years those arrangements have evolved to include an "incentive fee" provision, which helps to ensure that ETS will be financially rewarded for operating efficiencies. (The original simple cost-plus contract provided no incentive for ETS to keep costs down.)

Naturally, in a relationship as devoid of precedent as this one, other tensions occasionally flared up. On one such occasion another, later independent review committee began flirting with the idea of re-merging the two entities. Richard Pearson, president of the College Board at the time, and his fellow officers weren't about to sit still for that one. Visions of preoccupation with technical, psychometric matters, to the detriment of CEEB's associational activities, were enough to put an end to that incipient exploration. At another time two later presidents of the CEEB and ETS went so far, however, as to have joint vice presidencies in such areas as regional representation and a Washington presence, but decisions and interpretations by the courts and the Federal Trade Commission ultimately combined to move the two organizations into the businesslike, arm's-length stance that now characterizes the relationship.

Through all these fluctuations, the SAT remained very much at the heart of the negotiations. It had grown to become by far the largest of the ETS-administered testing programs, and its welfare was an important ingredient in the glue that helped keep the relationship between the CEEB and ETS from coming unstuck in those moments of stress.

As the CEEB activities became more varied and the services for which it contracted with ETS multiplied, the contractual relationships between the two enterprises became more complicated and different provisions related to different services came to be included. But in all the provisions, the CEEB had, and still has as the College Board, the right—as does ETS—to terminate the agreement after due notice. And that's not just for effect! The College Board has exercised its prerogative in this regard, sought bids from other suppliers, and awarded contracts for services to vendors other than ETS. Again, I make the point that although the College Board and ETS may appear to constitute a monopolistic combine, the fact is that preservation of the integrity of the SAT is enhanced by the separate authorities of its producer and its sponsor.

There is a second factor as well that helps ensure that the parties directly involved—the organization that sponsors the SAT, the colleges that use it in their admissions procedures, and the students who take it—are getting their money's worth. Because ETS is a part of the testing industry, it competes with other nonprofit and with for-profit testing companies for contracts to supply assessment services. In that marketplace ETS manages to win its share of the business, and that is a comforting sign to the College Board. Cost-center controls ensure that standard rates are being charged for similar services to different clients, and that circumstance in turn ensures that the rates being charged by ETS to the College Board for the development and administration of the SAT are generally in line with industry standards.

Entrance of American College Testing Program

Nevertheless, questions of sponsorship, control, and costs aside, the CEEB remained a monopsony dealing with a monopoly, ETS, in the college admissions testing business until 1957. At that point one of the best things that ever happened to the CEEB happened—the founding of the American College Testing Program (ACT). From 1900 until 1957 the College Entrance Examination Board, alone at first and later with ETS, had enjoyed a real monopoly as the only national college admissions testing program, serving in a sense as an unregulated public utility. Just as a family had to get its electricity, if it wanted it, from the local electric light company, so a college that wanted to use national admissions tests had to use the College Boards. Although the newness of the field and its opportunities for experimentation, when combined with the CEEB-ETS tensions noted above, served to ward off the complacency endemic to monopolies, the appearance of ACT meant that the College Board and ETS could no longer be assured that they would have unhampered access to the colleges' rapidly growing need for entrance examinations.

Superficially, the College Board and ACT instruments look very much alike in the sense that if test items from the ACT Assessment battery and from the SAT were put in a hat and drawn out at random, only a practiced eye could tell which items were from which test. But beyond that surface similarity, there have been significant differences in the two tests. The SAT, for example, produces two primary scores, in verbal and mathematical reasoning. Until recently, the ACT test has produced four primary sources, in English, mathematics, social studies, and natural sciences. For the assessment of subject-matter mastery in those subjects and others, the College Board offers its Achievement Tests. Another obvious difference is in the scales used to report the scores. The SAT and the Achievement Tests are reported on a scale that runs from 200 to 800; ACT reports on a scale from 1 to 36. Generally accepted tables of equivalences comparing ACT and SAT scores have been published for years, despite the protests of the psychometric purists. Such comparisons are usually not made, however, between ACT and Achievement Test scores because the latter are for instruments designed to operate at a higher level of difficulty noted earlier.

There are differences, too, in the philosophies underlying the construction of the tests. A belief important in the development of the ACT instruments is that capable psychometricians, by keeping current with what is going on in the classrooms of the nation's schools, can construct tests that accurately reflect what is being taught there. The philosophy on which ETS and the College Board operate is that practicing secondary school teachers and professing college professors should be involved in the construction in order to ensure congruence between what is being taught and what is being tested. That technique is, of course, more costly and more time-consuming.

There is another difference that sets the two testing programs apart and explains, in part at least, the differing geographic popularity of the two competitors. They come out of different traditions. Over the first 50 years of the twentieth century two distinct college admissions systems evolved. One, dominated by the CEEB, was a system of admission by examination. The other, promulgated by the University of Michigan, was a system of admission by accreditation. Under the first, as its name implies, admission to college was based on performance on entrance examinations, the original College Boards. By contrast, under the system of admission by accreditation, the operating principle was that if a student earned passing grades in an "accredited" school, he or she was admissible to public higher education in his or her home state; accredited meant that the teachers in that school had gone to a teachers college approved by the state's major public university.

These two systems developed in parallel over the years before World War I but in ways that brought them closer together as World War II approached. In the "examination" camp the early, written, free-response essay examinations were giving way to the much less curricularly restrictive, objective, multiple-choice tests. In those changing circumstances it was recognized that test scores were less likely to reflect a student's performance in school than were the old College Boards and that, therefore, test scores alone should not be used to determine whether an applicant should be admitted to college. At the very least, the student's school record should be taken into account.

By the opposite token, in the "accreditation" camp it came to be recognized that schools differed markedly in their grading standards. As a consequence, a number of states developed in-state testing programs to help in the placement of students when they arrived on a college campus. And so it was that by the end of World War II, the two systems had grown much more alike; the practitioners in each system used both school records and test scores in helping students make the transition from school to college. The American College Testing Program entered the college admissions testing field after this convergence had taken place. It did so by focusing its attention initially on the public higher education institutions in the Middle West, which had been in the admission-by-accreditation group.

The founder of ACT was E. F. Lindquist, a professor at the University of Iowa and the father of the Iowa Tests of Basic Skills (ITBS), used by many schools throughout the country. My own interpretation of events suggests that Lindquist's ingenious adaptation of technology to the testing process had created excess production capacity in Iowa City. With that capacity at hand and in the knowledge that the market for college admissions tests was bound to grow, he seized the opportunity to take advantage of this burgeoning market. His approach was not to try to talk neighboring universities into giving up what they were already doing but rather to suggest that the new ACT battery, an upward extension of the Iowa Tests of Basic Skills, be used to supplement existing procedures. In this way states with their own in-state testing programs, with all their built-in self-interests, could retain those programs and at the same time gain easier access to out-of-state markets by affiliating with the ACT.

To get their new venture off the ground, the American College Testing Program embarked on a vigorous sales campaign. Its greatest success was where one would have expected it—among the public institutions in the Middle West. But the marketing effort was not confined to that part of the country and was met with varying degrees of success in other areas. In the South, for example, the states along the East Coast aligned themselves with the SAT (Georgia had been using the SAT for some years), while those in the Deep South joined the ACT group. In the Southwest, particularly in Texas, the higher education systems went in different directions, some with the SAT and others with the ACT. In the Far West, the SAT and the Achievement Tests were already in use by the more selective institutions in California. There the ACT made its inroads in the community college market.

The fact that the SAT was the most firmly established in the Northeast didn't keep the American College Testing Program from telling its story there as well. On one such occasion, the director of guidance in the local high school our daughters attended arranged for me to be on a program for one of the New Jersey counselor groups with Lindquist, rather like David and Goliath, only more so and with far less success for David. The meeting was at Upsala College in East Orange, New Jersey. Dr. Lindquist approached it from Iowa via Newark Airport and was on time. I approached it from Manhattan, got stuck in the Lincoln Tunnel, and was late. The session had already started, although barely so, when I arrived and was hustled onto the platform from backstage amid snide remarks about my tardiness. As if that wasn't bad enough, my "friend" pulled out a pair of boxing gloves from under the table and suggested that Lindquist and I have at each other verbally. There I was, still very wet behind the ears psychometrically, invited to do oratorical battle with perhaps the most formidable test expert the country has ever known. (Lindquist made many contributions in many different fields; his talents were not confined to testing, but those are the ones with which I was preoccupied in East Orange.) Among his many other qualities, he was a gentleman and did much more to put me at ease than did our local guidance counselor. Thanks to him, I came through unscathed.

Although that confrontation was atypical in terms of the physical presence of boxing gloves, it was no different from many of the other opportunities we at the College Board were offered to debate the relative merits of the SAT and the ACT with our counterparts from Iowa City. The motivation, as it was at Upsala, was always to try to get a verbal fight going; the tactics for doing so were so unprofessional that the officers of the College Board and the ACT finally came to an unspoken but carefully preserved gentleman's agreement not to appear on the same stage at the same time. That was in the late 1950s. That informal pact remained in effect at least through my presidency at the College Board, with two exceptions, both in the early 1980s. In one instance Oluf Davidsen, president of the American College Testing Program, and I appeared before a special commission appointed by Florida's chief state school officer to consider problems in testing then facing that state. The second was at a meeting that was unique in other ways as well. It was the only meeting jointly sponsored by the College Board and the ACT, as well as the only one I know of that has had as its theme "assessment in the arts." It came about this way.

That long-standing agreement not to appear on the same program at the same time meant that Oluf and I did not get many opportunities to visit with each other. But normally once a year we got the chance to do so at the annual conferences held regularly around the world by the International Association for Educational Assessment (IAEA); there is more on the association in Chapter 8, "The International Connection." It was at a meeting in Sodertalje, a suburb of Stockholm, Sweden, that William Turnbull, then president of ETS, suggested to Oluf and to me that we might want to consider jointly sponsoring an IAEA regional conference on assessment in the arts. We liked the idea and we did hold a Western Hemisphere regional IAEA meeting in Miami, Florida, jointly sponsored by the College Board and the ACT.

It was at the meeting in Sweden that Oluf contributed to my realization that the world had indeed grown more complicated over the years. The theme of the IAEA conference in Sodertalje was assessment in connection with vocational education. One of the early speakers, from Great Britain, put the topic in historical perspective by pointing out that in the old days a man's occupation was more important than his name and that if you knew what a man's occupation was, you knew exactly what he did. Carpenter, physician, ferryboat operator—it was clear what that person did for a living. But today? Doctor—what specialty? Teacher—what subject?

Oluf brought the point home by recalling his personal experience in Denmark, where his family had come from. He and Mrs. Davidsen had been traveling through Denmark with his sister, who lived there, visiting family homesites and gravesites. The tombstones confirmed that what an individual did was more important than what his or her name was. A gravestone would read, for instance, "Carpenter Sven Davidsen," not "Sven Davidsen, Carpenter." After hearing Oluf on this subject, whenever people asked me what I did, I would answer, "I am a meeting-goer."

This interplay of name and role, not so incidentally, has managed to complicate life for the SAT. The word *aptitude* in its title is often mistakenly equated with *intelligence,* and the test itself with an intelligence test. But there is a world of difference between the SAT and an intelligence test. An IQ score on the latter is presumed to be an immutable measure of a person's intellectual capacity and as such should never change. The SAT, on the other hand, is, despite its name, a test of developed verbal and mathematical abilities that are expected to, and do, change over time. That's why high school seniors score higher on the average than sophomores do. Because the word *aptitude* can be misleading in this regard, some observers argue that the name should be changed. My own position has been to leave it alone, leave it as it is, in part on the grounds of tradition, in part on the grounds that no satisfactory substitute has been devised after years of trying, and in part in the belief that the test's critics would change only their tune, not their message, if the name became something other than the Scholastic Aptitude Test. On this last count, I am convinced that instead of berating the College Board for sponsoring a test with a misleading name, those critics would take it to task for trying to fool the public by simply changing the name. It's definitely a no-win situation.

The ACT, of course, doesn't face that problem. But since the ACT Assessment battery is a multiple-choice, objective, machine-scored instrument like the SAT, it does face the charge that it simply provides mechanically derived scores, devoid of the application of human judgment, and that is why the idea of a conference devoted to the exploration of assessment in the arts held such appeal for both organizations. As the participants in the regional IAEA conference in Miami pointed out, assessment of creative work in the arts is something that can not be accomplished through the application of modern technology. Like the grading of essays, it is a task that has to be carried out by human beings applying human judgment to what the artist or student of art has created: the picture drawn or painted, the music composed or played, the piece of sculpture crafted, the dance performed, the story written.

Ideally we might wish for a return to the good old days of the original written, free-response examinations of the CEEB, when such judgment was regularly applied; but, as suggested earlier, given today's numbers, the logistics would make it impossible. With over 2 million students taking the SAT and the ACT each year, the mechanics involved in assembling, training, and overseeing the work of the thousands of graders needed to score the tests if they were in a totally free-response mode would be horrendous and the costs prohibitive.

That statement, by the way, is not the result of uninformed speculation. It is based on the experience that ETS has had over the years in scoring approximately 100,000 twenty-minute essays annually composed by candidates taking the College Board's Achievement Test in English Composition with Essay each December and in dealing with the free-response answers to questions posed in 29 Advanced Placement Examinations in 15 fields each May. Large-scale essay testing is not dead!

And so it is that the creative tensions between the College Board and ETS on the one hand and the healthy competition with the ACT on the other involve not just the nature of the testing instruments themselves but the supporting services that can be offered by the application of modern technology to meet the demands of a mass market. In this respect the students and the institutions that use the SAT and the ACT are well served by those tensions and competition that exist in the nonprofit sector of the testing industry. (Not so incidentally in this context, Oluf Davidsen and I did appear together, after we had both retired, on the same stage at the same time when we were the 1988 recipients of the Excellence in Education Award of the National Association of College Admissions Counselors.)

Other Programs and Services

The above references to the Achievement Tests and the Advanced Placement Examinations properly suggest that the SAT also exists internally at the College Board within a set of other programs and services. Note has already been taken of the part it played together with the Achievement Tests in the transformation of the original College Boards into what is now known as the Admissions Testing Program (ATP). Today that entity includes other components as well.

Stimulated by competition from the ACT, the Board added the Student Descriptive Questionnaire (SDQ) to the ATP in 1971. In this self-report candidates voluntarily provide information about themselves in both academic and nonacademic areas—their abilities, goals, activities, and interests. The first major revision of the SDQ was introduced in the 1985–86 academic year and focused more sharply on academic aspects.

The availability of this information in the aggregate has proved generally valuable in understanding the changing characteristics of the candidate pool and was specifically useful in studying the reasons for the decline in national average SAT scores during the 1960s and 1970s. More practically from the colleges' point of view, the College Board is able, on the basis of what students report about themselves and with their permission, to provide through the activity known as the Student Search Service (SSS) the names of potential applicants having certain characteristics identified by the colleges. An institution may be particularly interested, for example, in increasing its pool of applicants who expect to go into engineering. But probably most important has been the ability of colleges to target specific populations of students in their efforts to attract more minority applicants.

PSAT/NMSQT

The pool of names available via the SAT or the Achievement Tests is greatly augmented by those who earlier indicate a willingness to let their names be used in the Student Search Service when they take the Preliminary Scholastic Aptitude Test/National Merit Scholarship Qualifying Test (PSAT/NMSQT). That instrument is a shorter, slightly less difficult, and considerably less expensive version of the SAT. As its name implies, it serves more than one function. As the PSAT, it gives students a chance to practice for the real thing, the SAT, and its scores provide useful information to students as they begin to think about specific college possibilities. As the NMSQT, it serves as an initial screening for students choosing to enter the competition not only for the regular National Merit Scholarships but also for awards available from other sources, such as the National Merit Scholarship Corporation's National Achievement Program for black students and the College Board's National Hispanic Scholar Awards Program. In both functions the test is less expensive than the SAT for two basic reasons. First, its parent, the SAT, absorbs most of the developmental costs; the PSAT/NMSQT's items come from old SAT forms. Second, it is administered by schools to groups of students rather than via individual registrations, which are required in the Admissions Testing Program. As for the numbers involved, over 1.5 million take the PSAT/NMSQT each year, and more than 2.8 million students who took the PSAT/NMSQT and the SAT chose to be included in the Student Search Service in 1989–90.

CSS and AP

This set of services built around the SAT itself fits within a still broader array of College Board activities. In this regard, 1954 and 1955 were watershed years, for those were the years when the association formalized the establishment of the College Scholarship Service (CSS) and assumed responsibility for the Advanced Placement (AP) Program. By then the College Board had succeeded in "refounding" itself, to use Frank Bowles's terminology, this time as a viable and respected education association, and this success had attracted these two new ventures to the Board. When a group of private-college presidents in the Northeast wanted to establish a mechanism for stretching their student financial aid dollars by making awards on the basis of demonstrated financial need, they sought out the College Board to take on the task. When The Ford Foundation had for several years successfully explored, with a small, select group of colleges and schools, the possibility of awarding college credit for college-level work taken in secondary school, the foundation turned to the College Board to provide a permanent home for what became known as the Advanced Placement Program.

Both CSS and the AP Program have proved highly useful and visibly successful over the years. The concept of need-based aid, which CSS pioneered, soon provided the rationale for the distribution of the massive amounts of state and federal student financial aid dollars that began to be pumped into higher education in the 1960s; what started out as a duplicating service for a common financial aid application turned into a sophisticated, computerized computation service handling on the order of 2.5 million financial aid application forms each year. Meanwhile, the Advanced Placement Program grew slowly at first and then took off. There were times in the late 1960s and early 1970s when the proponents of egalitarianism considered the AP Program, with its emphasis on the brightest from the best schools, to be antithetical to civil rights and called for its abolition. But good sense prevailed, and recently much of the Program's growth has taken place in schools that serve large minority populations. It always seemed ironic to me that the liberal white establishment (of which, doubly ironically, I was assumed otherwise to be a part), in its call for equality of educational opportunity, denied the likelihood that there are bright, academically able black and Hispanic students who can take advantage of the Advanced Placement Program. As to the extent of growth, 1,229 students took 2,199 AP Examinations in spring 1956. In 1988 nearly 300,000 candidates sat for close to 425,000 AP Examinations.

Funding

For more than 25 years, however, while both programs were getting established, they required subsidy in much the same way the SAT required underwriting in its early years. That subsidy of the SAT came, of course, from funds provided through the original essay examinations. Beginning in 1955, it became the SAT's turn to do the underwriting. Indeed, one of the great joys of working with the College Board is its ability to generate a few extra dollars to support promising programs like CSS and AP in their formative years, as well as such public service activities as the Educational EQuality Project and the Advisory Panel on the Scholastic Aptitude Test Score Decline, which are the subjects of Chapter 4.

This ability of the College Board generally, and its SAT in particular, to generate a few extra dollars isn't an unmixed blessing. For one thing, there are always many more good works the organization would like to create and direct than it can afford, and so, when we would seek foundation support for some of them, we could be turned away in good conscience on the grounds that the good old College Board could generate the funds if it had a mind to.

Another disadvantage is more subtle and therefore requires an explanation. When I joined the staff in 1955, the College Board was housed in a single, five-story brownstone on the Columbia University campus. That year, four of us became members of the professional staff, almost doubling it. But that was only the beginning of the rapid growth that was to force the College Board to make three moves over the next 30 years: first to the Interchurch Center on Riverside Drive in Morningside Heights, adjacent to Columbia; second to a green glass skyscraper at 888 Seventh Avenue in midtown Manhattan; and finally to its first owned home at 45 Columbus Avenue in New York City in an art deco landmark building across the street from Fordham University and Lincoln Center. (The Board's moves are described more fully in Chapter 10.)

Along the way serious consideration was given to the possibility of moving the Board's headquarters either to Princeton, New Jersey, or to Washington, D.C. Particularly attractive was an early offer from ETS to have the College Board establish its headquarters in Princeton on the new property ETS had just acquired. That possibility was rejected on the grounds that being so physically close to ETS might cause the College Board staff to become too preoccupied with operations at ETS to provide the desirable associational counterbalance in the conduct of what was then very much a joint enterprise. For me, one of the compelling reasons for not moving to the nation's capital was much the same as the one for not moving to Princeton—the possibility of having the staff's attention diverted from the business of the association by the political distractions of the Washington scene rather than those of the testing scene at ETS.

The Board's attitude in this regard did not go unnoticed by the education associations headquartered in and around Washington and served, I fear, to confirm the sense of aloofness on the part of the College

Board that the leaders of those associations attributed to the New York-based enterprise. And it didn't do anything, either, to lessen the jealousy I observed on their part over the Board's not having to rely on "soft money," which is to say philanthropy, for its support. For example, one evening when I was dining with a staff colleague in a Washington hotel, there were four associational leaders at the next table. When their bill came, the host of the group told the waiter, "Give the bill to Mr. Hanford over there. He's got all the money."

I've often wondered if that belief might subconsciously have had something to do with the less-than-friendly attitude toward the SAT displayed by some members of Washington's "educational secretariat." A number of them have indulged in SAT trashing in recent years, complaining that it is outdated or biased. It got a backhanded compliment from one member who said it had done its job (I was never sure what he meant by that) and ought to be retired. At the same meeting one of his apostles went so far as to opine that the SAT "deserved a decent burial." But here the SAT is, still alive and kicking.

CLEP

Considerations of headquarters location and associational jealousies aside, the College Board continued over the years to be an attractive repository for the good ideas of others. In the early 1960s, for instance, John Gardner, then president of the Carnegie Corporation of New York, tried to get Frank Bowles to have the College Board undertake the development of examinations at the college level that could be used by adults to receive college credit for knowledge they had acquired in nontraditional ways. Bowles did not believe the Board was ready to take on this added responsibility, and he declined. Gardner then turned to ETS and prevailed upon it to do the job while he looked for another sponsor. No sponsor as appropriate as the College Board presented itself, and Gardner returned to his first choice. By that time ETS had a product to offer and Richard Pearson had succeeded Bowles as the Board's chief executive. When Gardner and ETS approached him with a ready-made battery of test offerings, Pearson was willing, and the College Board became the sponsor of what has come to be known as the College-Level Examination Program (CLEP). It consists of General Examinations in five basic areas and Subject Examinations in specific subjects. Underwritten by the Carnegie Corporation of New York in its early years, and given a financial boost in the mid-1970s by the adoption of its examinations by the armed forces through the DANTES program, CLEP, like the AP Program and the CSS, has nevertheless required subsidy from the Admissions Testing Program and, thus, the SAT.

And so it is that the SAT is neither the property of ETS nor the sole test among the array of College Board services. It has a distinguished lineage and has dutifully provided support for a number of poor relations while they were getting their feet on the ground. It has done so without having a monopoly in college admissions testing and exists within an industry that gives it high marks and healthy, high-quality competition. It is from this background that the SAT, for nearly a third of a century, provided me with unparalleled opportunities for gaining insights into what was going on in education, in the nation, and in the world.

CHAPTER 3

Understanding the SAT

Early on in my life with the Scholastic Aptitude Test (SAT) I took part in a program on college admissions at Flushing High School in New York City's Borough of Queens, along with the admissions officer from City College of New York (CCNY) and the coordinator and director of college admissions counseling for the city schools. In those days CCNY was a highly selective institution and Flushing High School was inhabited by a good number of students whose parents aspired to the best in education for their progeny. With both students and parents in attendance, the atmosphere was less than relaxed as the three of us discussed the college admissions scene.

I learned two things from that experience. First, Harold Zuckerman, then not only director of college admissions counseling for the New York City schools but the only college admissions counselor for the city schools, warned me in advance that I would be besieged by parents the minute the formal session ended. He advised, "When you've had all you can take, suddenly look up, raise your hand as if you're waving at someone, and shout, 'I'll be right there!' " After our panel discussion was over, a group of anxious parents did surround me and when I'd had enough, I did look up and raise my hand, only to find Zuckerman doing the same thing on the other side of the room. That tactic, I have to say, served me well over the years.

The second thing I learned had to do with explaining the SAT. I'm convinced that when I started to speak in the Flushing High School auditorium, at least 97 percent of the parents in attendance believed that

SAT scores were the most important factor in gaining admission to a selective college and that a student with a 510 verbal score was by definition brighter than a student with a 490. When I finished demolishing those misconceptions in a few well-chosen words, I had the impression that the percentage had plummeted to perhaps 96. Was I a total failure? I don't think so; 10 or 15 minutes simply isn't long enough to get people to understand what the SAT really is and does. I often wondered if I could compose something that would explain it. This chapter represents one attempt.

Understanding the SAT and the perspective on society it gave me is aided by the fact that the test is a product of the industrial-turned-scientific-and-technical era in which it was conceived and grew up. In a very real sense it represents the application of industrial technology and science to what is essentially an art form, the assessment of human performance.

The evolution of the SAT has been marked by the interplay between the growing sophistication in the theoretical manipulation of numbers and the ability to do the manipulation by machine, or, in today's terminology, between the capacity to create software and the skill to develop the hardware to manipulate it. In the case of the SAT, as in other contexts, each has fed on the other. Most of this chapter deals with the software because that is where an understanding of the test can best be developed. But the sudden maturation of the SAT in the years immediately following World War II occurred because it was able to take advantage of the economies of scale that had fueled the industrial revolution. The original method of having college entrance examinations graded by individuals would simply have been too cumbersome and costly. The application of mass production techniques made it possible to adapt Carl Brigham's scientific principles, mostly statistical, to the examining process and to do so at a time when the number of students going on to college was increasing dramatically. But back to those hardware developments later. For now, the software side.

Kinds of Tests

Assessment of human performance comes in a variety of forms. There are hearing tests, eye examinations, drivers' tests, tests of endurance, and tests of will. Obviously, the SAT isn't one of those. It is, on the other hand, one of many tests and examinations used in schools and colleges to assess academic performance and potential. There are two types: free-response tests and forced-choice tests. The questions on a free-response examination are just that—questions that the persons taking the test are invited to answer freely in their own way. For example, the question "Why did David kill Goliath?" would require the examinees to write a personal interpretation of the encounter in their own words. Questions in mathematics can also be free-response. The examinees are expected, without any hints, to come up with the right number when asked, "How much is 9 times 6?"

By contrast, forced-choice tests are made up of questions for which the test takers are provided a choice of answers, from which they are forced to choose the best one. In the jargon of the testing world, what I refer to as forced-choice tests are called multiple-choice tests. The decision to use that terminology seems unfortunate. The term *choice* implies options and can mean more than one unless, of course, you mean a single choice as in former Russian elections, or you're talking about true/false or yes/no questions where you have one choice between two alternatives. The word *multiple* in the testing context seems redundant, and if *choice* is to be modified, I prefer *forced* because the test taker is forced to make one choice from several suggested answers.

The answers offered in the above biblical question (with apologies to the test-construction experts) might be

(*a*) because Goliath was big
(*b*) because David was small
(*c*) because Goliath was a Philistine
(*d*) because Goliath was ugly
(*e*) because David and Goliath were longtime enemies

The test taker is then asked simply to choose the best one, which in the foregoing example I intended to be (*c*). Most forced-choice tests used in schools and colleges today offer four or five possible answers. In the mathematics question posed above, the possibilities might be

(*a*) 48
(*b*) 54
(*c*) 56
(*d*) 64
(*e*) 72

Tests and examinations can be paper-and-pencil (or pen), oral, or computer-administered if they are forced-choice. Generally speaking, although there are many exceptions, "written" has come to be used with free-response examinations and "objective," "standardized," or "multiple-choice" with forced-choice tests.

Exercises that are administered by computers are usually referred to as "computerized," and they are "tests" because they are most often forced-choice. Oral exercises are usually free-response and therefore normally referred to as "examinations." In my lexicon, then, examinations are old-fashioned, people-scored, and written or oral, while tests are machine-scored and forced-choice. (For me, a short examination in class is a quiz, not a test.)

Therefore, the SAT can be said to be a forced-choice, paper-and-pencil test for which the test takers are asked to use a pencil to fill in a circle on the piece of paper that serves as an answer sheet, identifying their choice among the answers offered for a given question.

Grading Methods

Candidate performance on tests and examinations, like student performance in the classroom, is recorded in a variety of ways. The two most common are by letter grade (A to F) and on a numerical scale (0 to 100). The public seems generally to understand that on the letter scale A through D are passing grades and that 60 is normally the lowest numerical passing grade. Many tests involving large numbers of students measure performance (that is, report scores) on a percentage basis. In other words, when a student scores at the 80th percentile, it means that he or she performed better than did 80 percent of a reference population, or group of students. To figure out the number of right answers it takes to score at a certain percentile, the tests are normed; that is, they are administered experimentally to groups of students who are presumably like the populations of students who will later be taking the tests for credit. The scores are then ranked according to percentiles, and norms are established; the norm, of course, is determined by the experimental groups. To keep their tests up-to-date, test makers often vary the nature of the contents and configurations of their instruments and then renorm them to take account of the changes.

I recall a high school principal who complained that one testing company had asked his school to participate in the renorming of one of its offerings without giving adequate notice. He was from Cincinnati, and because its schools had taken part in an earlier renorming, the testing company wanted to produce a new set of norms based on the same population. The Cincinnati schools refused, and the company had to use another city with a population that was bound to be different. As a result, the norms (that is, the percentiles) were bound to be different from what they would have been if Cincinnati had participated. As a consequence, scores earned on the new forms of the test were certain to have a meaning different from that of scores earned on earlier versions, even if the content and configuration of the test had remained the same. The result? Scores on most tests are not exactly comparable over time. Such tests, however, are often referred to as "standardized" even though the "standard" changes over time.

Not so incidentally, the process of renorming explains, at least in part, why school systems sometimes change tests. If they play their cards right, their students' test performance as measured by the national norms of a different test is likely to appear improved without any real improvement in their academic achievement. Enough schools have done just that to the extent that one observer has recently been able to call attention to the fact that if the reported test results are to be believed, most students in most states are scoring above the national average, which, while politically convenient, is numerically impossible.

The concept of "average," I find, is often misunderstood. Many people, for example, think that 500 is the average SAT score because it is halfway between the lowest and the highest scores possible on the test. Some persons fail to realize that you can drown in a river that has an average depth of one foot. My predecessor, Sidney Marland, made the point by recounting the experience of a then fellow school superintendent. Marland ran the elementary schools; the other man, the local high school. He'd been visited by the father of one of the seniors, a graduate of the Massachusetts Institute of Technology, who wanted his son to follow in his footsteps. The father's complaint was that the guidance counselor had advised the son not even to apply to MIT. Marland's colleague tried to reason with the father, pointing out that MIT was extremely selective and that the boy was in the bottom half of his class. The father's rejoinder? "With the taxes we pay in this town, no student should be below average!"

Scoring the SAT

Although most tests are regularly renormed and thus have averages that change over time, the SAT isn't and doesn't. Its current score scale was produced by using the students who took the test in 1941 as the norming population. Before that, the SAT had been renormed each year. Using that 1941 population as the anchor, so to speak, a permanent score scale was established and a given score on every edition of the SAT has now had the same meaning for nearly half a century.

Its score scale is unique as well. So that the SAT scores would not be confused with letter grades or percentages or percentile rankings, the score scale was established to run from a low of 200 to a high of 800. No particular score could be interpreted as "passing;" a score of 500 simply meant, and means, that half the students on whom the test was originally normed scored above 500 and half below. But the populations taking the test each year have changed, and that half-and-half division is no longer true. The original groups of students taking the test were made up of select candidates who were applying to very select colleges. Over the years, as more and more students took the test in applying to a more diverse group of colleges, their average scores drifted down to the point where, today, the average scores of students taking the SAT are in the 400s. A score of 500 now is well above average, and a score of 650 (halfway between 500 and 800) puts a student not at the 75th percentile (halfway from the average to the top) but at something on the order of the 90th percentile for math and the 97th for verbal.

Two points bear emphasizing here. First, the 200-to-800 score range should not be thought of as similar to either the A-to-F letter grade range or the 0-to-100 percent range, and 500 is not the average score on the SAT today. Second, as noted above, SAT scores are unique in that they have the same meaning over time. On this second point, the first question asked by the Advisory Panel appointed in 1975 to study the then 10-year decline in national average SAT scores was whether the SAT had gotten "harder." The panel members satisfied themselves that it hadn't and that the SAT score decline was the result of other factors. Given the efforts expended by Educational Testing Service (ETS) to ensure the comparability of SAT scores over time, that conclusion by the score decline panel should not have been surprising.

If there are different kinds of tests and they use different methods of recording and reporting student performance, this is in part because tests and examinations serve different purposes. For the SAT the purpose is to predict how well students will do academically in college, and for that particular purpose the use of a scale that has no implied comparability with any other test or grading scale is important. It is important because SAT scores are intended to have a unique meaning for each college and university; there is no passing or failing score.

Reliability and Validity of the SAT

The question then becomes, "How well does the SAT do the job it is supposed to do?" Two criteria (that is, standards against which results are gauged) are most frequently used to answer this question about almost any test. In the jargon of psychometrics, they are reliability and validity. A test's *reliability* is a measure of the consistency with which it makes its measurements. A test's *validity* is a measure of how well those measurements do the job they are supposed to do.

The nature of the difference between these two criteria is sometimes described by reference to the statistically minded basketball coach who discovered that the average weight of his best players over the last 20 years had been 178 pounds. So the next season he picked his squad on the basis of weight. All the players weighed between 174 and 182 pounds and they lost every game. The point of the story, of course, is that while scales are consistent and reliable when it comes to measuring weights, they are not valid for choosing basketball players.

First, some words about the reliability of the SAT. A test is considered to be reliable if different editions, or forms, of that test are consistent in the measurements they make. Thus, for the SAT, reliability is a function of the answer to this question: "How likely would it be for a student who gets, say, a 520 on a particular form of the test to get a 520 if he or she had taken a different form of the test instead?" Psychometricians answer this question by referring to a student's hypothetical true score. I say "hypothetical" because a student's *true score* is the average of all the SAT scores that student would get if he or she took the test an infinite number of times on the same day, a feat only hypothetically possible. The degree to which a student's score on a given form of the test is liable to differ from the true score is the test's *error of measurement*. All tests have the error; tests simply aren't as consistent as weight scales in their measurements. The SAT's error of measurement is such that two times out of three, the score a student gets on a particular form, or edition, of the test will be within about 30 points one way or the other of the true score. That phenomenon may seem to suggest that SAT scores aren't all that reliable, but that's pretty reliable—indeed very reliable—for a test. If you won't take my word for it, listen to the statisticians. Whether or not they are fans of the SAT, they will at least reassure you that the test is reliable.

When you are considering the reliability and other technical aspects of the SAT, please keep in mind that it is the product of an era of rapid scientific progress and technical development. As such, in its early years it had an aura of mystery about it, a mystique that was the private property of the psychometricians (as the scientists beginning to explore this new means of human assessment were being called). The cloak of secrecy with which they surrounded the SAT continues to haunt the test today, despite the steps that have been taken to remove it.

Until the late 1950s, candidates were not allowed to know their own SAT scores. The scores were withheld on the grounds that their meaning was too complex to be interpreted by the psychometrically unwashed. Admissions officers could be taught to use the scores without having to understand them. As for students, what they didn't know couldn't hurt them. Callous-sounding today, yet an attitude that made reasonable sense in the 1920s, 1930s, and 1940s, when the psychometricians themselves were still feeling their way with this new approach to the assessment of human performance in the form of scholastic aptitude.

But as the test became more widely used, familiarity with the instrument bred not contempt but curiosity. The admissions officers who represented their institutions as members of the College Board began to wonder why students shouldn't know their scores. Wouldn't knowing their scores help them decide what colleges to apply to? It took nearly a decade of agonizing debate, following the separation of the technical, scientific, and research arm of the enterprise (ETS) from its constituent arm (CEEB), to come up with a final answer. In the end it was affirmative, and for more than 30 years students have known their scores.

As soon as the decision was made to release the scores, it became necessary to begin to remove at least some of the cloak of secrecy that had surrounded the test and to let students and the public know what the scores meant. The first and most ambitious step in that direction was the College Board's publication in 1971 of *The College Board Admissions Test Program: A technical report on research and development activities relating to the Scholastic Aptitude Test and Achievement Tests,* edited by William H. Angoff of the ETS staff. A technical manual in the best sense, it describes in detail how the SAT and the Achievement Tests were developed, administered, and researched. For the professional users of the tests it explains, among other things, the mysteries of equating, reliability, validity, and error of measurement. To hear the accusations of the critics that the SAT remained veiled in secrecy until the truth-in-testing folk came along in the 1980s, you'd never guess that such a document existed. But it has existed—it was revised, updated, and published in 1984 as *The College Board Technical Handbook for the Scholastic Aptitude Test and Achievement Tests,* edited at that time by Thomas F. Donlon.

Two other steps later took public account of the SAT's error of measurement. Small steps on the surface, they will undoubtedly turn out to have had greater public significance than did the publication of the technical manuals. Yet they were taken only after persistent efforts within the College Board constituency over a 20-year period, led by Emery Walker, then director of admissions at Claremont Mens College (later to become Claremont McKenna College), and Harvey Mudd College. The first step recognized the imprecision of SAT scores by rounding off the third digit to zero. Until that time students were getting scores down to the last digit—a 472, for instance, or a 638. Today those scores would be rounded off to 470 and 640, which admittedly sound less precise than 472 and 638.

But that step wasn't enough for Walker and his colleagues. Having eliminated the implied exactness of the third digit, they went after the error of measurement itself. As a result, a student's scores are reported in ranges that reflect the error of measurement. Reporting a 472 score in a 440 to 500 range instead of simply as 470 helps students gain a clearer understanding of the meaning of their test performance.

Finally, in understanding the concept of reliability, it is important to recognize that the SAT's high reliability is not a unique function of the stability of its score scale over time. Standardized tests that are regularly renormed can have, and some indeed do have, the same degree of reliability as the SAT does.

Nevertheless, that SAT scores are reliable and have the same meaning over time still doesn't prove they do the job they are supposed to do. Reliability is simply a measure of how consistently a test does what it does. Whether what it does is what it is supposed to do is another matter, one that concerns validity, the second major criterion by which tests are judged. The validity of the SAT, therefore, is a function of how well the measures it produces (its scores) predict the grades students will earn in college. Despite the test's error of measurement, it does its job of predicting surprisingly well. The College Board urges colleges to conduct what are called *validity studies* to determine how effectively the SAT predicts grades in their particular circumstances and to use SAT scores only to the degree that they help predict academic performance. Because each college draws from a different pool of candidates (that is, from a different set of schools with different grading standards) and each has professors who grade differently (remember those snap

courses), the predictions are bound to, and indeed do, vary from institution to institution.

In validity studies the colleges plot the SAT scores their enrolled
students received against the grades they earned in college. If SAT scores
predicted perfectly, the result would be a straight line (Figure 1). But
they don't predict perfectly, and the points plotted (that is, the points of
intersection of the line for the average grade earned by a given student
with the line for his or her SAT score) tend to be dispersed. If the points
are all over the lot (meaning that there was little or no relationship
between grades and scores and that, for instance, as many students with
high SAT scores earned low grades as earned high grades, and vice
versa), that would mean the SAT had no predictive usefulness for that
college and that the college shouldn't require the SAT for admission
(Figure 2).

Over the years many colleges have done many validity studies, and
most find that there is a marked relationship between SAT scores and
college grades—what the statisticians call a correlation. That is, they
find that the points of intersection between scores and grades cluster in

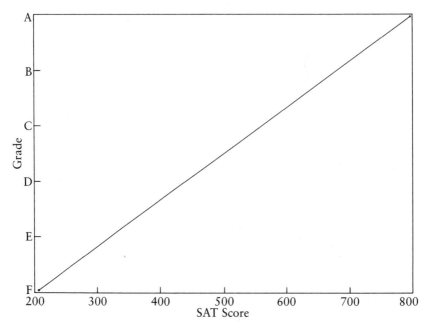

Figure 1. Perfect Correlation between SAT Scores and College Grades

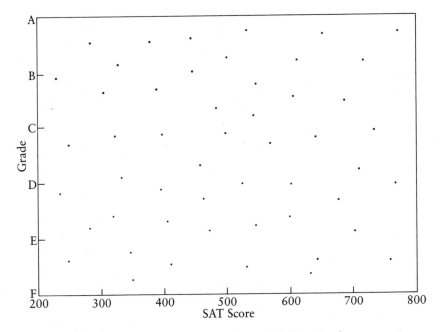

Figure 2. No Correlation between SAT Scores and College Grades

a roughly defined band, denser in the middle than along the perimeter, moving from the low-score–low-grade end of the graph upward toward the high-score–high-grade end.

Using standard statistical techniques, not psychometric mystique, the statisticians can then derive a mathematical formula for the hypothetical line that best represents that particular distribution of score-grade intersections (Figure 3, page 38).

That formula, produced on the basis of the SAT scores and college grades earned by students actually enrolled in a given college, can then be used by the college to predict the grades an applicant with a particular set of SAT scores is liable to earn in its classrooms. Of course, the narrower the band and the denser the points along the line produced by a given college's prediction formula, the better its predictions will be.

Despite the claims of some observers, colleges don't stop the prediction process at that point and make their decisions. In fact, they don't even start there. For most colleges the best single predictor of academic performance in college is academic performance in high school. But it, too, is far from perfect. (Remember Harvard's top-seventh experience

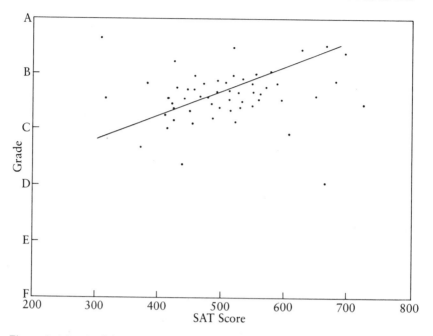

Figure 3. Meaningful Correlation between SAT Scores and College Grades

in Chapter 2.) Not only do schools differ in their overall grading standards, different teachers of the same subject in the same school often
grade differently. As a result, plotting school grades against college
grades usually produces a distribution (that is, a pattern of points of
intersection) not unlike the SAT score–college grade distribution. For
most colleges the school–college grade band tends to be a little narrower
and the cluster of points around the formula-produced line a little denser
than for the SAT score–college grade distribution, but not much.

The surprising thing to me is that for most colleges the SAT alone
predicts almost as well as do school grades alone. In other words, the
results of two hours of testing time do just about as well in predicting
academic success in higher education as do grades earned in three or
four years of secondary school—a sad commentary, I fear, on grading
pratices in the nation's schools. As a matter of fact, psychometric colleagues have suggested that if the phrase "for most colleges" was deleted
from the first sentence of this paragraph and the predictive power of the
SAT compared with that of school grades, the SAT would come out
ahead. Their suggestion makes sense to me in light of one study I recall

at one of the service academies several years ago. It demonstrated that SAT scores alone did a better job than school grades alone in predicting. They did so because the candidates for the Air Force Academy, Military Academy, and Naval Academy come from such a wide variety of schools each year. By contrast, many institutions attract applicants from similar if not always the same schools; in these institutions grades generally do a better job.

But while SAT scores and school grades are reasonably effective in predicting academic success in college when used alone, they do an even better job when used together. Here again, the statisticians have ways of combining the two to produce a single prediction formula reflecting a distribution of intersection points that form a narrower band and cluster closer to the prediction line than either SAT scores or grades alone do. In such circumstances, SAT scores represent a nationally comparable counterbalance to the effects of different grading practices in the schools. In the words frequently used by the College Board, they provide a "common currency" for measuring academic promise, and the able student from the school that grades "hard" can be assured of a fairer shake in competing with the less able student from the school that grades "easy" than he or she could without those SAT scores.

Despite this advantage, one of the favorite criticisms of the SAT is that the improvement in prediction it makes when combined with school grades is neither significant nor worth the time and money involved. I have jousted verbally on this subject in the *Harvard Education Review* (May 1985, August 1985, November 1985) with Professor James Crouse of the University of Delaware, one of the most serious and credible critics of the test. The reader who wants to delve more deeply into this matter is invited to review our exchange there, keeping in mind that while the *Harvard Education Review* did me the courtesy of permitting me to rebut Crouse's initial onslaught, it gave him the last word—the chance to re-rebut. So much for journalistic fair play!

In brief, while agreeing that there is some improvement in prediction from using SAT scores along with school grades, Crouse suggests that the improvement is minimal, that relatively few students would be affected, and that the use of school grades alone to predict academic success would produce just as good a class as using both SAT scores and grades. My response, crafted with the help of psychometrically sophisticated colleagues, was based on the assertions that the populations of students Crouse used to make his case weren't appropriate, that the admissions process didn't and doesn't work the way he apparently thinks it does (selective colleges don't simply rate students according to academic promise as indicated by the combination of test scores and school grades and then start selecting from the top down until the class is filled), and that any change that would have an adverse effect on students from schools with strict grading standards would be "significant." So there, in effect, is my last word.

One other aspect of the SAT's validity bears mention here. For reasons of currency and convenience, most validity studies are conducted using freshman grades as the criterion against which test scores and school grades are validated. This practice leaves both, the former in particular, open to the charge that they don't predict later academic success in college, and people are prone to level the charge. There are two problems with that assertion. First, freshman grades are excellent predictors of senior grades. Second, the studies using senior grades as the criterion demonstrate that SAT scores are just about as good at predicting them as they are at predicting freshman grades.

Homoscedasticity

Although reliability and validity are the most frequently discussed bases on which tests like the SAT are judged, there are other, even more technical aspects of the assessment process. For example, there is *homoscedasticity,* not to mention its obverse, *heteroscedasticity,* statistical concepts that measure how well or how poorly scores on a given test discriminate or make distinctions about student performance on different parts of a score scale. For instance, scores between 400 and 700 display more homoscedasticity (make more effective distinctions) than those between 200 and 400 or between 700 and 800. The test is designed to do so because that is the range within which most students score. And because they invariably do so, the SAT has to have more items that produce scores in that range in order to sort out the students whose scores bunch up in it—that is, to discriminate among them. Because fewer candidates score between 700 and 800, and because those who do are so bright to begin with that it is relatively less important that they be sorted out as precisely as those who cluster in the middle of the scale, SAT scores have less homoscedasticity in the 700-to-800 range than do scores between 400 and 700. At the same time, because distinctions among candidates at this level of performance (700 to 800) have more significance in the selective admissions process that the SAT was designed to serve than those, say, between 200 and 300, the test developers take into account the need to ensure that SAT scores between 700 and 800 at the top end of the scale have more homoscedasticity than do scores beween 200 and 300.

In composing the foregoing lay exposition of the concept of homo-scedasticity, I couldn't help being reminded of the pleasure noted earlier that those of us new to the College Board staff in the mid-1950s took in displaying the knowledge we were then acquiring about the SAT.

Technical Development of the SAT

The facts that each edition, or form, of the SAT is reliable, has validity, displays appropriate degrees of homoscedasticity along its score scale, and produces scores that have the same meaning as the scores on any other edition are in large part functions of the technical precision with which each form is developed. The items for each one are assembled according to exceedingly exact specifications. For example, there must be equivalent numbers of each item type (antonyms, reading compre-hension, quantitative comparisons, and so forth) at specified levels of difficulty. As a prior step, individual items are written to meet precise requirements and then pretested to see if indeed they operate at the intended level of difficulty.

Consider the item that is meant to discriminate between above-average and below-average performance on the SAT. Now assume that when the experimental item is administered, half the candidates get it right and half get it wrong. Good item? Not necessarily. If lots of candidates who score above average on proven items get it wrong and lots who score below average get it right, then the item isn't doing the kind of discriminating it is supposed to and it is rejected. Only if more of the above-average scorers get it right and more of the below-average scorers get it wrong will the item be used operationally in a regular edition of the SAT.

Items that discriminate at the upper end of the score scale are harder to construct than those of middle-level difficulty. That is so because questions designed to probe higher-order thinking skills (that is, in the SAT, to measure more highly developed verbal and mathematical skills) are difficult to construct, and it is only through pretesting that such difficulties can be addressed. Only if a difficult item performs consistently for high-scoring students (that is, they aren't thrown off by any ambi-guity and select the same best answer) is it included in an operational form of the test. Therefore it turns out to be fortunate that although more difficult questions are hard to construct, fewer of them are needed in the SAT because of the lesser need for homoscedasticity at that level.

In any event, the need to include questions of varying difficulty in each form of the SAT sets the stage for two of the more valid student criticisms of the test. Because the bunching of questions of middle-level difficulty around the center of the scale leaves room for relativley fewer items at the upper and lower ends, students performing at those extremes find themselves frustrated. Bright students are forced to spend most of their time answering questions that are really too simple for them, while those who are able to deal effectively with only a very few questions find themselves frustrated by phalanx after phalanx of questions that are beyond their comprehension.

In this situation we come to a circumstance in which developments in software have outstripped hardware capacity—not the technical capacity of computers to handle the software program but the numerical availability of terminals to handle the test takers. Psychometricians have known for some time how to deal with the frustrations of too many hard questions or too many easy ones. The process is known as "tracking." A student starts with a question of average difficulty. If it is answered correctly, the student is routed to a more difficult item; if answered incorrectly, to an easier one. Then the process is repeated. If the question is answered correctly, the student is routed to a still more difficult item; if incorrectly, to an easier one. With relatively few questions, the candidate can be routed to a set of items on that section of the scale that appropriately challenges his or her developed abilities in verbal and mathematical reasoning. In turn, those items produce a score that is at the very least equivalent to what the student would earn on a regular form of the SAT and do the job in a much shorter period of time than current administrations of the test require.

The obstacle to using this approach via paper-and-pencil technology is its gross inefficiency. To do the job right would require the use of test booklets of massive size, containing a majority of questions a given candidate would never use. It is a process, however, that modern computer technology can easily handle. The problem is that there simply isn't enough computer hardware (terminals) to accommodate the hundreds of thousands of candidates who now take the test on a given date. When people ask me how I could continue to work happily for a single employer for more than 31 years, I use this example to make the points that the challenges always keep changing and the new problems posed in these fluid circumstances kept my work at the College Board from ever becoming dull or routine.

Because the problems kept coming thick and fast, my speculation about the future tended generally to be short-run. But there was one occasion, in 1967, when I took a chance on looking ahead. It was at a colloquium on "College Admissions Policies for the 1970s," convened at Interlochen, Michigan. Using the now archaic "console" instead of "terminal" in a discussion of the "eternal verities of college admissions" in a paper entitled "A Look from the Twenty-first Century," I foresaw the computer hardware supply problems in these terms:

> Verity the third: College Board test dates will always be unsatisfactory to somebody. A generation ago, the burning issue was whether the then proposed November date would interfere with interscholastic football games. Today, Johnny's problem is that the testing consoles are all scheduled during the school days for the next month and he can get access to one only on the night of the dramatic club performance.

Today's shortage of terminals poses a challenge that is typical of what made my life with the SAT so fascinating. The challenge is whether to continue to rely on current practices until the supply of computer hardware catches up or to seek some interim solution using what I have called paper-and-pencil technology. One such approach might be to use ·tracking by parts instead of by items. Each SAT form would consist of three pairs of subsections, or parts, of increasing difficulty, perhaps as follows: A-level, hard and producing scores from 500 to 800; B-level, medium difficulty with scores from 350 to 650; C-level, easy with scores from 200 to 500. Each candidate would be instructed to start with a B-level subsection. On completing that, the candidate would be instructed to move, depending on what he or she thought about his or her performance at the B-level, to either an A-level or a C-level subsection. On

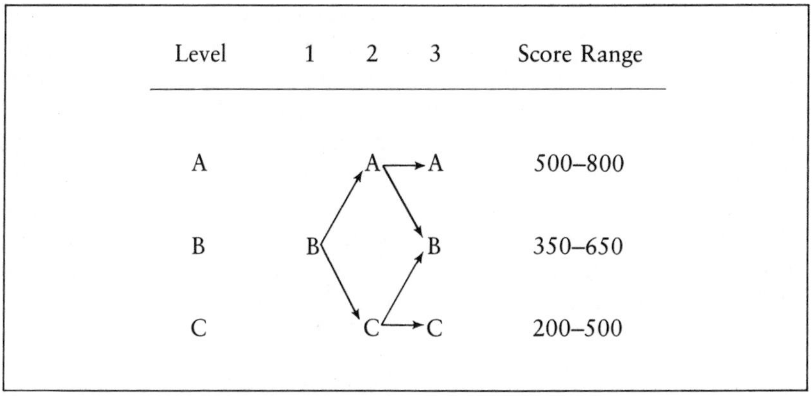

Figure 4. Possible SAT Subsections

completing this second subsection, the candidate would have the option of staying at the same level for the third subsection or returning to the B-level (that is, for the candidate who chose A-level in the second round and found it too taxing, moving back to B-level, or, for the candidate who chose C-level and found it overly easy, moving back up to B-level in the third round). Perhaps the diagram in Figure 4 will help.

Following this procedure, the candidate would be able to make a decision about the difficulty level and concentrate on questions that would generate verbal and mathematical scores appropriate to his or her developed abilities. Whether such an approach, or some variation of it, would prove to be practical, however, remains to be determined.

One matter that would have to be explored is *equating,* the process that ensures that scores on different forms, or editions, of the SAT are comparable. Currently each edition of the SAT contains an equating section, consisting of items of varying difficulty that have been administered previously and provide a psychometric anchor to earlier forms.

Criticism and Security of the SAT

The twin needs to include both experimental and equating sections in regularly administered forms of the SAT lead to two issues. One has to do with the generation of criticism and the other with the need for security. One of the frequently heard criticisms is that the process of development is circular: all that the scores on one form of the test really do is predict performance on other forms and have little to do with academic success in college. My response to that charge is to point to the high degree to which SAT scores correlate with grades earned in both school and college; in the case of grades in college, I point to the SAT scores' high degree of predictive validity (the extent to which they predict college grades). Indeed, one of the things that continues to amaze me is that SAT scores earned in fewer than three hours of testing are as effective as they are in predicting academic performance in college, particularly when compared with the predictive power of grades earned in secondary school over three or four years. For most higher education institutions, SAT scores don't do quite as good a job as school grades, in large part because, as noted earlier, most colleges and universities each year draw their applicants from pools of schools that, in the aggregate, maintain roughly comparable grading standards from year to year. But for some colleges, SAT scores alone do a better predicting job than do school grades alone. Remember the above reference to the service academies? This relatively high degree of *validity* on the part of

SAT scores says something about the *reliability* of secondary school teachers' grades. And what it says is that the academic standards of the nation's schools vary widely. Thus, I would argue that the critics who say that SAT scores are meaningless because the testing process is a closed circle are just plain wrong.

As for security, if items in either the equating or experimental sections became known, obviously they couldn't be fairly used in subsequent forms, which is, after all, their intended use. It is to protect those items and, equally important, to keep secret all items on any form of the SAT that is yet to be administered that ETS goes to great length to ensure the security of test items.

This process has been severely affected in two contexts: the long-standing controversy over the efficacy of coaching for the SAT and the more recent complications created by the so-called truth-in-testing legislation introduced in New York State in 1979. The answers to the question "Does coaching work?" have been evolving, never, as one colleague put it, "the last word, only the latest one." The College Board's trustees first issued a statement on the subject in the late 1950s. Based on evidence available at that time, the statement was unequivocal in its assertion that coaching for the SAT didn't help, although it did suggest that some review of mathematics might be helpful if a student hadn't been exposed to the subject recently. That position and all later modifications of it have been predicated on the assumption that test items would be secure, that "coaching" meant training students to answer questions similar to those that appear on the SAT, and that coached students would not have access to test questions they would be asked on a form of the SAT yet to be administered. This last assumption, unfortunately, isn't always valid. There are cheats in the world and some of them have used all kinds of nefarious schemes to get their hands on "live" SAT questions and even full forms of the test itself.

In one instance where a group of candidates apparently obtained a form of the SAT before it was administered, ETS properly refused to report the scores without calling attention to the alleged irregularity. The candidates' parents sued and lost; ETS's procedures in such cases are thorough and fair. In the course of the legal proceedings I was deposed by the counsel for the students. In preparing me for the deposition, the College Board's counsel had only one bit of advice. "As president you're not expected to know all the answers to all the questions and probably don't anyway. So don't try to answer questions to which you don't know the answer." I did my thing, and afterward, on the way down in the elevator, counsel paid me what I consider one of the most reassuring compliments I have ever received. "George," he said, "never have I heard anyone be so vague about so much!" But that episode involved cheating as differentiated from coaching. Obviously, if students get their hands on questions ahead of time from a coaching school, they are going to give lots of right answers. That's not what the College Board trustees' statements in regard to coaching have been about.

Coaching for the SAT

The original trustee position on coaching has had to be gradually modified over the years as circumstances have changed and new research evidence has become available. One of the reasons that it was comforting to be so unequivocal in the 1950s was the realization that the trustees' position would serve to protect candidates from poor families who couldn't afford to pay for special coaching. But as more research results became available and differences in the nature of the coaching or special preparation became more fully understood, the College Board's position has had to be altered to take account of the new circumstances. Because those findings always lagged behind the critics' perceptions of the benefits of coaching, it was always a challenge not to appear too defensive. Probably the most far-reaching single development on this score was the advent of the so-called truth-in-testing legislation, which served to put literally hundreds of used SAT items in the public domain for all to see and practice on. Currently, the College Board's position is a complex but studied one. What really continues to bother me, however, is not the issue of whether or not special preparation for the SAT, whatever form it takes, works, but the fact that such score gains as may be the result of coaching don't mean much at the highly selective colleges, where factors other than SAT scores play such an important role in admissions decisions.

If the College Board appeared to be dragging its feet, many of the coaching school entrepreneurs appeared to be engaging in flights of fancy. One of the more respectable, for instance, admitted that what he reported as "average score gains" for his customers were really only the averages of those whose scores went up and did not include the scores of those whose scores went down. Other coaching school proprietors will report average gains not on the basis of performances on the regular SAT under normal circumstances but on what students do on tests "like the SAT," which the coaching schools have developed themselves and for which their special preparation is particularly well suited. Still others will report that "some" of their clients have gained as much as, say, 250 points. "Come to us," they say, "and gain over 200 points." What is so troublesome about that approach is that the unsuspecting public is led to believe that high-scoring students are as liable to benefit as are low-scoring students. And that just isn't so. The statistical chances are much higher that a student with low scores, say between 200 and 400, will go up when that student takes the test a second time even without coaching. On the other hand, a student with scores at the upper end of the scale, say 650 to 800, is likely to see scores go down even with coaching. Again, the irony is that the low-scoring student isn't likely to change his or her chances of admission to a selective college with a suspect score gain on the SAT and that the high-scoring student isn't going to find his or her chances of admission to an Ivy League institution influenced by a few points on the SAT. Does coaching help? The experience of undergraduates at Harvard suggests that it doesn't.

Truth-in-Testing Legislation

The second context in which the test development process has more recently been severely tested is the effects of the so-called truth-in-testing legislation, which calls for the public disclosure of all items from SAT forms used to generate scores, after the tests are administered. Not only has truth-in-testing legislation resulted in the need to generate many more test items (because disclosed items can't be reused), it has also complicated the pretesting and equating processes. Fortunately, psychometrics is an evolving science and new ways of constructing and administering tests are constantly being developed and, ultimately, a solution may be found. For a while, a technique known as item response theory (IRT) was believed to hold promise of making elimination of the need for equating sections possible. (I was able to store it in my vocabulary of psychometric terms by relating it to the New York City subway system and its Interborough Rapid Transit line, the IRT.) But, like the subways, it isn't doing the job.

Hardware for Scoring the SAT

As suggested earlier, the application of the software concepts of reliability, validity, homoscedasticity, and equating has been made easier over the years by the development of ever more sophisticated hardware. My appreciation of that evolutionary process was enhanced by prior association with one of the most interesting characters I have ever met—Arch W. Shaw, a Chicago entrepreneur in the grand style. Shaw published the first business magazine in the United States and helped underwrite the start-up of the Kellogg cereal enterprise. He was one of Herbert Hoover's closest friends and knew Carl Sandburg well enough to get him to deliver a lecture for me at the North Shore Country Day School in suburban Chicago on Lincoln's birthday. But the base for his fortune was built on a simple revolutionary idea. Observing the practical utility of library cards in keeping track of books, he came up with the idea of adapting them for use in bookkeeping and accounting in place of the bound journals and ledgers then in use. That adaptation opened the way to the "keysort" concept, where information was entered by punching out the cards in appropriate places; the cards were then sorted by running spindles through holes in a template into the deck of cards to select those with the desired information. That approach was soon replaced by the familiar IBM card, on which information was entered by punching out the cards in the appropriate slots and processed by running the cards through an IBM machine. Today, of course, cards are passé and information is now entered directly into the computer for processing.

Scoring of the SAT followed much the same line of development. At first a template was prepared with holes punched out in patterns that would match the entries for the correct answers on an answer sheet. The template would then be placed over each answer sheet and the right answers counted, answer sheet by answer sheet, for each test taken. Faster than grading examinations by hand, this method still took an inordinate amount of time. To speed things up, the responses on an answer sheet were punched into an IBM card and the cards then run through a scoring machine. But as the number of students taking the test increased, this method, too, proved too time-consuming, and mark-sense scoring was introduced. This scoring technique required that test takers use special pencils with "lead" in them that would give off an electrical charge to activate feelers in the scoring machine. But again, technology was waiting with a still more rapid and even more accurate approach, optical scoring. Today literally thousands of answers sheets per minute are "read" by optical scanners. And now, as already noted, the technology (if not the supply of hardware) exists that makes it possible to do away with the answer sheet entirely and have the test taker enter his or her answers directly into the computer.

I observed these changes in the hardware with interest, always able to understand what the machine or computer did but, with one exception, never fully aware of how. The one exception was a machine they used in the mark-sense era. Educational Testing Service had to be sure that those special mechanical pencils with the special lead it sent out to the testing centers had enough lead in them, and ETS used an upside-down electric eggbeater to do the job. The eraser was put in one beater hole, which drove the lead up, and if there was enough, the eraser was then put in the other, reverse beater hole, which pulled the lead back down. That operation I could understand. Otherwise I made a practice of not learning how hardware operated. A little knowledge about a piece of mechanical equipment can get you into a lot of trouble.

Despite the technical advances made in the administration of the SAT, the old template approach remains in use. There was and always is the danger that the hardware will go haywire. To guard against that possibility, samples of machine-scored answer sheets are regularly subjected to template scrutiny as a quality check. It is used, too, when a student or a school or college representative questions whether the student's scores from a particular SAT administration are accurate. Invariably they are. But once in a while . . .

On one occasion a very bright young lad from a particularly strong high school received scores in the 200s. His school counselor questioned the accuracy of the scores ETS had reported. In making hand-scoring checks, the template is routinely moved off by one question (or answer) to see if the candidate might have gotten off the track by one place somewhere along the line. In this instance, the woman doing the checking discovered a nearly perfect pattern of answers. That meant that the young man would have scored in the 700s, not the 200s, if he had marked his answer sheet properly. Educational Testing Service reported this finding to the counselor who had initiated the inquiry. He in turn told the boy what had happened. The boy wasn't surprised. His family wanted him to go to an Ivy League college that required the SAT. He wanted to go to a public university that didn't. He figured that one way of getting his own way would be to score very low on the SAT and that an even better way of doing so than marking answers at random would be to mark the correct ones off by one place on the answer sheet. The reported scores remained the same and he went to his non-Ivy institution.

There are a couple of points to this story. First, the scores were the property of the young man, not of his school or of his parents; that is the contract the College Board makes with its candidates. Second, no matter how far technology takes the testing process, there will always need to be human verification of what the hardware turns out.

And there are a couple of points to this chapter. As a product of science and technology applied to an art form, the SAT is neither as precise as some believe nor as flawed as others appear to believe. But it does have the great advantage of having remained constant in the seas of economic, political, social, demographic, and educational ferment since World War II. Because little else did, the SAT provided a uniquely stable base from which to observe the changes that were taking place.

CHAPTER 4

Decline and *EQuality*

The national average Scholastic Aptitude Test (SAT) scores went down in the 1960s and 1970s. That decline was directly responsible not only for my most interesting single assignment at the College Board but also for what I consider two of the most significant achievements of my presidency. The assignment was staff coordinator for the Advisory Panel on the Scholastic Aptitude Test Score Decline. The achievements were the launching of the Educational EQuality Project and the Commission on Precollege Guidance and Counseling. They came about in this way.

The SAT Score Decline

In 1975 Gene Maeroff, then an education writer for *The New York Times,* observed that the national average SAT scores had been going down steadily since 1963. His front-page story to that effect was published on March 17, 1975. That simple statement of Maeroff's observation masks a complicated set of circumstances. A few years earlier the College Board had begun collecting biographical data voluntarily from candidates registering for the SAT. Because the data the students supplied in the aggregate looked interesting, we began publishing each fall a composite profile of the preceding year's high school senior class. In the information we provided were those seniors' average SAT scores. Checking back, Maeroff observed that the scores had been going down, and he wondered what they had been doing before 1970. We couldn't tell him exactly, because we hadn't begun collecting and reporting information by graduating class until then. Available, however, were the average SAT scores for all candidates taking the test in any given year—that is, for sophomores, juniors, seniors, and adults all lumped together. What those score data revealed was that the average scores of all SAT takers had been going down since 1963, and Maeroff correctly surmised that despite the lack of exact comparability in the figures, the average SAT scores of the nation's high school seniors had been declining since 1963.

Investigation by Advisory Panel

That finding got the nation's attention by providing statistical evidence of what many people were already beginning to suspect. The nation's schools were in trouble. In the face of such an inference drawn from the evidence supplied by one of their instruments, the College Board and Educational Testing Service (ETS) decided that a careful look should be taken at the reason for the decline. Was the inference correct, and if so, why? To take that look, the two organizations appointed the inevitable blue-ribbon panel, in this instance the Advisory Panel on the Scholastic Aptitude Test Score Decline. What wasn't inevitable about this panel and what really distinguished it were its makeup and its leadership. Its 21 members included three nationally recognized high school teachers—one each in social studies, mathematics, and English; five distinguished university professors—in psychology, education, sociology, science, and statistics; four well-known secondary school administrators—a high school principal, a big-city school superintendent, a chief state school officer, and the head of the National Association of Secondary School Principals; two proven higher education administrators—a college president and a university vice president; an expert in educational television; a foundation chief executive; the head of a firm specializing in human assessment; and three other educational statesmen in the persons of Ralph W. Tyler, Benjamin S. Bloom, and Harold Howe II, former United States commissioner of education, who served as the panel's vice chairman. The chairman, Willard Wirtz, former United States secretary of labor, was a statesman, period, and one of the most perceptive, thoughtful, and literate gentlemen I have ever known.

Working with this diverse group of gifted individuals and their chairman over the two years of the panel's life was a joy. The problem they were dealing with was especially complex, involving a wide range

X of social, educational, technical, and scientific issues. Watching them sort out those issues and then come to consensus under the skillful leadership of Bill Wirtz was a privilege.

Technical Issues

Early on in their deliberations the panelists decided there were really two considerations they had to deal with—a reasonably finite set of technical or test-related issues and an almost infinite variety of other possibilities that were being advanced as causes of the decline. Although the panel members proceeded to work simultaneously on both sets, they chose to concentrate first on the technical issues in order to make sure that the decline was not an artifact of the test itself. Here the panel relied heavily on the expertise of its mathematically, statistically, scientifically, and psychometrically oriented members. The first question they attacked in this arena was whether the decline in SAT scores had resulted from the test's having become progressively harder over the years. As became their practice in such matters, the panel members asked for research to be done; reviewed proposals from staff and others for doing it; approved, rejected, or suggested modifications in the submissions; authorized the research to go forward; and then took the findings into account in coming to consensus. Twenty-seven studies and background papers, commissioned by the panel, constitute 560-pages of appendixes to its basic report, *On Further Examination*, published by the College Board in 1977.

To investigate the difficulty level of the test, the panel requested two studies to supplement the study on the stability of the SAT score scale that had been completed just two years earlier, in 1972. One study explored the subject by comparing students' performance on pairs of 1963 and 1973 editions of the test. The second looked at the possibility that the questions repeated in the equating sections of the test may have become obsolete. These studies, plus one on the validity of the test, prompted the panel to conclude:

> In general, and after checking the technical and psychometric aspects of the SAT thoroughly, the panel finds consistent confirmation that the score decline has not resulted from changes in the testing instrument. The scaling and equating and item-obsolescence procedures that are followed are reliable, and the predictive validity of the test is slightly higher than it was before. The standard established in this test has remained substantially constant, and the decline the scores reflect is, if anything, slightly larger than the reported record indicates (*On Further Examination*, 10).

In other words, the decline was real and other reasons for it needed to be explored. It was when this conclusion began to take shape on the panel's horizon that the fun began.

On Further Examination is in five parts. The last part, "Summing Up," starts this way:

> If you turned to this concluding section for a quick and easy understanding of the panel's views on the decline of test scores, you are indulging in a practice like some of the educational shortcuts that may have contributed to the decline. This is a complex subject, and our views of it are filled with nuances, qualifications, and some doubts. The quality of our judgments is conditioned by the quality of the evidence. Without a reading of the report, the summary may suggest a simplicity that is unfair to an important subject (44).

It is with this caution in mind that I advise anyone who wishes to explore the SAT score decline in any depth to read both the panel's report and its appendixes. My impressionistic recollections of a fascinating exercise follow.

Other Issues

Having satisfied itself that the meaning of the test's scores had remained constant, the panel turned its attention to one of the other more intuitively plausible causes of the decline. Had the population of candidates taking the test changed in any significant way? One thing was clear from the start. The numbers taking the SAT each year had grown considerably. During the 1960s those numbers had tripled. What was not clear was whether the mix had changed as well. The College Board had not begun collecting biographical data about SAT candidates until the early 1970s, and the downward drift had started almost a decade earlier. One of the most complex and ambitious projects commissioned on behalf of the panel was designed to explore this issue.

Fortunately, the availability of data from two earlier studies made this exploration possible. As noted in the "Annotated List of Studies and Papers" in the panel's report, "Two major social science research efforts—Project TALENT in 1960 and the National Longitudinal Study in 1972—obtained extensive data on ability and other significant characteristics for national probability samples of high school seniors" (55). Data from these studies, together with data for SAT takers who had participated in Project TALENT, demonstrated that there had indeed been marked changes in the populations of high school seniors, college entrants, and SAT takers between 1960 and 1972. This finding, supported by information made available by the American Council on Education (ACE) and the American College Testing Program (ACT), led the panel ultimately to conclude that "most—probably two-thirds to three-fourths—of the SAT score decline between 1963 and about 1970 was related to the 'compositional' changes in the group of students taking this college entrance examination" (45).

I returned to this finding over and over again in the early and mid-1980s as the school reform movement was gathering steam. While most observers were interpreting what had happened in the nation's schools as failure, I used the panel's finding as evidence of success. My reasoning went like this: The very first table in *On Further Examination* shows that between the years 1963–64 and 1964–65, the number of 18-year-olds in the country jumped from 2,763,000 to 3,804,000 and then stayed well above the 3.5 million mark. As a footnote to that table observes, "This figure, which appears so high as to suggest error, is confirmed by reference to birth statistics (on comparable fiscal year basis) for 1945–46 and 1946–47" (4). What these figures reflected, of course, was that veterans from World War II were being reunited with their wives and were beginning to raise families that had had to be postponed during the war years. That conflict had another, related legacy as well, the GI Bill. It served to raise the educational expectations of an entire generation, the parents of those baby boomers who began to think about college for themselves in the early 1960s. The point I stressed was that the demands on the schools multiplied rapidly not only in terms of sheer numbers but also in terms of the proportions of those numbers who were staying in school longer and considering the possibility of going to college.

The baby boom wasn't the only source of numerical pressures on the schools. In 1954 the Supreme Court handed down its landmark decision in *Brown* v. *Board of Education*. In its aftermath, as the civil rights movement gathered momentum, more and more minority youngsters, particularly blacks at that point, also began staying in school longer and thinking about college. As far as the schools were concerned, I've always considered it a tribute to the ingenuity of the American people and their commitment to education that the nation's schools didn't collapse under the sheer weight of numbers imposed on them. That the schools weathered the double influx of the baby boomers and minorities is a story of a success, not of failure.

Pursuing these data further in terms of the information that began to be available about SAT candidates in the early 1970s, the panel discovered that the composition of the SAT candidate population had pretty much stabilized after 1972 but that the score decline had continued. The baby boom had run its course and the civil rights movement had had its fullest numerical effect on the schools. Yet the decline persisted, and the panel came to think of the 12- to 14-year slide as a two-part phenomenon. But while the panel was confident that the decline was real and that the first part of it could be accounted for in large measure by changes in the population of students taking the test, its members were far less certain about what was responsible for the second half of the decline, from about 1970 to 1977, and for the unexplained one-fourth to one-third of the first phase.

Much of the uncertainty was caused by the difficulty of subjecting most of the hypotheses, then being advanced to explain the decline, to statistical or other measurable analysis. But a few hypotheses could be, most of them relating directly to the test itself. In the aggregate the analyses confirmed that the decline was what the panel referred to as "pervasive"—for example, that the decline had occurred among high- as well as low-scoring students, in private as well as public schools, and in traditional as well as experimental schools. Another analysis, relying on student financial aid data in relation to SAT scores, demonstrated "an increased percentage of students coming from lower-income families before 1972, but no significant change since that time" (61). This finding was consistent not only with the two-phase interpretation of the decline but also with the fact that because students from low-income families tend to do less well on the SAT than those from more affluent families, more of them in the test-taking population would tend to bring the national average test scores down. (As noted in Chapter 5, there are a variety of reasons for this, such as attendance at schools with limited resources, having parents with lower levels of education, fewer books in the home, etc.)

During the panel's deliberations another explanation was advanced that lent itself to statistical analysis and has continued to surface from time to time ever since. Offered then, and repeated later, by Robert B. Zajonc, it suggested that the decline was caused by changes in family size. According to Zajonc's theory, which has been confirmed in other settings with other tests, children born later into a family do less well in school and on tests than those born earlier. Because family size was growing during the period of the decline, Zajonc speculated that the presence of more later-born children from larger families in the SAT population caused the lower scores. On the basis of research conducted for it in relation to that population, however, the panel concluded that, "while the Zajonc hypothesis seems sound, it could only account for a small portion of the total SAT score decline" (56). (Although the panel's report does not make reference to the possibility, I recall being intrigued at the time by the observation that when there get to be eight or more children in a family, the test performance of the youngest ones begins to improve as the early-born children apparently begin to take a hand in their youngest siblings' upbringing.)

The question still remained: if the test's meaning had remained constant and if changes in the population accounted for less than half the decline, what other explanations might there be? Two more possibilities, both having to do with the kind of preparation students had been getting in high school, also lent themselves to statistical scrutiny.

First, what about the course patterns the students had been following? After reviewing the available data, the panel found that those patterns had changed and that there had been an effect. For instance (I emphasize "for instance"), the panel noted that its "net conclusion is that there is almost certainly some causal relationship between the shift in the high schools from courses in the traditional disciplines to newer electives and the decline in SAT-verbal scores," but hastened in the same sentence to "warn against any oversimplistic interpretation of this finding" (26). In the next paragraph the panel warns, "In our view, 'returning to the basics' would be wrong unless it included full reappraisal of what the right basics are. . . ." (26). That thought profoundly influenced my thinking in regard to the development of the Basic Academic Competencies in the Educational EQuality Project, discussed later in this chapter.

The panelists also said, "It is perhaps relevant that there has not been the proliferation of electives in high school mathematics that has been characteristic of the verbal skills area" (28), but again they issued a caution, this time against overinterpreting this last observation as *the* reason for the greater falling off of SAT-verbal scores in the latter stages of the overall decline.

The second hypothesis subjected to rigorous research analysis in relation to the preparation students were receiving in high school was that the standards of performance to which they were being held were deteriorating. One of the major research efforts commissioned on the panel's behalf explored this possibility in terms of the difficulty of the reading levels found in widely used primary and secondary school textbooks. Here in particular, as in the panel's report generally, no brief summary can do justice to the complexity of the issues involved.

With that caveat, I note two passages from *On Further Examination* relating to the study by Jeanne Chall and colleagues at the Harvard Graduate School of ·Education. First: "The study develops in statistical form the fact that a constantly increasing percentage of textbook space is taken up by pictures, wider margins, shorter words and sentences and paragraphs; the amount of exposition is decreasing, the amount of narrative going up" (31). Second: "The study [which used 'various indices of difficulty and challenge,' including the Dale-Chall Readability Formula and Chall's Reading Stages] confirms what we know from the reports of textbook writers enjoined by publishers to 'make it simple' and from the echoing reactions of better students that what they are reading at school is 'simpler stuff than we read in the newspapers' " (31). In all likelihood, the panel found, the educational standards to which students were being held during the period of the decline, and before, weren't what they used to be.

There was abundant evidence to this effect in a variety of other contexts, but such evidence, even that relating to course patterns and textbook difficulty, the panel was inclined to characterize as "circumstantial." One of the appendixes to the panel's report, "List of Hypotheses Advanced to Explain the SAT Score Decline," lists 87 hypotheses, including those already described. As to the charge of lower standards, the list contains such entries as the increased use of "audiovisual equipment," a "decline in modern foreign language study," the "stress on independent study," "automatic promotion," "less homework," the "encroachment of the labor movement on the teaching profession" resulting in "fewer contact hours between pupils and teachers," and the "influence of the soft pedagogical left." The panel refrained from direct comment on many of the possibilities advanced but in the end did come to the point of reporting that "in general we find that there *has* been a lowering of educational standards and that this *is* a factor in the decline in SAT scores" (31).

The panel also found, however, that these different standards had evolved within a changing environment and social context. The influence of one such major change continues to intrigue me. It was the advent of television. Mass availability of that medium first occurred during the years when the students whose SAT scores produced the decline were growing up and going to school. The entry in the "Annotated List of Studies and Papers" regarding the 1976 paper by panel member Wilbur Schramm on "Television and the Test Scores" begins with this sentence: "There is no conclusive evidence as yet that television has been a sufficient cause for decline in test scores, although it may be one of several elements in a complex causal system" (62). It ends with this: "The trend of the evidence is that television viewing patterns belong to a group of strong variables that interact with each other and with school (and, therefore, test) performance, probably with negative effect" (62).

Although I continue to agree with this last observation, I do not believe (and, I suspect, most of the panelists would in retrospect agree) that this finding necessarily has long-term negative connotations. Although many commentators on the SAT score decline perceived television as "the thief of time," I see it, in postpanel parlance, as a "new means of processing information," one that opens up myriad new ways for people, young and old alike, to learn. My point is this: Men and women were able to accommodate to the advent of the printing press and to the educational opportunities it opened up; I am convinced that the same thing can happen in television. Human beings don't have to give up anything to take advantage of the learning potential of this new technology. All they have to do is learn how to take advantage of it.

This topic subsequently came up again in the process of defining the six Basic Academic Competencies for the Educational EQuality Project; later in this chapter there is a fuller treatment of this development in that context. The point to be made here is that there was a proposed competency, "observing," which didn't quite make it as a seventh basic competency. Most people saw it then either as a skill related primarily to the visual arts and the laboratory sciences or as part of what came to be known as the "reasoning" competency. I saw it, and still see it, as a separate skill related not only to art and science and reasoning but to the visual media like film and television as well. There is, I am sure, a competency in the processing of visual information that is somehow different from that involved in reading and listening and reasoning, one that needs further exploration in the teaching-learning process. The panel's report put it more felicitously: "Traditional education and television are currently out of kilter, and the stakes in correcting this quickly seem to us higher than is generally realized. Yet if television's abuses have made it a 'vast wasteland,' its potential is of becoming learning's most fertile grove" (37).

But if television was still primarily a distraction, it was only one of many influences. The panel's report calls attention to a number of factors in a variety of contexts: more one-parent families, more working mothers, the military draft, the unpopular war in Vietnam, political assassinations, Watergate, the threat of atomic war. The panelists wondered about the effect of these and other distractions on student motivation. As the panel put it, this was "a period, covered by the score decline, which has been an unusually hard one to grow up in" (43).

In leaving the topic of the score decline at this point, I am compelled to return to the caveat I voiced early in this chapter. My approximately 20 paragraphs on the subject in no way do justice to the more than 270 (75 pages) in *On Further Examination* or to the 560 pages of the 27 appendixes. The report itself is a masterpiece of clarity and purpose, of literary style and cohesion, composed in its entirety by the Advisory Panel chairman, Willard Wirtz. I only hope that my brief references to that work and the elegance of the quotations from it will prompt readers to revisit one of the most important and truly seminal documents about education in the United States to appear in this century.

Addressing the Challenge

The report was certainly seminal and originative as far as the College Board was concerned. It called attention to the lowering of standards in the schools and challenged the association to take action appropriate to its mission. Unfortunately in one way—although, as it turned out, fortunately in another—circumstances intervened that delayed our decision about exactly what to do. What was unfortunate was the loss of time. Sidney P. Marland, Jr., who was president of the College Board during the panel's life and on the occasion of the formal presentation of its report to the College Board and ETS, was committed to mounting a response to the panel's challenge. I worked closely with him in trying to figure out just how broad the follow-up effort ought to be. Should we attempt to embrace all aspects of the need for reform or focus on one or two aspects? And what form should our response take as a consequence?

Those questions were rendered moot when President Marland took everyone by surprise by deciding to retire in 1978, a year earlier than expected. His successor, Robert J. Kingston, was similarly committed to responding to the panel's challenge but was understandably cautious about undertaking an effort of such magnitude and importance in his first year. He resigned in 1979, near the end of his first year, and I've always assumed because the trustees probably didn't want to go through another time-consuming presidential search, they asked me to take the job. When I did, the challenge set by the panel on the SAT score decline was much on my mind, too, but another, more immediately pressing problem—at least as far as the College Board was concerned—was on the agenda. It was the pending so-called truth-in-testing legislation being proposed in Albany. Dealing with that issue as I assumed my new responsibilities preempted most of my time during 1979–80. It wasn't until the summer of 1980 that we were able to get our act together in response to the panel's challenge.

By that time our idea of establishing a commission to study the issues raised in *On Further Examination* appeared to have passed us by. Everyone, it seemed, had already gotten into the act, including the Education Commission of the States, the Carnegie Foundation for the Advancement of Teaching, the National Academy of Education, and the United States Department of Education. That is why I say we were fortunate in not having been able to respond earlier. Now we were forced to come up with a different approach. So, rather than choosing to study the reasons for the lower standards in the schools, we decided to concentrate on determining what those standards ought to be in relation to college admissions. If they were too low, what should they be?

We were initially aided in coming to this conclusion by a group of "wise persons" whom we convened in September 1980 to help sort out the options open to us. (In an earlier time I suspect we would have called them "wise men," even though not all wisdom has ever been reserved exclusively for males.) Although not unanimous in their opinions about what we ought to do, they were convinced that the College Board had an obligation to do something, and their deliberations helped immeasurably in setting us finally on our track. In a sense, their collective advice echoed that of another wise person whose advice I had sought, Stephen K. Bailey, then head of the National Academy of Education, which was itself embarked on an exploration of the deteriorating quality of our nation's schools. I told Bailey that we were finally getting around to thinking about what action we might take but wondered if, with all the other players already in the field, it made sense for the College Board to get involved. His answer was that "The schools are in so much trouble, they need all the help they can get!" The question for us, then, was where and how to help.

Discussions then and later tended to focus on four major topics: curriculum, teaching, administration, and external factors variously interpreted to include government, community, society, and the economy. Of the four major topics, curriculum was obviously the area in which the College Board was most directly involved. But in deciding to concentrate there, we recognized that success in that area could provide useful leverage in support of reform efforts in the other three fields. Teachers would have a better idea of what to teach and of the standards to which they should hold their students. Administrators would have curricular goals around which to rally their faculties. And the public at large could be reassured that the teachers and administrators knew what they were doing. A bit of literary exaggeration for effect, I realize, but the concept of leverage was useful because it kept our effort from being, and from being perceived as, totally self-contained. We realized that curricular reform alone wouldn't cure the schools' ills, but we knew too that curricular change was essential to overall improvement. What came as a surprising revelation to me was that, since the 1930s, there had been no attempt to come up with a comprehensive definition of college admissions standards in the United States. There, we decided, was where we should begin—with a definition of academic preparation for college expressed in terms of subject-matter coverage and standards of performance.

Academic Competencies

We began at home, so to speak, with our own constituency, the school and college teachers who help create the College Board tests. We asked our Achievement Test and Advanced Placement examiners what they thought young people going on to college should have studied in high school and what standards they believed those students ought to be held to. They began the process by agreeing that there are six subjects that should be an essential part of academic preparation for college: English, the arts, mathematics, science, social studies, and foreign language. The inclusion of the arts came as a surprise to some, but it was the teachers in the other five subjects who insisted on it. The examiners were unanimous in their conviction that study of all six subjects is necessary for a college preparatory program of quality. Please note that their emphasis was—as we asked it to be in response to the public concern about standards—on quality.

Nevertheless, that emphasis, by itself, bothered me. The College Board had spent 25 years responding to the call for equality of educational opportunity, and its member institutions were committed to that effort. As a consequence, I believed that we had to balance any renewed attention to quality with a concomitant focus on equality. To get some idea of what the focus should be, we turned to another part of our constituency, represented by the Advisory Panel on Minority Concerns. Its members were convinced that the greatest learning handicap faced by educationally disadvantaged minority young people thinking about the possibility of going to college was a lack of the basic academic skills necessary to do college-level work. In setting about the task of determining what those skills should be, the panel was aided considerably by the contribution of its one "majority" member, John Monro, former dean of Harvard College, who had dramatically given up that post in the late 1960s to become a teacher of freshman English at predominantly black Miles College in Birmingham, Alabama. That Monro should play such a pivotal role in this new College Board effort was not surprising; he had played a similar role in an earlier effort. Considered by many the "father of the College Scholarship Service," he had been instrumental in developing the concept of student financial aid awarded on the basis of need—the concept on which the CSS operation was established in the mid-1950s and on which, during the 1960s and 1970s, the federal government's massive infusion of student aid dollars was based.

In preparation for the meeting of the Advisory Panel on Minority Concerns in the fall of 1980, we asked its members to think ahead about the kinds of academic skills, or competencies, they believed students going on to college should have. As expected, they thought in terms of reading, writing, doing math, and studying. Others, such as speaking, listening, using the library, and taking examinations also came in for consideration. Monro's unique contribution was his belief that one of the aptitudes needed for college-level work is the ability to make connections among ideas. He demonstrated what he meant by bringing to the meeting essays that some of his students at Miles College had written. Their assignment had been to write about what they observed in tables showing changes in the ethnic populations of several states over time. (The tables reflected the migration of blacks from the rural South to the industrial North.) Some of the essays were excellent. Some were mediocre. Some were not so good. Monro's point was that the better papers demonstrated that their authors had the ability to make connections and thus the ability to draw conclusions from statistical information. The panel agreed, and the skill Monro had identified was included in the original list of what came to be known as the Basic Academic Competencies. It was listed under the name "drawing conclusions from data."

To assist in the definitions included in that first list, we called on the services of Dennis Gray of the Council for Basic Education. What surprised many of us at the time was the absence of any earlier effort to bring such definitions together; Gray created his first draft from a variety of sources. We then convened a series of seven "urban dialogues," as we called them, to discuss the definitions of the competencies Gray had teased out of the literature. They were held in cities that had large minority populations, particularly blacks or Hispanics or both. For the discussions we brought together teachers and others from the high schools that served those populations and from the higher institutions in the area that tended to enroll the majority of the local high school graduates. Our goal, of course, was to discover what academic skills they, as practitioners dealing with the "new populations" identified by the Advisory Panel on the Scholastic Aptitude Test Score Decline three years earlier, believed college-bound young people should have.

As a result of those deliberations, a number of competencies were restructured, redesigned, or reworded. For example, the abilities to use library resources properly and to prepare for examinations were subsumed under an expanded definition of studying. But the most fascinating and, I believe, significant result of those urban dialogues was that at each one of them, without knowing what had transpired at any previous session, the participants broadened the draft definition of "drawing conclusions from data" by describing it as "reasoning." What happened in each instance was this: Informed at the outset about the origin of the concept, the English teachers claimed it was related to writing, and the mathematics teachers observed that it concerned numbers and therefore involved their field. As each discussion progressed, however, the participants came to realize that it was a competency that had to do not only with writing and mathematics but also with reading, speaking, and listening and with the comprehension of specific subject matter as well. They determined that it was a separate competency in its own right and that it should be called reasoning.

The *Educational EQuality Project*

Meanwhile, the effort on which we had embarked the preceding summer got a name. It fact, it got three names, only one of which survived. I suggested the first one when I announced the project to the College Board membership at the National Forum in October 1980. I spoke of it tentatively as the Excellence and Equity in Education project and, using the initials, referred to it in mathematical terms as the E^3 (that is, E to the third power) or the E-cubed project. I'm glad I was tentative. In the first place, the name was long and unwieldy. In the second place, subliminally or otherwise, my choice was probably responsible for inspiring one of my senior vice president colleagues, Merritt Ludwig, to come up with a catchier name. My diction had been poor; I had mumbled the "bed" in "cubed," and "*E*-cubed" had come across to many as "*E*-cue." In any event, taking account of the College Board's dual interest in excellence and equity, Ludwig substituted "equality" for "equity" and "quality" for "excellence" and came up with Project EQuality with its capital *E* and its capital *Q*. That was the name under which our effort was launched. As it turned out, however, there was an affirmative action employment program by the name of Project Equality (without the capital *Q*) already in existence. Wanting to avoid the possibility of dispute, despite the unique *Q* in our title, we regrouped and came up with the Educational EQuality Project as the formal name for our endeavor and the EQuality project as the short form or popular designation.

Defining the Basic Academic Competencies

Finding an appropriate name was, however, only a minor diversion from the task of consolidating and reconciling the findings of our academic constituency on the one hand and the minority panel on the other. We decided to do that by bringing about 50 participants from our subject-matter discussions and competency-related dialogues together with an equal number of persons with similar backgrounds who had not taken part in the first round of discussions. We did so at a symposium in St. Louis in May 1981. It turned out to be, as one participant described it, "something of an academic Woodstock."

I went to the symposium convinced that the members would conclude there should be two sets of college admissions standards—one for selective and one for open-door institutions, with the first patterned after the findings of our academic constituency and the second based on the outcomes of the urban dialogues. As it turned out, I was wrong. What happened was that the group unanimously agreed that all young people aspiring to higher education needed to develop the competencies identified by the urban dialogues and to study the six subjects called for by the Achievement Test and Advanced Placement examiners. In effect, the St. Louis symposiasts agreed that students needed to have the competencies to learn the subjects and needed to study the subjects in order to develop the competencies.

What was equally surprising was that they came to agree on precise definitions of the competencies. After Dennis Gray's latest statements were presented to the entire assemblage, the participants were divided into four groups for intensive discussion. The group reactions were then combined, consolidated, and refined overnight by a small working group and returned to the committee of the whole, as it were, where the final wording of the competency definitions was adopted.

The foregoing paragraph makes the exercise sound pretty cut-and-dried. It wasn't. There was, for instance, heated debate over whether the proposed competency "observing" (referred to earlier in this chapter in the discussion of television), should be included. I obviously thought it should, but the participants were divided in their opinions and it ended up in the Green Book as Appendix A, titled "Observing: A Competency to Consider." (The Green Book is the familiar name of the EQuality project's first publication, *Academic Preparation for College*.) Also, anybody who has ever witnessed a large group of people trying to edit a bit of text that is important to them can attest to the difficulty of such an effort. There was animated wrangling over the use of particular words and nuances of sentence structures, over the relative emphases given to aspects of a given competency, and over what should be left in and what should be left out. Voices were raised and feathers were ruffled but in that curiously intimate way that leads to mutual understanding.

Where there is tension, there is often humor. One of the discussion groups reported a dispute over the inclusion of a theretofore unrecognized competency dubbed "squinting," a subcompetency of listening. As the group described it, it is the practice of sitting in the front row at college lectures, leaning forward expectantly, and squinting knowingly. Properly done, it gives the impression of hanging on the professor's every word when in fact the squinter is quietly dozing.

As we began the task of trying to reach closure on the definitions of the competencies, I tried to add a bit of humor to the occasion by falling back on the tried-and-true story of the man, his son, and the donkey they were taking to sell at the county fair. As they started out, the father put the boy on the donkey. As they were going along, they met a group of people who complained, "Look at that healthy young boy riding on that donkey while his poor father is trudging along in the dust!" So the father and son traded places and soon met some more people who were heard to remark, "Look at that man riding that donkey, while that poor young lad is trudging along in the dust!" So the father got off the donkey and he and the boy walked along beside the donkey. But sure enough they met some more people on the road who observed, "Look at that silly man and his son trudging along in the dust while they have a perfectly healthy donkey to ride!" So the father and son both got on the donkey and were riding comfortably along when they met still another group of travelers who, you guessed it, said, "Look at those two healthy people weighing down that poor donkey!" And so, you guessed it again, the father and son got off the donkey, picked it up, and started carrying it to the fair. At the edge of town they came to a bridge over a stream. The father, who was in front, tripped on a loose board on the bridge and the donkey was catapulted into the river and washed away. That's the story. Of course, the moral is "If you try to please everybody, you'll lose your ass!"

The St. Louis symposium proved to be the exception when we reached closure on the competency definitions, which have remained unchanged to this day.

Reaching agreement on the necessary outcomes to be identified for the six Basic Academic Subjects proved to be more time-consuming than we had thought. We left St. Louis with some general conclusions about the form they ought to take but no specific wording. That process took two years. More about it below. In the meantime, we published the statements defining the competencies and were amazed at the positive reception they received.

One unexpected reaction was from the business community. When, in the course of polite conversation, friends asked what was going on at the College Board, I would describe the EQuality project, the St. Louis symposium, and the competencies. Business people among them often remarked that they would like their new hires to have essentially those same skills. To test this attitude further, we convened some "business dialogues" involving representatives of the business community and the schools. Those discussions tended to confirm what I had picked up informally, but with two interesting shifts in emphasis. First, the participants properly noted that much of education today tends to be a pretty lonely process, while many jobs in the workplace require teamwork. As a consequence, in business more stress would be put on speaking and listening—in other words, in learning to get along with others. Also, in business job-holding skills would be substituted for study skills. At one of the dialogues I attended, the owner of a McDonald's franchise described the most basic requirements as being neat, polite, on time, and able to follow directions. Those participants in the business dialogues, who were for the most part in charge of hiring new employees for entry-level jobs, certainly had a perspective different from that of the chief executives then making headlines with their pronouncements about wanting liberally educated young men and women who can change with the times.

At about this time I discovered that the nation's business leaders weren't aware of the manpower problems facing their enterprises a few years down the road. David Packard, the chief executive officer at Hewlett-Packard, somehow got wind of what we were doing with our EQuality project and suggested that I visit the headquarters of the National Business Roundtable a few blocks away from the College Board's office in New York City. He thought the staff there should know what we were up to. I did and was shocked to learn that manpower wasn't on the roundtable's then current agenda. This was 1982! After finally convincing the chief of staff that I wasn't there to raise money, I was finally able, after three abortive attempts, to get him and his colleagues to understand that the demographics were changing dramatically; that while the cohorts of young people who would be graduating from high school would be getting smaller, both the proportion and the absolute number of minority youngsters in those cohorts would be getting larger. The numbers finally sank in.

Now I don't presume to suggest that my visit to the National Business Roundtable headquarters was responsible for attracting industry's and the business community's attention to their stake in education, although I do like to think that it may perhaps have served as one of many catalysts. In any event, manpower considerations and the education imperatives related to them were soon on the business community's agenda, and its endorsement of the Basic Academic Competencies provided a boost to our EQuality effort.

Defining the Learning Outcomes

Meanwhile, back at the College Board, staff colleagues and faculty members from the constituency were engaged in the arduous and demanding task of fleshing out the outlines, formulated in St. Louis, of the learning outcomes—what students planning to go on to college should have learned about the six Basic Academic subjects. As had been done earlier for the competencies, statements of the outcomes were drafted, subjected to intensive discussion in the field, refined, reviewed again, and finally presented for adoption to the College Board's academic advisory committees in the six subjects. The results, together with the competencies, were published in May 1983 under the title *Academic Preparation for College: What Students Need to Know and Be Able to Do,* published by the College Board in 1983. It is difficult for me objectively to assess the impact of the Green Book, as it has come to be known, on American secondary education, but I do take pride in that there are half a million copies in circulation and that external evaluators, Abt Associates, Inc., observed in their 1989 *Executive Summary: Edu-*

cational EQuality Project External Evaluation, 1980–1989, that "of all education reform documents, the Green Book was the one most often used to illustrate the substantive implications of state regulatory reform initiatives. . . . It formed an important niche in state policy-making and was used by more than half the states" (11).

We publicly announced the availability of the Green Book at an 11 a.m. press conference in Washington, D.C. I recall listening to a local rock station on the radio in a cab on the way to National Airport after lunch. One item in the 2 p.m. news report went like this: "The College Board, sponsor of the SAT, says you have to be able to act, dance, and sing to get into college." I wanted to call up and say, "You're wrong! It's 'or,' not 'and.'" But that was before car phones became popular. What I wasn't so anxious to publicize was that I'd never have made it to college under the standards called for in *Academic Preparation for College.* I can *not* act, dance, or sing.

Successful as the Green Book was in helping state and other authorities (principals, superintendents, school boards, and the like) establish goals and set standards, it wasn't enough. Teachers wanted more specific advice on how they might help students achieve the desired outcomes. And so another two-year, as it turned out, round of intensive discussions was initiated—discussions intended to produce suggestions but not to provide prescriptions. My personal engagement in this second round, as in the steps leading to the publication of the Green Book, was peripheral, and I found myself frequently frustrated again by the slow progress. In retrospect, however, I am amazed at the achievement of our staff in the Office of Academic Affairs in producing in the span of just five years documents of such lasting value. In my time at the College Board two subject-matter commissions, one in mathematics in the late 1950s and one in English in the early 1960s, each took more than two years to fulfill their missions in their subjects.

Sequels to the Green Book

In our latter-day EQuality effort the final product was a series of six sequels to the Green Book, one in each of the six Basic Academic Subjects. Published by the College Board in 1985 and 1986, they are titled *Academic Preparation in English* (1985), *Academic Preparation in the Arts* (1985), *Academic Preparation in Mathematics* (1985), *Academic Preparation in Science* (1986), *Academic Preparation in Social Studies* (1986), and *Academic Preparation in Foreign Language* (1986). Because the cover of each book is a different color, they soon became known as the Rainbow Books or the Rainbow Series.

Two aspects of the series gave me particular pleasure. First, in each Rainbow Book, Chapter 5 suggests how the Basic Academic Competencies might be taught in relation to the book's subject, giving further credence to the St. Louis finding that both the subjects and the competencies are essential to academic success in college. Second, the observing competency was rescued from the appendixes to the Green Book and received prominent attention in most of the Rainbow Books. It wasn't so much its expected mention in relation to science and the arts that pleased me as the consideration it received in connection with the other four subjects. I remain convinced, now even more than at the St. Louis symposium, that observing is an important skill that needs further exploration and attention, particularly as it relates to "viewing." In the span of human history, the audiovisual media are in their infancy. As I noted earlier in this chapter, men and women learned to live with the output from the printing press; they can equally well learn to live with, and benefit from, the output of television. That is why I heartily subscribe to the observation of the Advisory Panel on the Scholastic Aptitude Test Score Decline that television has the "potential . . . of becoming learning's most fertile grove" (*On Further Examination,* 37).

While the observing competency finally made it in through the back door, so to speak, note should be made that another competency made it in through the front door and into the Green Book, where it is described as the "Computer Competency: An Emerging Need." The text states that "a revolution in communications and information technology is making the computer a basic tool for acquiring knowledge, organizing systems, and solving problems. As such, it is having a profound influence on learning and on the world of work" (*Academic Preparation for College,* 11). That is why it joined reading, writing, speaking and listening, mathematics, reasoning, and studying as one of the now seven Basic Academic Competencies.

In the early years of the EQuality project there were those who recognized the danger of its being used either to justify or to influence the College Board's tests. Therefore, from the outset I insisted that no consideration be given to the testing implications of what we were about, at least until what turned out to be the Green Book was in place. But I must admit that I found one of the early conclusions of the project reassuring as far as the SAT was concerned. That was its identification of reasoning as central both to the development of the competencies and to the achievement of the Basic Academic Subject outcomes, because verbal and mathematical reasoning (remember the debate at those early urban dialogues over "drawing conclusions from data") is what the SAT is all about.

The final publication effort of the EQuality project takes this connection explicitly into account. Much attention has been given in recent years to the importance of developing students' critical, or higher-order, thinking skills (the "hots" as they have come to be known); SAT scores have been offered as evidence that young people, particularly minorities, aren't developing these skills as proficiently as they should. One problem is that by the time many students reach the senior year in high school, it's too late to help them achieve the level of sophistication in reasoning called for in the Green Book and in the Chapters 5 of the Rainbow Series. Taking account of this fact, the project developed a second series of books—known in their formative days as "grandchildren of the Green Book," and now as the "Thinking Series"—which offer suggestions, again not prescriptions, for teaching rudimentary reasoning skills throughout high school. These suggestions are designed to help provide students with a base for the later development of the higher-order thinking skills called for in *Academic Preparation for College* and required for success on the SAT. Therefore, in the interests of symmetry, it can be said that the EQuality project began with the decline in SAT scores and ended more than 20 years later with suggestions for more effectively developing the competencies those scores reflect.

I leave it to others to assess the accomplishments of the Educational EQuality Project. When we started the project, we didn't have specific goals in mind, least of all the publication of another commission report. We knew only in the most general terms what we wanted to accomplish and didn't have a game plan for doing so. That was, I believe, one of the project's greatest strengths. It was free to evolve as one set of accomplishments provided the base for mounting a next stage. Nevertheless, although we fostered flexibility, the absence of stated predetermined goals made the task of evaluation that much more difficult. Yet, difficult as it may have been, I take comfort from the external evaluators referred to earlier who, in commenting on "the overall impact of the EQuality project," observed that it "played a critical role in the education reform movement of the 1980s."

Commission on Precollege Guidance

After the EQuality project was sucessfully launched and we had time to assess other current needs on the college admissions scene, it became apparent that one aspect of admissions was being almost entirely ignored in the school reform movement. That was the precollege guidance and counseling of students, particularly of minorities. Under the able chairmanship of Harold Howe II, former United States commissioner of education and the vice chairman of the Advisory Panel on the Scholastic Aptitude Test Score Decline, the dedicated members of the Commission on Precollege Guidance and Counseling spent two years assessing the situation. They then issued their findings in a two-volume landmark report published in 1986 by the College Board under the title *Keeping the Options Open*. Please note that unlike the circumstances that led to mounting the EQuality project, here no one had been studying the problems, no commissions were already in existence, and the field was being overlooked.

At the other commissioners' request, I served as one of the members and therefore am comfortable in relying extensively on excerpts from *Keeping the Options Open* to summarize its investigations, its findings, and its recommendations. But again, as in the activities of the SAT Advisory Panel, no brief summary on my part can do justice to the two volumes of the commission's full report.

In my Foreword to the second volume of *Keeping the Options Open*, subtitled *Recommendations*, I spoke of the reasons for the appointment of the commission in these terms:

> The Commission on Precollege Guidance and Counseling extends a long-standing tradition of the College Board. When a significant problem related to its mission is identified and no other agency appears to be addressing it, the College Board appoints a commission of knowledgeable individuals to wrestle with it independently and in the public interest. The Commissions on Mathematics (1955–59), English (1959–64), Tests (1967–69), and Non-Traditional Study (1970–72) are cases in point.
>
> The problem that this latest Commission was asked to study is the uneven quality that characterizes precollege guidance and counseling services available to high school students today. That condition was identified in 1983 in the aftermath of a series of reports on the sorry quality of secondary education in the United States. Those reports focused on what their authors considered the essentials of education—administration, teaching, and curriculum. Guidance and counseling services, if mentioned at all, were treated as peripheral, outside the mainstream of schooling. Yet it would be ironic if the current efforts at reform generated by those reports succeed only to find many students denied the benefits of the new-found quality because of inadequate counseling services.
>
> It was in the hope of being able to avert this outcome that the College Board's Trustees authorized the appointment of the Commission on Precollege Guidance and Counseling in 1984 (vii).

In the opening section, titled "Setting the Stage," under the heading "A Special Imperative for Guidance and Counseling," the commission's report noted:

> Schools should be caring environments in which students are respected and supported both as learners and human beings. All young people need such schools, but particularly the increasing number who suffer disadvantages from poverty, discrimination, and family stress or disruption. Yet, we have not heard from educational leaders about the importance of this basic need as much as we have about new requirements, more tests, and longer school hours. The Commission believes that many students become discouraged as a result of the ways schools are now operated, and that improved guidance and counseling in the schools can contribute significantly to reducing the considerable waste of human talent noted in our initial report.
>
> We are told by many thoughtful analysts . . . that the nation's economic future depends upon higher levels of educational attainment among those now at the bottom of the economic ladder. In the years immediately ahead, the traditional age group providing college applicants will decrease in number, while the proportion of the age group that is economically disadvantaged will continue to grow and include more black, Hispanic, and immigrant children. Unless students from these segments of society are prepared and encouraged to enter higher education, the percentage of college graduates among the adult population will decline. Such a decline poses a threat to our standard of living, the development of our communities, and the nation's ability to compete successfully with other countries.
>
> The country's future economic health provides a powerful imperative for improvement of guidance and counseling functions in the schools. We would add what we believe is another equally important argument—the entitlement of children to a public education that meets their abilities and needs. Flagrant violations of justice too often have been inflicted on minority groups in this country. The promise of equal educational opportunity has been made, but not kept. Better counseling and guidance services in schools constitute an important element in making that promise a reality for *all* children (1, 2).

Particularly poignant was a meeting the commission held in Kansas City with representatives from different parts of rural United States. The other commission dialogues had been held in large urban settings, where national attention to the educational disadvantages of minority students tended to be focused and where problems of inadequate schooling tended to be more fully documented. Hearing about the problems of rural schools was a new experience for me. In some respects the difficulties faced by urban and rural young people seemed to be the same. But there

were differences: The American Indian students, who never have to
handle money on the reservations, finding themselves suddenly on a
college campus with financial aid dollars in their pockets to spend and
no prior advice from a school counselor about how to deal with it. The
young people from rural communities whose parents don't want guidance for their offspring for fear they'd be enticed away from the chores
at home—the brawn drain, as I later came to think of it. I learned for
the first time about the Black Belt in the impoverished rural South,
peopled mainly by blacks whose schools can't afford counseling services
for their young.

One of the participants in Kansas City was a school superintendent
from a rural district in the Southwest. He made the point that in districts
like his, school personnel had to assume multiple responsibilities. He
doubled, among other things, as a plumber. I'll never forget his story of
the time when the school cafeteria fed the students undercooked Spanish
rice. In disposing of the stuff, the students filled the waste lines with
uncooked rice; when water was run to wash it down, it expanded and
plugged the drains. He drove to his father's shop, where he had once
apprenticed as a plumber, to get the tools to cope with the problem.
Like plumbing services, such guidance services as could be made available had to be add-ons to teachers' and other staff members' regular
responsibilities.

We found from the experience of one rural community in Iowa that
not all rural communities are poor, lack counseling services for their
young, and worry about losing their sons and daughters to "a better
life" somewhere else. Life in rural Iowa sounded pretty inviting!

On the basis of information gleaned from its dialogues, from the
College Board constituency, and from the research conducted for it, the
commission issued the following major findings in *Keeping the Options
Open:*

- Adequate counseling and guidance services are essential for all
  students, particularly for those who suffer disadvantages from
  poverty, discrimination, and family stress or disruption. . . .
  Learning failures among students frequently are caused by lack
  of support from school and family rather than by lack of ability.
  [Changing circumstances are] placing more of the burden on the
  schools and other community agencies.
- Counseling is a profession in trouble. . . . This erosion of support
  for guidance and counseling is occurring at a time of urgent
  concern about the increasing school dropout rate and numerous

calls for dropout prevention programs that involve counseling and a wide range of support services in and out of the schools.

- Provision for guidance and counseling follows an all too well-established pattern in the distribution of public services: Those with the least at home often get the least help from public institutions and programs. . . . Specifically, we have found that those students who come from families and communities where knowledge of the consequences of different course and curricular choices is limited are least likely to have access to informed guidance and counseling in school. When the relative need for guidance and counseling is considered, this maldistribution is especially damaging. The resulting waste of human potential is indicated by a rising school dropout rate . . . among black and Hispanic students (2, 3).

To deal with the problems it had identified, the commission made eight specific, far-reaching recommendations in the report, four for "action in the schools" and four that "involve a variety of actors and institutions outside the schools":

1. Establish a broad-based process in each local school district for determining the particular guidance and counseling needs of the students within each school and for planning how best to meet these needs.
2. Develop a program under the leadership of each school principal that emphasizes the importance of the guidance counselor as a monitor and promoter of student potential, as well as coordinator of the school's guidance plan.
3. Mount programs to inform and involve parents and other members of the family influential in the choices, plans, decisions, and learning activities of the student.
4. Provide a program of guidance and counseling during the early and middle years of schooling, especially for students who have not been well served by the schools.
5. Strengthen collaboration among schools, community agencies, colleges, businesses, and other community resources to enhance services available to students.
6. Establish a process in each state to determine the guidance and counseling needs of specific student populations and give support to local initiatives that address these needs.

7. Increase support of federal programs that help disadvantaged students to enter and remain in college.
8. Revise the training of school counselors to include the specific skills and knowledge necessary to enable them to take a more central role in schools (5, 6).

Keeping the Options Open has served to draw national attention to an aspect of education that is too often overlooked. It has provided a platform for a profession in need of recognition and has operated to reaffirm the College Board's stake in precollege guidance and counseling. In this latter sense, as in the reaffirmation of the association's interest in academic affairs via the EQuality project, the fallout from the decline in SAT scores served not to lessen the College Board's commitment to the mechanics of the college admissions process but to revitalize its commitment to the educational and human aspects of the process as well. And it seems to have served the same end for education in the United States generally.

CHAPTER 5

Minorities and the SAT

In the spring of 1941 the Harvard lacrosse team made its annual trek south during April vacation to play the University of Pennsylvania, the University of Maryland, and the United States Naval Academy. Lucien V. Alexis and I were members of the squad. Alex was black. The rest of us were white. The games in Philadelphia and College Park went without a hitch, but when we got to Annapolis, the Academy refused to play us as long as Alex was in uniform. Because lacrosse was a "minor" sport at Harvard in those days, we all provided our own transportation, by car. Alex didn't want to deprive the rest of us of the game we'd come so far to play, and he took the first train back to Boston. We lost, just as badly as we would have if Alex had been there. He wasn't a star. But the incident did make the papers and so, when we went up to West Point to play the Military Academy a couple of weeks later, the entire contingent of black cadets was on hand to greet our bus. I forget now whether there were two or three of them.

I told this story often during the 1960s and 1970s. In those years the protesters and the civil rights movers were clamoring for reform and they wanted it fast. I used the story about Alex to assure them that society was moving in the right direction, even though it wasn't doing so very rapidly. And I urged them to be patient and to persist.

Desegregation

Indeed, the progress has been slow and full of many ironic twists as well. Three instances make the point. One, integration became the law of the land in the expectation that it would immediately add new populations to the melting pot. Instead, it led to cultural pluralism. Two, the courts did act to integrate restaurants, rest rooms, swimming pools, and buses. But our society chose to put the heaviest burden of desegregation on those without a vote, the nation's children. Three, we still haven't figured out how to integrate. The Department of Labor reports employment test results by ethnic group to help employers in their affirmative action efforts. Yet the Department of Justice says that practice is against the law.

Association with the Scholastic Aptitude Test (SAT) provided a fascinating perspective from which to observe that slow progress and those many ironies. I joined the College Board staff in 1955, a year after the landmark decision by the Supreme Court in the case of *Brown* v. *Board of Education*. That action, calling for an end to racial discrimination in the schools, served as the stimulus for a nationwide effort to put an end to that practice not only in the schools but in housing, transportation, and all other public aspects of American life.

At the outset, although the Board of Education in the case was in Topeka, Kansas, the problem of segregation with which the Supreme Court's decision dealt was seen as a regional one focused on the schools in the South, which were segregated by state law. Ironically again, as it was to turn out, well-meaning white liberals from the North sallied forth to join their black brothers and sisters in the South in protest against segregation in public facilities. They allied themselves with Martin Luther King, Jr., and they joined in the march on Selma.

But the Supreme Court's decision wasn't confined to de jure segregation, a separation of the races called for by (state) law. And the law of the land was being violated by de facto segregation in many northern cities, a separation of the races by schools that had developed there for other reasons. "To bus or not to bus?" became the question of the day. Meanwhile the levels of rhetoric and violence escalated. The effects of an unpopular war in Vietnam fueled the fires of protest and spilled over not only onto the nation's campuses but also into its cities' streets. The plight of the urban poor and their educationally disadvantaged children came into focus, and steps began to be taken to provide equal educational opportunity for all young people. The national effort to end discrimination in all our schools was under way, and the world of the College Board and the SAT was never the same again.

Desegregation of Test Centers

At the College Board that effort began without fanfare in the late 1950s, well before the civil rights movement got moving. It began with steps taken to desegregate test centers in the South. Although the administration of test centers is routinely handled by Educational Testing Service (ETS), the responsibility in this instance was assigned to the Southern Regional Office of the College Board. There the task was put in the hands of two Southern gentlemen on the staff, Ben Gibson from Georgia and Jim Buford from Tennessee. Working out of the College Board office in Sewanee, Tennessee—"Now wait a minute," you say. "Sewanee? What was the College Board doing with an office there? Isn't that on the mountaintop where the University of the South is? How come? Why, with all the other regional offices in or near urban centers like Boston, New York, Chicago, and San Francisco, is the Southern Regional Office a couple of hours' drive from both the Nashville and the Chattanooga airports?"

The reason was simple. It was there because the man we wanted to run the office, Ben F. Cameron, Jr., insisted on living there. He'd been a professor at the University of the South. That's where his home was. And that's where he wanted to live.

Despite its geographic isolation, the office in Sewanee had its advantages. Four come to mind. For one thing, you had to pass by a pond on the way from the local motel to the office. If you left early enough in the morning, the director of the regional office gladly supplied fishing gear. It was the only locale I ran across where I could go fishing on the way to work.

Another advantage was that the director's wife was a doctor, a pediatrician who spent not an inconsiderable amount of time visiting sick children in the hollows and earning the affection of their backwoods families. One of the ways they expressed their gratitude was to provide her with corn liquor. I'd heard of the stuff and was leery of imbibing. Reports were that if it didn't kill you, it would make you go blind. The doctor saw the fear in my eyes when the potion was offered and undertook to reassure me. "I sampled this batch yesterday," she said. "It's safe." Safe or not, I thought I was going to gag when I put a couple of drops on my tongue. It just plain burned all the way down. You don't drink corn liquor straight; you've got to cut it with something. That evening it was orange juice. But it wasn't simply the availability of the doctor or the availability of yet another intoxicating beverage that constituted the full advantage. It was a bit more complicated than that. I had arrived in Sewanee with a miserable cold. The doctor prescribed what she described as a sniffle pill, which I washed down with corn liquor and orange juice. Never before or since has a full-blown cold disappeared so quickly!

A third advantage of having the Southern Regional Office on the mountaintop was that it gave the staff what we called a lightning-rod issue in dealing with the Board of Trustees. Anyone in his or her right mind knew that the office ought to be in Atlanta, and the trustees were all in their right minds. They wanted to discuss "the location of the Southern Regional Office." And they discussed it—passionately—so thoroughly that we knew their pent-up frustrations would be thrown into the dialogue so completely that they would be relieved of any further tensions and the next couple of items on the agenda would have clear sailing. Therefore we would put the issue of location just ahead of any matter of business that seemed likely to arouse the trustees' concern.

Ultimately, Cameron became a College Board vice president and commuted weekly from Sewanee to New York. We engaged another director, who had the wisdom to see the writing on the wall and to move the office to Atlanta. But meanwhile the Sewanee location had provided its fourth advantage, a suitable headquarters for the sensitive task of desegregating the test centers in the South. Keep in mind that it was undertaken in the years before the protests and demonstrations had begun. In any event, it wasn't an effort to which the College Board and ETS wanted to attract a lot of attention in the first place; we simply believed that it was the morally proper and legally right thing to do. Off-the-beaten-track Sewanee was a fine location in which to avoid attention.

The trials and tribulations Gibson and Buford endured in those days to find suitable testing facilities are a story in themselves. Most of the cities and larger towns in the South had at least two high schools, one white and one black, and if there were any black SAT candidates in the area, there were two test centers, one white and one black. Buford and Gibson's assignment was to find facilities that would accommodate both blacks and whites. The public high schools couldn't do it; they were segregated by local law. So, too, were most local public buildings such as town halls and auditoriums. Churches and federal government facilities usually seemed to offer the best solutions, but sometimes even these turned out to have potential disadvantages. In some locations, the quarters available from the more usual federal agencies that dot the national landscape simply weren't suitable. They were too small or they didn't have the right furniture or they were in particularly noisy surroundings. The fallback position in such instances was occasionally to use Strategic Air Command (SAC) bases. The trouble with them was that there might suddenly be an alert on one of those Saturdays when the SAT was being administered. The base would have to be secured and all candidates confined to it until the alert was over. Luck was with us. There were no alerts. And desegregated test centers were on their way to becoming a way of life in the South. They remain so today, but back again in the public schools, which have since become integrated.

To leave the topic at this point, however, would be misleading. There was an intermediate development leading to the eventual desegregation of test centers that calls attention to one of the most difficult dilemmas that have plagued the efforts to open up access to higher education. You would think that having succeeded in doing what it thought was morally proper and legally right, the College Board would have been able to rest on its laurels, at least as far as test centers were concerned. Not so! It wasn't long before young blacks and their civil rights champions were complaining about what they called hostile test centers. They contended that black students were being disadvantaged by having to take examinations in unfamiliar surroundings under the supervision of test administrators who were predominantly white. With the passage of time and with the eventual desegregation of the schools, that problem appears pretty much to have disappeared. But the implications of that turn of events persist in hampering efforts to achieve equality of access to higher education for blacks.

Those implications were addressed directly at a conference on "Educating Black Children," which I attended in 1986. One of only two or three whites at that meeting of leading black educators, I listened to a speech by one of the recognized spokeswomen for black interests in the United States. She reminisced nostalgically about growing up in a supportive black community. Her parents were interested in education and the education of their children. There were books in the home and they were used regularly. Homework was recognized as important and it got done. She went to a segregated school. Like the children, the teachers were black. They cared about their students and provided a sympathetic environment for learning. The spokeswoman called for a return to that kind of support for black children today.

After that session, I commented to one of the participants on the eloquence of the talk we had just heard. The superintendent of a major city school system, he agreed with my assessment of the speaker's eloquence but then went on to point out that integration had destroyed at least part of her dream, the part that had to do with the schools. He was saying, in effect, that the same thing that happened in the aftermath of the desegregation of test centers had happened more generally in the aftermath of desegregation in the schools. If not hostile, the learning environment for black youngsters in many settings had become less sympathetic.

Whether the civil rights movement had the same negative effect on the black family and the support it gave to its youngsters I am not prepared to speculate, although the early tendency in the civil rights movement on the part of many blacks was to blame the white majority for the poverty in which most of them lived. This may well have served to take some of the pressure off the black family's impulse to encourage the pursuit of academic excellence on the part of its children. "You deserve a college education," they might have implicitly been suggesting to their young people. "Whitey should give it to you."

Whatever the reason for the lack of family support to which the black spokeswoman called attention, the conference at which she spoke was encouraging evidence of a growing recognition by the black community that it, too, not just the white majority, has a responsibility for helping its young people achieve equality of access to higher education. Association with the SAT provided a unique vantage point from which to view that quarter of a century it took for black leadership to move from the whitey-owes-it-to-us stance to the we-have-a-responsibility-too attitude.

What I think happened was this: Court-ordered integration destroyed the cultural isolation of many of the nation's blacks. Going to college was encouraged, and as more young blacks went on to integrated colleges and universities, they sought out each other and collectively struggled to find their common heritage. Courses in Afro-American history and black literature became the order of the day, and a common cultural base within the melting pot began to slowly be built. Now, that base of ethnic identity and cultural pride has been carried into the black community and assumed by its leadership.

Equal Access to Higher Education

But to return to the test center desegregation: it was one of two quiet efforts undertaken without fanfare in the late 1950s. The other was an exploratory one, an experiment involving JHS 43, the local junior high school serving that part of New York City in which the Board's central office was located. The premise being tested was that with the help of additional guidance and related services both in and out of this predominantly black school, its dropout rate could immediately be reduced and the college-going rate of its graduates could later be increased. Known as Project 43, this early effort not only proved the validity of the premise but also formed the base on which the later citywide and national Higher Horizons projects were built. The College Board's contribution in this instance was minimal and in essence provided dollars for the support of activities for which public funds could not be spent. Those dollars, then, went toward social service agency fees, field trips, tickets for museums and cultural events, and the like.

Encouraged by the success of these two low-key efforts, the College Board, under the leadership of President Richard Pearson, initiated its public effort to promote equality of access to higher education on behalf of minority students. In undertaking that effort, the Board relied at the outset on the experience gained in Project 43. For example, there was Project Opportunity, conducted in cooperation with the Southern Association of Colleges and Schools (SACS) with help from the Danforth and Ford foundations, and there were Project Open and Project Access, each designed, like Project 43, to deal with an abnormally high dropout rate and an abnormally small proportion of students who continued their education after high school. Also in those early years of the civil rights response, the College Board assisted in enterprises conducted under other auspices such as HARYOU-ACT and Harlem Preparatory School.

Those of us on the staff realized from the outset that participating in such projects in particular and promoting equal access to higher education generally would require input from the communities we were seeking to serve. And so the College Board sought actively to involve blacks, particularly black educators, in our deliberations. It was from all these contacts, within the College Board constituency and without, that I came to know firsthand the depth of the resentment toward the SAT that pervaded the black community at that time.

Charge of Discrimination

The SAT seemed to serve as a symbol of the repression blacks believed they had endured over the years. Taking advantage of the release that the decision in *Brown* v. *Board of Education* seemed to promise, they attacked the SAT with enthusiasm. Some years later, again in one of those curious twists of fate, Ralph Nader in his frontal attack on the SAT criticized the test for being ineffective and unfair. He claimed that the ineffective use is calculated and the unfairness deliberate, that the main purpose of tests like the SAT is to perpetuate an unfair social system by denying opportunities and rewards to those who rightly seek them.

Discrimination, then, was the fault with which the SAT was charged, and to listen to the rhetoric of the 1960s and 1970s, you'd think it was a fault only recently charged. Not so! In the years right after World War II, discrimination was something that some people claimed was being practiced against Jewish students from New York City. And, it was claimed, the SAT was being used in that practice by some of the Ivy-League-type institutions. If a college found itself with more Jewish applicants than it wanted, all it had to do was tell those whom it didn't want that their SAT scores were too low. (In those days candidates for admission were not allowed to know their scores.) If that charge of discrimination was true, there were bound to be some pretty high-scoring students who were being discriminated against. But because they had earned high scores, it wasn't the test itself that discriminated but rather the way its scores were being used.

That distinction tended to get overlooked as the civil rights movement took hold and discrimination in college admissions came to be perceived as a practice to deny black and Hispanic youngsters their right to higher education. As it had before, the SAT came in for a lion's share of the blame. Those days were the beginning of tough times for those of us at the College Board, wanting to help but associated in people's minds with something that was seen as getting in the way of equality.

At first the circumstances were complicated by the secrecy surrounding the test. From the SAT's beginning and through the 1960s, the College Board did not publish data about the ethnic background of students who took the test because the Board didn't collect that information. Even after the information began to be gathered in the early 1970s, the College Board didn't publish the ethnic data it had assembled. It didn't, on the advice of black leaders in the College Board constituency, on the staff, and elsewhere. Their concern was that the public release of data that showed that blacks, on the average, were scoring about 100 points lower than whites did on the SAT would only serve to harden stereotypical attitudes about the academic ineptitude of black youngsters. I took a contrary position almost from the outset, believing that the differences in scores were a measure of the educational disadvantage being experienced by minority young people. One of the first efforts on which I embarked after becoming president of the College Board was to convince the trustees and then the leaders of the black and Hispanic communities that the interests of their young people would best be served by the Board's publishing the data and displaying, for everyone to see, the extent of the educational deficit the nation had to help these young people overcome. In the end I succeeded in convincing the leaders of the black community and those of the National Urban League and the National Association for the Advancement of Colored People that I was right. But the point to keep in mind here is that as the efforts to increase the minority presence in higher education gained momentum in the 1960s, the secrecy surrounding the scores that different student populations obtained on the SAT served to heighten the suspicion of the test itself.

Although there were no formally published data to confirm the surmise, it was generally believed that blacks did indeed, on the average, score about 100 points lower than whites did. Because the test was surrounded by secrecy, it was popularly and quite naturally assumed that the reason blacks scored lower was that the SAT was biased and that it therefore discriminated against them. Without published data about the performance of blacks on the SAT in relation to their performance in college, it was hard to refute the change. When the data were finally published, however, it became clear that the SAT did the job it was supposed to do for blacks as well as for whites. In other words, validity studies showed that SAT scores predicted academic performance in college as well for blacks as it did for whites. But the rhetoric persists to this day to the effect that the test discriminates against blacks, when in fact it no more discriminates against blacks now than it did against Jewish students from New York City 40 years ago.

The question then becomes, "Has the SAT been used to discriminate against blacks just as it was allegedly used to discriminate against Jewish students from New York in the years after World War II?" That's a different question from "Does the SAT discriminate against blacks?" My answer to the first quesiton would have to be that it occasionally has. For instance, there was one early statewide adoption of an SAT requirement in the South that I suspect had as one of its motives the exclusion of blacks from higher education. (If it did, it backfired.) But in my judgment the instances were rare and the great majority of higher institutions did not use the SAT to keep out black students. Yet the fact remains that blacks and Hispanics have continued to score well below whites on the SAT. And that fact raises the question, "Does use of the SAT in college admissions result in discrimination against minority youngsters regardless of what the intention of individual institutions may be?" That question, please note, is different from the first two questions. The problem in responding is that people who make the charge that the SAT discriminates against minorities are seldom clear about which question they are dealing with. The College Board has been trying to sort out the questions and the answers to them ever since it became involved directly in trying to respond to the intent of the Supreme Court decision in *Brown* v. *Board of Education*.

Today, if he were consistent, Ralph Nader would be claiming that the SAT was also rigged over the past 25 years to ensure that Asian American candidates would outperform the majority candidates. Baloney! It's not that the SAT was or is rigged to be biased for or against any cultural, ethnic, or linguistic group. What the SAT does is predict how well students from any background will do in courses taught in the standard middle-class American English used in the nation's colleges and universities.

Nevertheless, one piece of advice we received from our black constituents was that it would help if questions using vocabulary unfamiliar to most poor, black, or other minority students could be eliminated from the SAT. To try to ensure that result, many years ago ETS initiated what have come to be known as sensitivity reviews. Blacks and Hispanics are asked to review all items slated for inclusion in an operational form of the SAT to make sure that any that appear biased in the sense I have described are eliminated. That effort seems to have been successful. Today's most strident critics keep going back to one single item that was last used in an operational form of the test in 1975 (out of several hundred thousand) to support their claim that the SAT is biased. It involved the words *oarsmen* and *regatta,* which they contend are strictly upper-middle-class. I question even that contention on the grounds that most blacks I've asked have said that the youngsters in their communities with any expectation of going to college, and therefore taking the SAT, wouldn't have had any trouble with those two words. And I reject on two grounds their more general claim that the vocabulary of the SAT is biased against minorities: first, so few items have been called into question; second, validity studies persistently demonstrate that the test predicts as well for minority as for majority students. But those reflections deal only with the first of the three ways in which the SAT is presumed by its critics to discriminate against minorities—that the test itself is biased.

Our black constituents were also prone to make a second charge against colleges and universities—that the SAT is used to discriminate against blacks. This charge is harder to treat. I can recall discussing the problem with admissions officers somewhat along the following lines: "Look," I'd say, "you contend that you want to admit more blacks but that you can't because their test scores are too low. If you want to enroll more blacks, why don't you simply ignore SAT scores in their cases?" "Certainly we want to admit more blacks," they'd say, "but if we admit students with SAT scores that are too low, they'll most likely flunk out."

Colleges were indeed faced with a tough choice. Should they protect blacks from the likelihood of failure by keeping those with low scores out? Or should they admit some lower-scoring students on the chance that with a little special help they might make it? By and large, colleges bent over backward in choosing the latter course. But when pressed about why they didn't admit more, they fell back on an affirmative answer to the first question ("Has the SAT been used to discriminate against blacks?"). When they did, the blame was put on the good old SAT. "Obviously," they would say, "use of the SAT discriminates against blacks." As they said it, they were overlooking the many blacks with marginal scores who were being admitted. In my opinion, despite those inconsistencies, most colleges and universities did a conscientious job of trying to find the proper balance between keeping out those students who obviously couldn't make it academically and taking a risk with those at the margin who might have a chance.

The circumstances I describe were most prevalent at selective institutions, where much more than SAT scores is taken into account in making admissions decisions. Indeed, I have the clear impression that the more selective the institution, the more likely it would be to make exceptions in favor of minorities. At some public universities, the allowances for exceptions were publicly announced. At the University of California, for example, an applicant had to stand in the top 12.5 percent of his or her high school class or achieve a minimum combined verbal and mathematical score on the SAT. But there was, and is, an allowance for exceptions—that is, in special circumstances such as the need to increase black or Hispanic enrollment or to fulfill male or female intercollegiate athletic requirements. That backdoor approach was later to turn out to be anathema to the Hispanic community. (Its leaders want their young people admitted through regular channels; they do not want all Hispanic students on a campus to be perceived as having gotten in through the back door.) In the final analysis I have to say that, allowances, exceptions, and back doors aside, the admissions practices of some colleges acting in good conscience and with the best of motives gave the appearance of using the SAT to keep blacks out.

My third question was, "Does use of the SAT in college admissions result in discrimination against minority youngsters regardless of what the intention of individual institutions may be?" The answer has to be yes. The fact that minorities, on the average, don't score as well as whites do requires that affirmative response to that question. Look at the circumstances: The psychometrician is convinced that the SAT doesn't discriminate against minorities because its items aren't biased and its scores predict as well for blacks as for whites. The admissions officer knows that he or she isn't using the SAT to discriminate against minorities because the same standards are being applied to blacks and to whites. The black knows that he or she is being discriminated against because blacks score 100 points lower on the SAT and aren't admitted to selective colleges in the same proportion as whites are. Everyone is right! Which is not surprising in a nation where the Department of Labor and the Department of Justice disagree on appropriate affirmative action.

As suggested earlier, most selective colleges in those early years of the civil rights movement bent over backward to increase black enrollment, either through backdoor admissions policies or by giving black applicants preference at the margin. This practice posed the problem of how to accommodate these new populations. Some colleges ignored them and left young blacks to fend for themselves as part of an integrated community. Other colleges sought ways to provide special support services. One admissions dean reflected the attitude of a number of his colleagues when he spoke of the need to provide a "critical mass," enough black students to provide a congenial environment for themselves within the larger student body. Here colleges faced the same no-win situation faced by the College Board in its test center desegregation effort—desegregation leading to the presence of black students in what were perceived to be "hostile environments."

Like it or not, likes tend to associate. When I was on the staff of the North Shore Country Day School in suburban Chicago in the early 1950s, the school used to have "play days" with the University School at the University of Chicago, located in the midst of the city's predominantly black South Side and enrolling a considerable number of black students. A play day is an occasion when the student bodies of two schools get together for sports and recreation, not opposing each other with school teams but being united so that youngsters from both schools are playing together on teams against each other. Thus the athletic competition provided an opportunity for the all-white North Shore students to play with and against blacks from the South Side. But when it was time for lunch in the cafeteria, the blacks always reestablished their own critical mass and ate together. In another of those ironic twists of fate, the action of those black youngsters presaged the emergence of cultural pluralism in the aftermath of society's attempt to integrate itself a decade later.

The University School students were always polite and well behaved. The same couldn't be said about some of the critical masses that coalesced on some of the nation's college and university campuses in the late 1960s and early 1970s. Demonstrations, sit-ins, and takeovers were the order of the day as young blacks sought redress for the many grievances their communities held against the "white establishment." As other causes aroused students' emotions, the protests were not confined to blacks. In the aftermath of one widely reported building takeover, the dean of a well-known college, one of the most able educational administrators I have been privileged to know, resigned, saying, "I thought I'd signed up to help young men and women with their educations, not to serve as a military tactician."

We were never quite sure in those days at the College Board whether student protest would spill over into our meetings. Thanks to the initiative of protest-hardened veterans like Arnold Goren of New York University, however, we had contingency plans for dealing with disruptions at annual meetings. We knew who was going to turn off the microphones, who was going to turn off the lights, who was going to have access to the bullhorn, and who was in charge of giving the signal to initiate those responses. As it turned out, we never had to put our contingency plans into effect, but knowing they were there helped.

Occasionally a single student could generate a crisis. One example was an inner-city black freshman enrolled in a major state university. He went into the registrar's office to change a course and got wound up in typical establishment bureaucratic red tape. He finally became so frustrated that he threatened to "burn the goddamn building down." The registrar was alerted and called the minority affairs officer for advice. "What should we do?" The response? "Call the fire department." Now, more than a quarter of a century later, that able black minority affairs officer is a full-fledged, fully integrated, highly respected dean in that same university, helping young men and women of all races and color with their educations and not having to serve as a pyrotechnic tactician.

But while the selective public and private universities were being reasonably successful in recruiting, admitting, and retaining black students, the major increase in minority enrollment was taking place in the open-door institutions, the community colleges, and the onetime teachers colleges turned state universities. For whatever reason—perhaps because many were essentially commuting colleges or because they, like the blacks, were seeking identity as champions of affirmative action or because they provided fewer support services for the new populations—their black students tended to protest less and to drop out more.

Higher education as a whole, however, took understandable pride in its response to the civil rights movement, to federal legislation in the

Johnson administration, and to executive regulation in the Nixon era, all calling for desegregation. The proportion of blacks in the population going on to college began to approach that of the majority. But then in the 1980s, the numbers began to fall off. Why? It didn't happen in the more selective institutions. The numbers enrolled in them have remained relatively stable as they continue to recruit, enroll, and support the more academically promising minority students. The decline, therefore, had to have occurred primarily in the open-door institutions, where the open door frequently became a revolving door. Students who were already educationally disadvantaged found themselves underprepared and pro- grammed for failure. So they dropped out, shared their disappointment with their younger brothers and sisters (in both the familial and racial senses), and generated a chain reaction that has turned many promising young blacks away from college.

Roles of the SAT

Through all this flow and ebb of minority numbers in higher education, the SAT played three important roles and one nonrole. First, through its offshoot, the Preliminary Scholastic Aptitude Test/National Merit Schol- arship Qualifying Test (PSAT/NMSQT), as well as in its own right, the SAT served as the most widely used and possibly the most important single talent search device the country had. The National Scholarship Service and Fund for Negro Students (NSSFNS) turned to the PSAT/ NMSQT when it was transformed from an effort focused on the aca- demically elite to a broad-based talent-search enterprise. The National Merit Scholarship Corporation (NMSC) used the PSAT/NMSQT as the initial screen for its National Achievement Awards to black students and the SAT as one factor in choosing the ultimate award winners. In more recent years, after the College Board began collecting ethnic data about test candidates, colleges have been able to use this information, which is supplied voluntarily through the Student Descriptive Questionnaire (SDQ) in connection with the SAT and on the PSAT/NMSQT answer sheet, to recruit minority candidates through the mechanism of the Student Search Service (SSS).

On this score note should be taken of the widely reported an- nouncement in 1984 by Bates College, in Lewiston, Maine, that it was giving up its requirement of the SAT for admission and was asking instead for College Board Achievement Test scores. Bates gave as one of the reasons for its action the assertion that the SAT is biased against minorities. That explanation must have been offered for effect. It certainly couldn't have been for cause, for two reasons: One, because the Achievement Tests are designed to assess the knowledge acquired by students in what might best be described as advantaged schools, they are pitched at a higher level of difficulty than the SAT so that the more selective colleges may use them to help make choices among high-scoring students. Two, each year about 1.8 million applicants take the SAT. Roughly 20 percent are minority, which provides a pool of something over 350,000 minority candidates. About 250,000 students take the Achievement Tests annually. Roughly 5 percent of them are minority, which produces a pool of some 12,500 applicants. To imply, as Bates did in its announcement about giving up the SAT and using the Achievement Tests instead, that by that action alone it would be eliminating discrimination against minority applicants was misleading. Bates certainly had every right to do what it did, but I was appalled by the reasoning it offered, and I said so publicly at the time.

Another reason offered by Bates for abandoning the SAT, one that is widely echoed by critics of the test, is that because the SAT is thought to be coachable and because minority youngsters are most often poor and thus can't afford coaching, colleges requiring the SAT are by definition discriminating against minorities. (The subject of coaching is dealt with in Chapter 3.) My comments on the matter are twofold: While the College Board's official position on coaching has evolved over time as new evidence has become available, the original trustee pronouncements, based on data from the late 1950s, were influenced by the desire to assure minority students that without coaching they would not be at a disadvantage, and the Board took a strong coaching-doesn't-help position. My second comment is that regardless of the time, minority students weren't going to be disadvantaged anyway. At open-door institutions the question was moot; SAT scores weren't used for admission. At selective institutions seeking to increase the number of black and Hispanic students, that goal would take precedence at the margin over whatever few points on the SAT score scale coaching might conceivably, on the average, produce.

The second role that SAT scores played as the number of blacks going on to college increased was, of course, its traditional role of helping colleges make admissions decisions, helping them make judgments. For instance, a college may question whether a given black applicant could make it academically, whether courses were offered at a level of difficulty that student could reasonably be asked to assume, and whether support services, if available, would be needed.

That these questions were raised about many black applicants to selective colleges had an unfortunate side effect. All blacks, including the most academically talented whom colleges would have been glad to admit under any circumstances, were perceived as having been admitted at the margin or through the back door. Under those conditions many, who in an earlier day would have become integrated in the student body, drifted instead into the critical mass and lent their not inconsiderable talents to arguments of protest.

The third role played by the SAT in the cause of increasing minority enrollment in higher education was helping minority students make choices about the course levels they should challenge and about where they might appropriately be placed in course sequences. The Bates decision to abandon its SAT requirement followed a somewhat similar one by Bowdoin College, in Brunswick, Maine, in 1969. These actions by two small liberal arts colleges in Maine 15 years apart were played up by the press as a massive movement away from the SAT. (If that isn't evidence of bias against the SAT by the press, then I don't know what bias is.) What the news stories in 1969 and 1984 failed to note was that although Bowdoin had stopped requiring the SAT for admission, it still required it for matriculation. If an admitted student hadn't taken the test, he or she had to take it for course placement. The availability of the SAT and other tests for that purpose made it possible for colleges, if they chose, to fit minority students into appropriately demanding sequences and to minimize the likelihood of failure and dropout.

My interpretation of events is that one of the main reasons minority enrollments have held up in the more selective institutions is that they chose to use evidence from the SAT and other sources wisely to recruit, carefully to admit, and sensitively to place black and other minority students.

And then that nonrole of the SAT: It was played out, or not played out, in less selective four-year and open-door community colleges and in institutions that sought to increase their minority enrollment on a sink-or-swim basis. They were less inclined to use SAT scores either to recruit applicants or to place newly admitted students. If they had used the scores, the success rates might conceivably have been higher, the dropout rates might have been lower, and the ebb in minority enrollments might not have followed the flow.

Involving blacks no matter what the cost was not peculiar to higher education. In the late 1960s the rush to employ blacks resulted in the appointment to positions in business and in education of persons who simply got in over their heads. Like educationally underprepared students going on to many open-door colleges, they were programmed for failure. The College Board itself was not immune. We employed some promising young blacks in positions for which they simply weren't ready. Most, given time and experience, have gone on to fulfilling careers elsewhere. Unlike the black students who failed in college and dropped out, they got a second chance.

For me personally there was a flip side to the minority representation coin. Involving blacks in College Board affairs resulted in my getting involved in theirs. It was a learning experience for me. By my own acronym, I am a SWAMP (that is, a suburban white Anglo-Saxon male Protestant), a minority anywhere these days but particularly so among blacks then. I sat on the governing boards of two organizations concerned with the education of black students, the United Board for College Development (UBCD) and the National Scholarship Service and Fund for Negro Students (NSSFNS), mentioned above. The UBCD was a consortium of predominantly black church-related colleges loosely allied with the National Council of Churches. Through participation in its activities, I came to know many presidents and administrators of the nation's predominantly black church-related colleges and to work with them in a difficult period, when predominantly white colleges and universities were scrambling to attract the best and the brightest not only of black applicants but of proven black faculty members.

The NSSFNS began as an effort to attract bright black (then still called Negro) students to selective colleges but was transformed in the 1960s into a national talent search effort on behalf of academically promising black students generally. As a member of its board of directors, I had the opportunity to be in touch with activist members of the black community and others interested in opening up access to college for young black men and women.

Given the College Board's commitment in this regard and my own direct involvement in the UBCD and the NSSFNS, I found myself on a number of occasions one of a small minority of whites, or the only white, in a gathering of blacks. I was fortunate to remain in communication with the blacks in those early protest years, that period of the most vocal confrontation. I am inclined to believe that the reason I was able to do so was that I didn't back off.

The College Board and ETS even invited confrontation. I recall one meeting that the two organizations jointly sponsored in the middle 1960s. It was held at ETS but the participants, mostly blacks, were housed in downtown Princeton. The meeting, frankly, was a disaster.

Sadly, we hadn't yet learned how to deal with blacks and they hadn't learned how to do more than get our attention. Later on, after the frustrations had been aired and productive communication between blacks and whites established, being a minority white in a predominantly black meeting was like being a fly on the wall. I recall particularly Andrew Young, between his stints as United States ambassador to the United Nations and as mayor of Atlanta, talking at a UBCD meeting in Atlanta to a group of presidents of historically black colleges. He really gave them the business, pointing out unique opportunities for service that their institutions could provide, opportunities that were being overlooked but could be taken advantage of if only those presidents would put their minds to it. Young, it seemed to me, was trying to help his brothers and sisters strengthen the critical mass that the black community represents in America's culturally pluralistic society.

Today I contrast those two meetings with a hearing conducted by the National Commission on Testing and Public Policy at predominantly black Howard University in December 1988. There an audience that was perhaps two-thirds black heard articulate black scholars—sociologists, psychologists, psychometricians, and administrators—present and react to papers on testing in education and employment as the process affects blacks. Those speakers weren't attacking or defending tests. They were seeking to help the commission understand how testing affects the black community. It was an exercise in consultation, not confrontation.

Those three meetings—at ETS in the 1960s, in Atlanta in the 1970s, and at Howard University in the 1980s—serve for me as benchmarks for what has been happening in the black community generally over the last 25 years: first, the verbal and sometimes physical attack on the establishment in order to stake out its civil rights claim; second, the development of its own critical mass by taking counsel within itself; third, its entry into the mainstream. But that process of evolution doesn't mean that the job is now done. Far from it!

Edmund Gordon, the brilliant black Yale psychologist, put it in words like these for me at lunch during the meeting at Howard. "A lot of blacks like me have made it into the mainstream, but there are still many, many more who haven't been as fortunate. They are the ones we need to help." The leadership in the black community is now coming from those in the mainstream, and I am heartened that they are taking a hand in helping their younger black brothers and sisters on the road to college. I like to think, too, that many of those leaders got into the mainstream, as Gordon said he did, because the SAT helped them somewhere along the way.

Higher Education for Other Minorities

As these developments in the national search for equality of educational opportunity were unfolding, others emerged, and the view from my SAT window expanded. For education the initial focus of the civil rights movement was on the plight of the nation's black minority, in large part, I suppose, because *Brown* v. *Board of Education* was primarily a black issue. But federal statute and executive regulation later defined disadvantaged minorities to include Mexican Americans, Puerto Ricans, and American Indians—populations that suffered many of the same problems encountered by blacks, albeit in the early years of the civil rights movement in less focused and less publicized fashion. As a result, a whole new set of challenges was presented.

As in the test center desegregation in the South, the College Board was into the Hispanic act before it became popular. The Board's entry into this arena via the establishment of its office in Puerto Rico in 1963 is described more fully in Chapter 8, "The International Connection." For the present purposes, however, it should be noted that there were three primary motives at play in the establishment of a College Board presence in the Commonwealth. One was service to the colleges and universities on the island, initially through the development of a Spanish SAT, the Prueba de Aptitud Académica (PAA). The second was the use of the PAA by universities in Central and South America for their own internal admissions purposes and by Spanish-speaking students from the southern hemisphere seeking entry to higher education in the United States. The third, most pertinent here, was helping young minority Spanish-speaking Americans, wherever they lived, make the transition from school to college.

This early experience with a Spanish-speaking constituency kept us from later being surprised by the differences that exist within what is loosely referred to as the "Hispanic community in the United States." Believe me, in the Caribbean there are rivalries among the Puerto Ricans, Cubans, and Santo Domingans that carry over to their populations "in the States" or "on the mainland." (As a point of clarification here, when Puerto Ricans refer to the United States in Spanish, they use the term *el continente,* but when speaking in English, they use the word mainland, for which there is no direct translation in Spanish.)

My wife Elaine's mother, Ellen, had a favorite singer in a favorite nightclub in Miami, Gypsy's Pub. Cleo, the singer, was from Santo Domingo. Elaine's mother was Irish. Whenever Ellen entered Gypsy's Pub, Cleo would sing "My Wild Irish Rose." This byplay led to an exchange of home visits. Once Elaine and I went with her mother and brother to Cleo's for dinner. In the course of our dinner table conversation, Cleo's father let it be known that he was the champion portable sauna salesman in the United States.

"What?" I asked. "In Miami?"

"Yes!" And he produced documents to prove his claim.

"How?" I asked.

"I concentrate on the upper-middle-class Cubans," he chuckled. "I tell them, 'You wake up in your air-conditioned house, go to work in your air-conditioned car to your air-conditioned office, have lunch in an air-conditioned restaurant, go back to your air-conditioned office, then head home in your air-conditioned car to eat and sleep in your air-conditioned house. You're Cuban! You need to sweat!' " His put-on obviously worked.

If there are rivalries between the Cubans and the Santo Domingans, they also exist among the Spanish-speaking nationals of Central and South America as well as the Caribbean, rivalries that carry over to the communities they form in the United States. Colombians, for instance, speak a Spanish Spanish and are scornful of the rapid-fire Puerto Rican Spanish of the Commonwealth. And on the island the longtime residents speak disdainfully of the "New Yoricans," persons of Puerto Rican lineage who have moved back to the island of Puerto Rico from the island of Manhattan and the other boroughs of New York City.

Mexican Americans constitute the largest population of Hispanics, or Latinos, in the country. Unlike the Puerto Ricans on the mainland, who by and large consider themselves Puerto Ricans first and citizens of the United States second, Mexican Americans tend to think of themselves as Americans with a Mexican heritage. Also, there is the uninformed assumption that people of Hispanic origin are all Roman Catholic, when in fact a large segment of the Mexican American population is Presbyterian. Most mainland Puerto Ricans live in large cities along the East Coast. Mexican Americans, on the other hand, who are located primarily in the Southwest and in California, are apt to be either urban or rural dwellers. These cultural and geographic differences have the effect of fostering social agendas with similar goals but different approaches to them. They also made it harder for the College Board to mount a concerted effort to help increase the number of Hispanic students enrolled in higher education.

Before the civil rights movement got under way, the Hispanic presence in the nation's colleges and universities consisted mostly of students from upper-middle-class families in Central and South America, and most of the few Hispanic college faculty members came from those same backgrounds. The other major source of Hispanic teachers was created by the higher education institutions in the Commonwealth and by the University of Puerto Rico in particular. Until Caesar Chávez Community College was founded in the midst of the civil rights effort, there was not a truly Hispanic higher education institution on the mainland, although some might argue that Hostos Community College within the City University of New York would qualify.

In any event, the small cadre of educated Hispanic elite produced under these circumstances was in sharp contrast with the numbers of college-educated blacks available to provide leadership to their brothers and sisters at the start of the civil rights movement. While the black presence in predominantly white institutions had been minimal up to that point, the nation's historically black colleges had for years been training black teachers and preparing other students for graduate liberal arts and professional school programs. On their faculties there were experienced professors whom predominantly white colleges could steal in their efforts to follow the law to integrate, men and women wise in the ways of university life who could serve as models for their students and colleagues and provide an intellectual base for the formulation of the black agenda.

But these human resources simply did not exist within the Hispanic communities in the immediate aftermath of *Brown* v. *Board of Education*. This circumstance explains in large measure why attention to the need to increase the number of minority students in higher education came so much later to the Hispanic than to the black population.

The College Board's first activity focusing on the special needs of Mexican American students was a 1969 regional conference convened in the Southwest to discuss those needs. A year later Thomas P. Carter's seminal voume, *Mexican Americans in School: A History of Educational Neglect,* was published by the College Board in 1970. A sequel, *Mexican Americans in School: A Decade of Change,* published by the College Board in 1979, reflected 10 years of slow, unspectacular but steady progress in the efforts to open up access to higher education for this largest segment of the nation's Hispanic community.

As in dealing with blacks earlier, the College Board sought actively to involve Mexican Americans and Puerto Ricans in its councils and on its committees. Our first Hispanic trustee was the Puerto Rican president of one of the colleges of the City University of New York; our second was a Mexican American community college president who later became the first chairman of the Board's Advisory Panel on Minority Concerns.

Externally, too, we sought to work with the minority leadership, but, again, this was more difficult with the Hispanics than it had been in dealing with the blacks. The National Association for the Advancement of Colored People (NAACP) and the National Urban League provided national foci for the black agenda, while, in contrast, Hispanic activities were divided among such community agencies as ASPIRA and the Puerto Rican Legal Defense and Education Fund (PRLDEF), headquartered in New York City; the League of United Latin American Citizens (LULAC) and the Chicano Council on Higher Education (CCHE) in Washington, D.C.; the Latino Institute in Chicago; the Mexican American Legal Defense and Education Fund (MALDEF), which, to my recollection, has been headquartered in San Antonio, San Francisco, and Los Angeles; and the National Hispanic Scholarship Fund (NHSF) in San Francisco. All had, and still have, different constituencies and different goals. But all their agendas included issues pertaining to education and all were united in their conviction that the SAT was unfair to bilingual youngsters like theirs. They continue to be convinced of that because Puerto Rican and Mexican American candidates on the average score lower than the majority, although not as low as blacks do.

But, I insist, it isn't the SAT per se that is biased or unfair. What the lower scores reflect is that bilingual Puerto Rican and Mexican American students apparently don't handle the standard middle-class English used for instruction in colleges as well as do the essentially monolingual majority. For some Hispanic students, having control of two languages is an educational advantage; for others, it is a handicap. What admissions officers need to do in evaluating the SAT scores of Hispanic applicants is to take account of the linguistic circumstances in which they grew up. They are bound to be different from those of the majority.

I've heard leaders of the Hispanic community wax eloquent on the problems faced by bilingual students in taking tests like the SAT. I can sympathize with their problems. It must be very hard to shift back and forth from one language to another, and their learning styles must be affected in the process. Nevertheless, I've heard people of other ethnic, non-English-speaking backgrounds describe how they went to school to learn English and then went home to teach it to their immigrant parents. They have little sympathy with what the Hispanics consider the plight of their children. In odd moments I've often wondered in this context why it is that so many people think children should study a second langauge in school if bilingualism is a handicap.

My mother's hometown, a small mill town in central Massachusetts, has for many years had a large Polish population, made up of immigrants brought in to work in the woolen mills and their descendants. In the 1930s my mother, who was a student of languages, studied Polish with the Polish nuns. She later astounded the ambassador from Poland during a visit to Harvard by greeting him and conversing with him in his native tongue. She was most proud, however, of her ability to recite the Lord's Prayer in impeccable Polish. Those nuns were able to teach her so effectively because in those days they were regularly teaching school-age children from the Polish community the language of their forebears. As in many Jewish congregations today, the Polish parents were then keeping their linguistic as well as their cultural heritage alive for their own children and did not insist on special treatment for their children in the public schools.

That small mill town had and still has Yankee, Irish, and French Canadian residents as well. Trilingualism was a problem in the schools, involving English, French, and Polish. My eighth-grade music teacher was Hector Choiniere from my mother's hometown. When she went to school with him, his name was Sweeney, but not because he was Irish. The teacher was and on the first day of school, when she found she couldn't get her Irish tongue around Choiniere, she told him, "In this class your name is Sweeney."

Here again is the reflection of a problem affecting the world of the SAT—the hostility of Mexican Americans and mainland Puerto Ricans toward a test using English, a hostility that is symptomatic of a fundamental problem facing our society at large. Are we to continue as a heterogeneous monolingual society or not? The dilemma is real. The Puerto Rican and Mexican American populations are growing steadily, particularly in the Northeast, the Southwest, and the West, and their influence can be seen in many ways—for example, in the instructions in English and Spanish in city subways. They weren't there when I was growing up in the 1920s and 1930s, or even a decade ago. However the nation decides ultimately to deal with its Hispanic populations, precedent for accommodating the burgeoning Asian American population will have been set. And the SAT is inevitably bound to get sideswiped in the process.

I don't presume to know the right way to deal with bilingualism, but I do know that so long as higher education continues to be conducted in standard middle-class English, and I predict it will be for a long time to come, the SAT or other criteria like it will be used in the college admissions process. In this circumstance the most effective educational approach to the problems of bilingualism on behalf of Hispanic youngsters who have the potential for college would appear to be the tried-and-true method of beginning where the students are. If large numbers of them are more comfortable in Spanish than in English in a particular school setting, then Spanish should be used as the language of instruction until the students can be weaned from it. But, this approach, which sounds so sensible in theory and on paper, has one major drawback. Because many, if not most, Puerto Rican and Mexican American youngsters aren't fluent in either language in the early years of school, they end up behind the verbal eight ball long before they get to high school.

For this reason, among others, I became convinced that much earlier intervention was needed to help achieve equality of access to higher education for Mexican American and Puerto Rican students—earlier, that is, than had been available to black students in the junior and senior years of high school through activities like Project Opportunity and Project Open and Project Access. An opportunity to explore this possibiliity presented itself in the early 1980s through the initiative of the Andrew W. Mellon Foundation.

The Mellon Foundation approached the College Board about exploring ways to encourage the educational development of the most academically able Hispanic students. It chose to approach the College Board rather than any one of the Hispanic agencies, at least in part because of the diversity among them. Convinced that the mounting of any such effort would require the support of the major Hispanic community action agencies, the College Board undertook to bring together the leaders of the agencies mentioned above. This undertaking was not as easy as it sounds. The agency representatives were suspicious of the College Board and its motives as well as wary of each other. Just getting them to agree to meet together in the same room was considered something of a diplomatic triumph in and of itself. I can take credit only to the extent that I was wise enough to engage the interest of Arturo Madrid in the process.

Madrid was a professor and an administrator at the University of Minnesota when he was called to head the Fund for the Improvement of Post-Secondary Education (FIPSE) in the Carter administration. In that position he was the highest-ranking Hispanic in the federal government, and indeed the first to hold such rank. He was so effective that he even lasted a few months into the Reagan years. Finding him suddenly available, I sought his help, and we managed to bring together leaders from ASPIRA, CCHE, LULAC, NHSF, MALDEF, PRLDEF, and the Latino Institute. We spent a couple of years working with this group, trying to devise a strategy that would be acceptable to all parties.

This task wasn't easy, either. A natural concern of our Puerto Rican and Mexican American colleagues was that any proposal we came up with under College Board sponsorship might divert foundation funds away from projects higher on the individual agencies' agendas. In other words, they didn't want the College Board getting in the way of their fund-raising activities. We worked our way through this thicket by coming up with a plan in which each agency would play a unique role of its own devising through its local offices.

The basic idea of the plan was to start at the junior high school level to decrease the high rate at which Hispanic young people drop out between junior high and high school and to increase the proportion of those going on to high school who choose a college preparatory course of study. In other words, instead of identifying a few able students early in their high school careers and focusing attention on them for three or four years, which was the initial approach considered, we opted to attack the problem early in junior high and thereby increase the entire pool of college-bound Hispanic youngsters. We talked about "enlarging the base of the pyramid" instead of taking an "obelisk" approach.

The Mellon Foundation followed our discourse carefully and, while maintaining its traditional interest in recognizing particularly able academic talent, encouraged the College Board and the Hispanic agencies in the development of the pyramid approach and in our efforts to raise funds from other philanthropic sources to launch the project. We thought we had finally succeeded when, in the later stages of our deliberations, the program officers of two major foundations (not Carnegie or Ford) expressed sympathetic and enthusiastic interest in what we were trying to accomplish. But they hadn't reckoned with their boards of trustees. When the proposals were presented, their trustees simply said no.

Nobody ever did tell us why the idea didn't fly after the encouragement we had received. Perhaps the program officers had misread their trustees' expressed interest in "doing something for the Hispanic community." My own reading is that "other interests" devoted to providing salvation for the Hispanics didn't want the College Board or anybody else upstaging them. The jealousies over turf within the world of philanthropy are often of no less intensity than the rivalry between Cubans and Santo Domingans.

Having at this point exhausted the Mellon Foundation's patience and our own, we decided in the end to focus on the foundation's interest in the best academic talent the Hispanic community had to offer. The result was the highly successful and universally popular National Hispanic Scholar Awards Program (NHSAP). By this time the Hispanic agencies with which we were working were no longer suspicious of the College Board and had come to respect Mellon's interest in the academically talented. They figured that the National Hispanic Scholar Awards Program would not divert funds they might otherwise be able to tap.

Under this program, 500 National Hispanic Scholars and 500 semifinalists are chosen each year from a pool of candidates who have taken the PSAT/NMSQT, voluntarily identified themselves as Hispanic, and indicated that they wish to enter the NHSAP competition. Those who qualify on the basis of their PSAT/NMSQT scores are then asked to submit application materials very much like those required by selective colleges. There are, however, two special considerations that are taken into account in the final selection process. One is evidence of a candidate's recognition of his or her Hispanic heritage; the other is evidence of a candidate's having had to cope with disadvantage, whether it was economic, social, educational, or otherwise. Each National Hispanic Scholar receives a $1,000 award, each semifinalist $100. The names of all are made available to colleges and universities seeking to recruit Hispanic students.

The results have been reassuring, to say the least. First, they confirm that there are a lot of bright Hispanic students in the nation's high schools. Second, the National Hispanic Scholars are serving as role models for younger students to emulate. Third, the program has apparently had the effect of inducing more Hispanic young men and women to think about the possibility of college. Fourth, colleges and universities have been helped in their efforts to recruit minority applicants by the increased number of Hispanic high school students taking the PSAT/NMSQT. And all this has the general approbation of the Puerto Rican and Mexican American community service agencies, an outcome that certainly couldn't have confidently been predicted at the beginning of the decade.

One of the early stumbling blocks would have been the reliance on the PSAT/NMSQT to create the initial pool of candidates. One of the long-standing objections to such use by the minority communities, black and Hispanic alike, has been based on the College Board's often-stated position that, in most circumstances, test scores alone should not be used to make decisions but should always be used in combination with other critiera. Early objects of this complaint were the regular and the National Achivement programs of the National Merit Scholarship Corporation. Like the National Hispanic Scholar Awards Program, both Merit programs use PSAT/NMSQT scores to create their initial pools of potential candidates. At first blush, those complaints appeared to be justified. The problem, however, was that the complainants failed to take public account of the College Board's qualification that they be so used "when other information of equal or greater relevance and the resources for using such information are available." I must say they could easily have overlooked that caveat in light of the College Board's failure to emphasize the point in its zeal to ensure that in any final selection process (that is, in any high-stakes decision), SAT scores were not the only criterion. Therefore, another important benefit from the creation of the National Hispanic Scholar Awards Program was the implicit acceptance by knowledgeable minority representatives of the need to have some mechanism, such as the PSAT/NMSQT, for creating a manageable pool of final candidates to consider in depth.

Just as the PSAT/NMSQT played a significant role in the national talent search and scholarship selection processes of the NMSC, NSSFNS, and NHSAP, it has also been part of a number of other efforts designed to increase the pool of Hispanic students considering college. The most significant of these was Options for Excellence, a three-year, $1 million project underwritten by the Minnie Stevens Piper Foundation in San Antonio, Texas, and conducted by the College Board. One of its two major goals was to increase the college-going rate among the Mexican American students in the high schools of Bejar County. (The other, also successfully achieved, was to increase participation in the Advanced Placement Program by all students.) With the public encouragement of Mayor Henry Cisneros, high school students were advised to take the PSAT/NMSQT, free of charge. Take it they did, in surprisingly large numbers. As it turned out, there was much more academic talent among them than might have been expected, particularly among the students not enrolled in bona fide college preparatory programs. The San Antonio experience has provided a role model for other communities seeking to achieve equality of access to higher education for their minority young people.

My personal understanding of the educational problems faced by American Indian young men and women became much clearer during my afterlife with the SAT (that is, after I retired as president of the College Board) as a member of the National Commission on Testing and Public Policy. Just as experience on the commission served to enhance my understanding of the linguistic problems faced by young people who grow up speaking both Spanish and English, so, too, it brought me a clearer recognition of the hurdles that inhibit the college attendance of American Indians.

As far as I can tell, the policy of the federal government into the

1980s was to destroy the cultures of the American Indian nations with which it had made treaties in the nineteenth century. At least its treatment of the American Indians was having that effect. Very recently, however, that stance appears to have changed, and actions have been taken that permit just the opposite. Included among the changes is the return to the tribes of responsibility for educational policy in the schools serving students on the reservations. That change in attitude reflects, I believe, further evidence of society's implicit but as yet hardly recognized espousal of cultural pluralism. For American Indian students the problems associated with going to college will be exacerbated—the problems of having to live in two cultures, the tribal and the broader societal ones; of learning two languages, their native language and English; and of learning to live with money. Their American Indian ways are different from those of society-at-large. They do think differently, more intuitively (or less logically as some would put it), but who's to say not as effectively. How to help young people in these circumstances will indeed continue to pose a real challenge to society and to the College Board. That is why, in 1987, I was encouraged by the initiation of the series of dialogues dealing with that challenge under the auspices of the American Indian Science and Engineering Society (AISES) and the College Board's Educational EQuality Project.

Meanwhile other minority-related problems have arisen on the college admissions scene. Today Asian Americans claim that their young people are being subjected to the same kind of discrimination that was allegedly practiced against Jewish students a half century ago. Harvard and the University of California, they say, have deliberately been controlling the number of Asian American students they will admit. Conditions have not come full circle, however, for today these students know their scores and are using them to make their case, calling attention in the process to applicants with lower scores than theirs who are being admitted. Like James Crouse, an SAT critic (see Chapter 2), they simply fail to recognize how admission to selective colleges works. Institutions don't rank students according to any one criterion—grades, SAT scores, or a combination of both—and then start selecting from the top down. They try to get a viable mix.

But suppose for the moment that their claim was upheld. What then would happen to colleges' affirmative action efforts to enroll more educationally disadvantaged students from the other minorities? Carried to the extreme, one of two outcomes would emerge. Either colleges would have to abandon their affirmative actions and stop admitting those students from other minorities at the margin, or they would have to admit high-scoring Asian Americans at the top of their rankings and then bypass the group of majority students in the middle in order to be able to admit low-scoring blacks, Hispanics, and American Indians at the margin.

Having to deal with dilemmas like that made my life with the SAT so fascinating and working at the College Board so rewarding!

CHAPTER 6

Athletes and Women

The life of the Scholastic Aptitude Test (SAT) has been plagued over the years by fallout from the misuse of it and its scores. One of the earliest alleged misuses, of course, was by those colleges said to be hiding behind SAT scores in order to limit the number of Jewish students admitted in the years following World War II. In recent years athletes and women have been among the most publicly prominent alleged victims. The problem for athletes was the adoption by the National Collegiate Athletic Association (NCAA) of eligibility rules for freshman participation in intercollegiate athletics based in part on SAT or ACT scores. For women it was the use by the New York State Regents of SAT or ACT scores alone as the basis for awarding state-sponsored scholarships. In both instances the outcomes had disproportionately adverse effects on the students involved. And in both instances the fallout was the repeated charge that the SAT is biased against minority athletes and against women. So here again is that subtle distinction between the existence of bias in the test itself and the biased outcomes that result from the improper use of SAT scores. Result? The usual. The existence of bias in the test was improperly inferred from what happened when its scores were improperly used.

Report on Intercollegiate Athletics

In another of those strange turns of fate, I had earlier participated in an endeavor that not only involved the interests of athletes and women but also served to prepare me for the reactions to the misuse of the SAT by the NCAA and the New York State Regents. During the academic year 1973-74, I devoted a six-month sabbatical leave from the College Board to an exploration of the need for a national study of intercollegiate athletics on behalf of the American Council on Education (ACE). The Carnegie Corporation of New York initially put up $15,000 to cover my expenses, and The Ford Foundation followed with $57,750 for me to enlist the help of nine part-time consultants. One of the accomplishments in which I take special pride was submission of our 182-page final report, accompanied by more than 400 pages of appendixes, the day before my six-month leave ended.

The fate of the report and its appendixes was something else again. At first, things looked promising. As a result of my inquiry, I had recommended the establishment of a Commission on Collegiate Sports to seek solutions to the problems I had identified. The staff at Carnegie was sufficiently taken with my rationale to encourage me to propose an underwriting of between $1.5 million and $2 million for such an effort. I compromised on $1.8 million over three years and cut the verbal dimensions of the proposal to fit that dollar cloth. In fact, the foundation staff was so taken with my idea that they invited me to tell their trustees about it before the actual proposal had been subjected to the normal in-house staff review, an unusual procedure to say the least. The common practice is for proposals to be carefully massaged by staff and meticulously prepared for trustee scrutiny. But my proposal was presumably so hot that the usual protocol was violated and I was asked to appear before my ink had time to dry. That the Carnegie Corporation of New York should be interested in a study of intercollegiate athletics was not surprising. After all, it had sponsored—indeed, one of its officers had conducted—the last major study of the field in the late 1920s. That its trustees nearly 50 years later should be uninterested was another matter.

My misgivings began at lunch before my "appearance" before the trustees. To my right at the luncheon table a businesswoman early on professed a total lack of interest in sports in general and thereafter conversed with the man to her right. To my left, another trustee explained her dim view of big-time college sports in more detail. Her son was, or had been, a member of the rifle team at Harvard and that institution had been negligent about replacing burned-out light bulbs in the rifle range, although it was floodlighting football practice.

My spies in attendance at the postluncheon session tell me that my performance was articulate, compelling, and animated. But it obviously left the trustees unmoved and the staff, I can only assume, chagrined. I was advised a day or so later that the ACE would be lucky to get a tenth of the amount from any one foundation, particularly the Carnegie Corporation of New York, and that the only hope lay in attracting the support of several foundations.

Accordingly, the $1.8 million proposal was pared down to about $750,000 by cutting out much of the research I had suggested, and it was eventually submitted half-heartedly on behalf of the American Council on Education to several philanthropic enterprises. Carnegie and Ford expressed continuing interest and talked in terms of their combined support providing a bit less than half the then current asking. Carnegie, however, made its dollars contingent on ACE's ability to find additional funding outside the Northeast; New York-based Ford, of course, did not qualify. The task of finding additional support anywhere proved difficult for ACE. The proposal was then trimmed to $500,000 by cutting out all the research, and later to $400,000 by reducing the size of, and length of service for, the staff proposed to serve the Commission on Collegiate Sports.

For better than two years the trustees of ACE regularly affirmed their concern over the state of intercollegiate athletics, confirmed their interest in "doing something" about the sorry state of affairs therein, and encouraged the president of ACE to continue his pursuit of the elusive dollars needed to do the job.

Why did the dollars prove so elusive? I think there were four reasons. First, I do not believe they were pursued as vigorously as they might have been. Despite the affirmations, confirmations, and encouragements, ACE at that time chose to treat the national problems of intercollegiate athletics in exactly the same way that college and university presidents generally were dealing with the local problems—that is, by doing just enough to ease their own consciences and pacify the complainants without doing anything but paying lip service to those problems. I simply refuse to believe that if the college and university presidents of the country had put their collective mind to the task (and keep in mind that the ACE is their club, so to speak), they could still not have raised the additional $50,000 that was necessary to complete the underwriting of that $400,000 proposal. But ACE and its presidents had other fish to fry; ACE lives mainly off "soft money" (foundation grants) and had other, more important, so they thought, projects to worry about.

Finally, a couple of years later, The Ford Foundation virtually shamed ACE into doing something by making a $200,000 grant. To cut the project down to this size, however, the idea of a blue-ribbon panel of distinguished public representatives who could speak with authority both to and for higher education was discarded, and a typical ACE in-house commission composed primarily of college and university presidents was appointed. This body soon used up the $200,000 in inconclusive meetings and went quietly out of existence, only to be replaced by an equally unproductive but even less influential continuing committee. That committee got swept into the underbrush when the furor over big-time college sports in the early 1980s led ultimately to the establishment of the NCAA Presidents Commission, discussed later in this chapter.

The second reason that the dollars proved elusive in the mid-1970s was substantive albeit complicated. It was based on the judgment by many that my inquiry had included all the studying that was needed. The introduction to my report recommended "that a Commission on Collegiate Sports be established . . . to formulate and oversee a program of studies designed to illuminate . . . the problems affecting college athletics in the United States in the mid-1970s." After the first cut in the asking price from $1.8 million to $750,000, however, the proposal that went to those other foundations assumed that my inquiry had comprised those studies and called for the proposed commission to review, and then base its recommendations for reform on, the results of my presumably preliminary investigation. Any foundation that received both the proposal and the report was bound to be confused. On more than one occasion the president of ACE told me that some foundation or other had tempered its rejection with the observation that the study had already been done and indicated that it wasn't in the business of funding commissions. For me the situation was both reassuring and ironic. It was satisfying in that some persons thought my brief but intensive sabbatical effort had done all the defining of the problems that was needed, but frustrating in that this very success ended up complicating the process of trying to find solutions.

The third reason the proposal didn't fly was that despite my identification of the problems, the report on which the proposal was based didn't, as my wife, Elaine, put it, "make enough waves." Only one of those 182 pages was devoted to specific recruiting and related violations of NCAA rules, and they had already been reported by the press. That litany included bomb threats to a high school principal who refused to alter an aspiring athlete's transcript and grades for a football player in a course he never attended. But for some reason, bringing all those violations together without editorializing about them or sensationalizing them simply failed to arouse public opinion. As Richard J. Margolis put it in the November 1974 issue of *Change*, vol. 6, no. 9, p. 59:

> He [Hanford] is less polemicist than administrator . . . which may be one reason why he presents us with a "balanced" analysis that never flies. . . . Hanford is thorough. He goes far beyond [the] themes of shoddy recruitment and big-time finances, grappling with such dilemmas as racism in sports, women's liberation, and the impact of television on college athletics. . . . Despite the writer's rounded and sometimes gifted prose . . . [it] seems to glide . . . atop smooth, artificial ice with nary a bump or an opinion to alter its course. . . . we get page upon page of pros and cons, all equally weighted. No maladies are isolated or deplored; no remedies are prescribed.

In any event, not the public or the media or those ACE college and university presidents or, for that matter, those trustees of the Carnegie Corporation were excited enough by my findings to support the proposal for the establishment of a commission to "do something" about the situation.

The fourth reason my idea wasn't supported was, as Margolis described it, "women's liberation." The motivation for my sabbatical effort was, of course, concern over the excesses being practiced in the recruitment and on-campus maintenance of male athletes in the big-time sports. But in putting my original request for Carnegie support together in 1973, I somehow managed to have the good sense to realize that women's athletics also deserved attention. After all, the passage of Title IX (pertaining in part to equal treatment of women in intercollegiate athletics) of the Education Amendments of 1972 was bound to have some effect. As a result, I engaged the services of Mary McKeown, then a graduate student at the University of Illinois, as one of my nine consultants and asked her to take a look at women in intercollegiate athletics; her findings constitute one of the appendixes to my report. When I submitted that document to ACE and the Carnegie Corporation a year and a half later, in 1974, it contained this italicized statement: "The most important and far-reaching recent development on the college sports scene has been the movement to achieve equal treatment for women in the conduct of intercollegiate sports." My judgment on this score proved to be correct, and it was the question of how to achieve equality of treatment for women in collegiate sports that preoccupied the Ford-underwritten commission and the other subsequent ACE committees that ultimately were put in place as a result of my sabbatical inquiry.

This sequence of events confirmed a conclusion I'd come to earlier: higher education in the United States is capable of dealing with only one serious issue at a time in any given field. In this instance, the legal necessity of responding to the requirements of Title IX pushed the problems associated with the shoddy conduct of men's big-time sports into the background. Certainly it was the issue of equity for women in sports that preoccupied higher education as far as athletics were concerned in the late 1970s. At the same time, I like to think that my effort did serve to plant the seed of greater involvement by college and university presidents in the conduct of intercollegiate athletics. Not only was the precedent of presidential involvement established, but the interest of the ACE leadership was engaged. The consultant who handled the financial aspects of sports for my inquiry was Robert Atwell, then president of Pitzer College in California. Atwell soon went on to become second-in-command at ACE and then its president; therefore, when things really got out of hand and into the public eye in the early 1980s, and college and university presidents finally decided that it was time to step in, they had an interested and informed pivot man to provide leadership for their effort.

Now these events, which seemed so remote from the world of the SAT when they began to unfold for me in 1973, suddenly came to have direct relevance to it in the early 1980s. With the passage by the NCAA of Proposition 48 in 1982, following the action by the New York State Regents to award certain state scholarships solely on the basis of SAT or ACT scores, the special interests of women and athletes began to complicate my life with the College Board. As they did, my sabbatical experience provided a very useful perspective from which to view the complications.

Propositions 48 and 42

First, about the athletes. By the early 1980s the excesses in the recruitment and retention of athletes competing in big-time college sports had reached the point of coverage in the media where a nucleus of concerned university presidents decided that some notice had to be taken of the circumstances. The reputation of higher education was being sullied, and they began to put pressure on the NCAA through the ACE. Mind you, they didn't take advantage of the established route—that is, the latest ACE committee on collegiate sports; it was manned primarily by the chief executive of lesser institutions—lesser, that is, in terms of athletic aspirations. Instead, the university presidents set themselves up in the beginning as a temporary ad hoc ACE body to deal with matters on a crisis basis. In time, and with the results of their influence on the conduct of NCAA affairs beginning to take effect, this body became transformed into what is now the NCAA Presidents Commission.

The process went something like this: What bothered those university presidents most was the harm being done to the academic reputations of their institutions. Athletes with submarginal academic records in secondary school were being recruited and admitted. Once they were enrolled, their eligibility was maintained by all manner of devious means. And in the end, too few were completing their studies and graduating. The presidents' remedy? Make sure that aspiring athletes take regular academic courses in high school and those admitted pursue a normally prescribed regimen of courses leading to a bachelors degree. Cliff Sjogren, then in charge of admissions at the University of Michigan, came up with a formula for achieving the first goal. It called for a program of preparation for college that included a passing average in a carefully defined core of real academic, not snap, courses. The presidents liked the idea but saw two flaws in it. Not only do high schools have different grading standards, they could not be trusted to present, nor could colleges be trusted to accept, legitimate transcripts. What could be trusted, however, were SAT and ACT scores. As a result, their proposal, which became NCAA Proposition 48, contained both Sjogren's plan and minimum scores on either the SAT or ACT.

When this proposition was put to the NCAA membership, it came under immediate attack. Representatives of predominantly black colleges in particular decried it on the grounds that it discriminated against minority athletes because, as they claimed, SAT (and ACT) scores are biased against blacks and Hispanics. I attacked it on the grounds that a national standard ought not to be imposed in place of the diverse entrance requirements of the nation's variously selective institutions. I applauded the intent of those university presidents but took issue with the means they chose to implement it. I advised the College Board's trustees of the public statement I intended to make to that effect, and they didn't object. Note that I didn't ask them to approve what I was going to say or to adopt it as College Board policy; that would have proved awkward for them. They were, after all, the elected representatives of the College Board membership, which included many of the NCAA institutions that had voted for Proposition 48. But the Board's trustees weren't about to keep me from saying what most of them as individuals believed to be appropriate.

I don't presume to suggest that if the Commission on Collegiate Sports I was calling for in 1974 had come into being, the conditions that prompted the adoption in 1982 of Proposition 48 would have been avoided and the SAT would not have become involved in intercollegiate athletics. But I do find it ironic that the SAT ended up under attack because it could be trusted to deal with some of the problems of institutional untrustworthiness I had earlier identified in my sabbatical inquiry.

Then, as if Proposition 48 wasn't already anathema to those espousing the cause of minority athletes, the SAT got socked again, this time in 1988 by Proposition 42. Proposition 48 said simply that a freshman athlete had to meet its requirements in order to be eligible to compete in intercollegiate sports. Students could be admitted whether or not they met those requirements, but if they didn't meet them, they couldn't compete. This meant that colleges were free to admit and award financial aid to students academically unqualified under the terms of Proposition 48, to deal with their academic deficiencies in the freshman year, and then, it was hoped, to get them into a regular degree program so that they could take to the field. A number of promising athletes were enrolled and awarded financial aid under this arrangement. But then somebody got the idea that athletes admitted in this way shouldn't be allowed to get financial aid. That was the gist of Proposition 42. In a close vote, in which I sense a number of NCAA representatives really didn't know what they were voting for or against, the proposition was adopted and the roof began to fall in. In a dramatic gesture demonstrating his disapproval, John Thompson, the highly respected Georgetown University basketball coach, boycotted two of his team's games. Other coaches and athletic directors also voiced their strong disagreement with the NCAA action. Sensing the rising tide of opposition being generated by those words and actions, the NCAA put the idea on hold. But the damage to the SAT had been done. When someone as highly regarded as John Thompson said he was against Proposition 42 because the SAT is biased against blacks, lots of people were certain to take his comment as confirmation of what they'd already heard in other contexts.

Actually, I staged a walkout of my own at this point. Because of my experience in the athletic arena, I was scheduled to take part in an accrediting team visit to Temple University for the Middle States Association of Colleges and Schools in March 1989, two months after the furor over Proposition 42 had broken out. But Temple's athletic director and its basketball coach had been so outspoken in their denunciation of the SAT that I became convinced they would be skeptical of any findings that might be made about their program by someone as closely associated with the SAT as I had been. So I withdrew from the Middle States Association evaluation team. I like to think I could have carried the assignment off objectively, but I must admit I get frustrated when well-meaning people mistake the discrimination that results from the misuse of the SAT for bias in the test itself. I found it ironic that the Georgetown and Temple basketball coaches, for example, were attacking Proposition

42 on the grounds that its use of SAT scores would have deprived low-scoring black athletes of financial aid as ineligible freshmen, and yet they were willing by their own admission to live with Proposition 48, which deprived low-scoring blacks from participating in intercollegiate sports. I don't see the distinction; if Propostion 42 deserved a boycott, so did Proposition 48.

In my book, use of the SAT in both propositions is inappropriate. Students should be admitted to colleges and universities according to each institution's own individual entrance requirements. Fortunately, my sabbatical experience prepared me for the SAT's encounter with the sad condition into which intercollegiate sports had fallen. With something over half the NCAA's Division I-A members (the big-time operators) having been cited for violations of NCAA regulations over the last decade, I really wasn't surprised that those university presidents believed they had to turn to a mechanism with the integrity of the SAT. They certainly couldn't trust their own institutions.

Athletic Equity for Women

My six-month leave of absence also made the fallout from the New York State Regents' use of SAT scores as the sole basis for the award of certain state scholarship funds easier for me to comprehend and to deal with intellectually. As I have suggested earlier, the issue of how to accommodate the requirements of Title IX in regard to the equal treatment of women in the conduct of intercollegiate athletics was the most pressing problem facing colleges and universities in the sports arena in the mid-1970s. Oversimplified, the question was whether to give women's athletics programs a chance to get established under their own auspices or under the aegis of the NCAA. Aware as I was of the shoddy practices existing in big-time men's intercollegiate sports, I championed the cause of the Association of Intercollegiate Athletics for Women (AIAW). I did so in the belief, first, that women deserved a chance to develop their own cadre of experienced coaches and administrators before being integrated with the men's athletic establishment and, second, that the women's emphasis on the noncommercial aspects of sports would have a beneficial effect on men's sports when the inevitable integration took place. And so it was that I became a sought-after spokesman for the AIAW in its struggle for recognition in the face of the NCAA's campaign to absorb responsibility for women's intercollegiate athletics.

As it turned out, I was on the losing side. As the NCAA took over, administration of women's sports came to be dominated by men, and men became coaches for many women's teams. I recall, for instance, the extremely able woman who had proved her worth as the assistant athletic director at a major Division I-A university. When the longtime athletic director left his post in the late 1970s, just about everyone at the institution and in the profession agreed that she clearly had the ability to succeed him. But she didn't get the job. The authorities argued that it would be unwise to expose a woman to the possibility of failure in such a publicly visible post. Although it is true that women are slowly being included in increasing numbers in the councils of the NCAA, and more and more women are gradually taking on responsibility for coaching women's teams, the fact is that women remain pretty much second-class citizens in the world of intercollegiate athletics.

In relation to the SAT, the point of this brief recital of the women's struggle for equality in the conduct of college sports is that parity has its price. The integration of women's athletics in the NCAA has meant, and will, I fear, continue for some time to mean, second-class status. Similarly, the integration sought, and to an ever-increasing degree being achieved, by the women's movement generally is having its price as well.

Sex Differences in SAT Scores

When I joined the staff of the College Board in 1955, boys scored higher on the mathematical sections of the SAT than girls did, and girls scored higher than boys on the verbal sections. Yet, at that time no one was suggesting that the mathematical questions were biased against girls or that the verbal questions were unfair to boys. The then current outcomes seemed eminently reasonable. In general boys are thought to be more interested in scientific and mechanical matters and girls are assumed to be more interested in literary pursuits. Thirty-five years later, however, the outcomes have changed, and males are performing better than females are on both parts of the test. The data, if not people's revised instincts, seem to support my conviction that the gradual deterioration of the SAT-verbal experience of females has to some degree been caused by the advances made in the search for social equity for women in our society. But social equity, like athletic equity, has only partially been achieved. As more women, like the nation's ethnic minorities, have sought to upgrade their status through education, they have become a larger portion of the SAT-taking population, and increasing numbers come from the less academically able end of the spectrum. Not only that, but the subjects girls take in secondary school have tended to be different from boys' course patterns. It's not that men are inherently more academically able than women and thus have higher SAT scores; it's that society and therefore education give them preference. Over the long haul women will achieve parity with men in athletics and in SAT scores.

For now, however, on the average the scores of males and females on the SAT are different, and that New York State judge who ordered the New York State Regents to cease using SAT scores as the sole criterion for awarding state scholarship dollars was correct. As in Propositions 48 and 42, the SAT came in for some hard knocks because it could be trusted. In New York State, when the costs of administering their state scholarship program seemed to be getting unreasonably high, the Regents sought to simplify the process. They could have used high school grades but they didn't, I presume because they couldn't trust the comparability of grades from one school to another. So they opted for an equally simple criterion that could be trusted, SAT scores. The College Board protested that decision at the time because, as the reader will now realize, the Board doesn't look with favor on the use of test scores as the sole criterion in any final, high-stakes decision. But the protest fell on deaf ears, at least until the judge's finding. He wisely ruled that other criteria should be applied along with SAT scores. But to read the headlines, the press reports, and the critics' comments, you'd think he'd ruled that the SAT is biased against women and shouldn't be used at all. He didn't. He observed that the use of SAT scores alone resulted in more awards to men than to women and ruled that outcome unacceptable. Here again we have a circumstance in which bias resulting from the misuse of the SAT is misinterpreted to mean that the test itself if biased.

Athletes and women are the subjects of this chapter. Despite its SAT-related flaw, Proposition 48 is slowly working in favor of athletes; and despite the misguided judgment of individuals like the New York State Regents, women are gradually achieving equal rights. But until the desired ends are achieved in both contexts, I fear the good old SAT will continue to come in for more of that undeserved criticism.

CHAPTER 7

Politicians, Public Servants, and the Media

If athletes and women have individually been victims of the misuse of Scholastic Aptitude Test (SAT) scores by the NCAA and the New York State Regents, politicians, public servants, and the media have been responsible for some of the widespread mass misuse and misunderstanding that attend the test. Three basic impulses seem to have been at work here: the will to win, the press for accountability, and the pursuit of controversy. Politicians look for issues that will help win elections, and once elected, they want to be able to ensure their own reelections by assuring the electorate that its tax dollars are being spent responsibly. School administrators want to demonstrate accountability for their schools by having them appear to "be ahead" in comparison with other educational institutions. In turn, the media, in vying for readership and playing the role of society's watchdog, thrive on stories involving competition, accountability, and controversy. It was, after all, the press that put the spotlight on SAT scores as measures, first, of accountability and, second, of comparability. And it is the media, through their penchant for controversy, that generate much of the public misunderstanding that afflicts the test.

SAT Investigations by the Press

The front-page story by Gene Maeroff in *The New York Times* started the accountability ball rolling in 1975 (see Chapter 4). Ironically, it came about as an indirect result of competition in the nonprofit college admissions testing market from the American College Testing Program (ACT). One product of that competition was the Student Descriptive Questionnaire (SDQ), introduced by the College Board in 1971 in response to an initiative taken by ACT. As noted in Chapter 2, the SDQ is the self-report instrument on which students voluntarily provide biographical and other information about themselves when they register for the SAT. Although accepted as a matter of course today, the introduction of the SDQ was debated almost as vehemently, if not as extensively, as the release of scores to candidates had been a decade earlier. The issue was privacy. In the end, however, the members of the College Board voted to initiate the service, and the collection and aggregation of data about SAT and Achievement Test candidates via the SDQ made it possible for the Board to publish information about the characteristics of the SAT population and how those characteristics were changing over time. Were there more or fewer minorities and women? What majors were the candidates thinking about? What kinds of activities had they been engaged in? How many of them worked? What were their SAT scores? It turned out that by 1975, the aggregate average SAT scores earned by candidates had been going down since 1963.

Use of Scores for Accountability

As noted above and recounted in Chapter 4, Maeroff took note of this phenomenon, and his *New York Times* story struck a national nerve. Concern over the quality of education in the nation's schools had been growing, and the evidence provided by the decline in SAT scores was interpreted by the critics as the result of a lowering of academic standards. In the process, national average SAT scores with their neat three-digit numbers became the surrogate for the educational counterpart to the economic gross national product (GNP), a measure I choose to call the gross educational product (GEP). Its scores suggested that the educational enterprise in the United States wasn't being fully accountable to the tax-paying public.

This role was not one that either the College Board or ETS had been seeking for the test. Rather, it had been thrust upon the SAT by external circumstances. As sponsor of the test, the College Board found itself in something of a dilemma. On the one hand, there is the old public relations maxim for dealing with the press that says, "I don't care what you say about me as long as you spell my name right!" Any publicity is good as long as you get your name in the newspapers. Indeed, one respected observer of the educational scene, who later served on the Advisory Panel on the Scholastic Aptitude Test Score Decline and fully subscribed to its findings, was at first convinced that the decline was an artifact perpetrated on the public by the College Board and ETS to keep the SAT in the news. On the other hand, there was the realization that the test's results had never been intended to be used for institutional accountability and that such use of the test scores alone as a measure of anything was in violation of the very principles of the proper test use the College Board espoused. But once having released the data, the College Board found it impossible to suppress them, and the annual fall press conferences called by the College Board to announce how the previous year's high school senior class had performed became popular media events. Trying to keep the data secret until the press conference proved to be something of a challenge.

A couple of years after Maeroff had taken his initiative, another reporter thought it would be interesting and controversial to compare average SAT scores by state. Which states were being more accountable than others? Which were winning the SAT sweepstakes? He asked the College Board for the data, and we refused to provide them. We refused on the grounds that just as a student's test scores belong to that student and a school's belong to that school and a district's to that district, so a state's aggregate average SAT scores belong to that state. Accordingly, we told the reporter he'd have to get the information from the offices of the individual state superintendents. In response, he called the 50 state departments of education; in assembling the state scores, he got some of the data wrong. After that, the state superintendents, through the national council of Chief State School Officers (CSSO), asked the College Board to do the publishing. Here again, the College Board found itself performing a task it had not sought and its SAT trapped in a role it was never intended to play.

Not so incidentally, we were not singling out the press, in the person of that reporter, for special treatment. Bill Honig, the chief state school office in California, once asked the College Board to supply him with the SAT scores for the high schools in his state to help him in his education reform movement. We told him he'd have to get clearance from each individual school. He did, and he got the scores.

Uninterpreted as they were that first year, the state-by-state data were grossly misleading. The uninitiated could easily assume that because Iowa scores were higher than Connecticut's, Iowa's schools were better than Connecticut's, when the real reason for the difference was, in fact, something else. Most college-going students in Iowa take the homegrown ACT (based in Iowa City), while only those few aspiring to selective colleges out-of-state take the SAT. Because the latter are normally among the better students, their SAT scores tend to be high. In Connecticut most college-going students take the SAT, and because their scores reflect a wide range of abilities, their average scores tend to be lower. When the College Board began publishing state data, we took great pains to issue all kinds of caveats and cautions for interpreting the meaning of the scores.

Not only did we try to forestall the Iowa-versus-Connecticut kind of comparison, we also continued to stress the point that SAT scores taken as a measure of either the GEP or state accountability are suspect because they are produced by only a percentage of the students attending the nation's or a state's secondary schools. Nationally the SAT is taken by about a third of the graduating high school seniors in any given year, and the scores earned by them have nothing directly to say about the academic promise or performance of the other two-thirds. The one-third that does participate, however, represents a significant and an important sector of the nation's young people, and what happens to their scores in the aggregate does bear watching.

Politics and Test Scores

One of the persons who did some watching in the early 1980s was Terrel Bell, the United States secretary of education in Ronald Reagan's first administration. President Jimmy Carter had created the Department of Education in payment of his political debt to the National Education Association (NEA) for its support of his candidacy in the 1976 presidential election. When Reagan was elected president four years later, he was determined to dismantle the new department and appointed Bell to oversee the dismemberment. But Bell had other ideas and surprised everyone, including himself, I gather, with his success in championing the campaign for school improvement that had been generated in the wake of the SAT score decline disclosure. As part of his effort to sustain that movement and in order to goad the states into taking part in it by demonstrating how they were doing academically, he began the practice of annually unveiling a "wall chart," which compared the states' average SAT and ACT scores with each other and over time. At first the comparisons were pretty raw, but as time went on, Bell and his successor, William J. Bennett, echoed the same caveats and cautions that accompanied the College Board's publication of national and then state SAT scores and took pains to put SAT and ACT scores in the context of other measures.

In 1984, however, Secretary Bell made me angry. The College Board regularly extends to the secretary of education, as well as to the nation's chief state school officers, the same courtesy it extends to school district superintendents and high school principals—that of providing average SAT scores for their respective populations before the national averages are publicly announced. We don't want those public servants to be surprised and therefore give them a chance to get ready for the good news or the bad. In some cases the executive directors of the College Board's six regional offices personally deliver the data to the chief state school officers to help them prepare for the public reaction. The time Secretary Bell made me angry was when, in full knowledge of our plans for release of the preceding year's scores, he insisted on holding a press conference in Washington to announce the news at precisely the same hour the College Board was holding a press conference for the same purpose in New York City. The news of a slight increase in the scores was obviously so hot that the Department of Education couldn't hold off even for half an hour. By making our good news his good news, the secretary was able, by implication at least, to take credit on behalf of the Reagan administration for the improvement in SAT scores.

That implication bothered me, too. *A Nation at Risk* was published in spring 1983 by the National Commission on Excellence in Education. The turnaround in SAT scores soon thereafter was not the result of a Reagan administration quick fix. One year wasn't enough. Rather, in my judgment, it represented the long-term payoff from the reform efforts that had gotten under way in the aftermath of the work of the Advisory Panel on the Scholastic Aptitude Test Score Decline and the appearance of *On Further Examination* in 1977. But by that comment I wouldn't want to take anything away from the impact of *A Nation at Risk*. It served not only as a focus and a stimulus for the national school reform movement but also put a stop to President Reagan's plans to abolish the Department of Education.

In fact, the news was getting so good that SAT scores made their way into State of the Union addresses and into the rhetoric of the 1984 presidential campaign. Now they were getting public attention at the highest level of government, and the name was being spelled correctly. One of my favorite quips in the course of that 1984 campaign, fed to me by one of my colleagues who helped me prepare some of my speeches, went like this: "We are in the closing weeks of a national presidential campaign and it appears that the main education issues boil down to these two—first, how much the federal government should contribute to education costs and second, school prayer. In other words, who pays and who prays? The first is much too complicated to deal with briefly, but when it comes to the second, and here I want to maintain a non-partisan position, I can assure you that as long as there are tests like the SAT, there *will* be prayer in the schools." Regardless of how that punch line comes across in print, it got a rousing reception in the middle of a luncheon speech to the Los Angeles Rotary Club. I am thankful that education is now important enough on the national agenda to be a topic for a Rotary Club luncheon address, and the SAT can rightfully claim some of the credit for getting it there.

Public Servants

Other, less prominent public officials have played a part as well. As a matter of fact, they got the competition and accountability balls rolling well before the reform movement got under way. Forerunners of those making it their practice to toot their own schools' horns on the basis of SAT scores were those high school principals who made much of the number of National Merit scholarships awarded their students. To demonstrate to the local taxpayers how accountable they were, they showed that their students were outperforming youngsters in other, similar schools. That practice was adapted for use in connection with the annual release of SAT scores. Above-average scores made the news. Below-average scores didn't. In one case, a big-city school superintendent was so pleased with the improvement his students had shown over the preceding year that he simply couldn't contain himself, broke the embargo date we had put on the release of the data, published the national scores as well as his own district's a couple of days ahead of time, and then went fishing.

As suggested, trying to keep the data secret until our press conference date always proved frustrating in one way or another. Eager school superintendents and principals weren't the only transgressors. A Philadelphia newspaper, for example, put our news release with its embargo date into its computerized file for retrieval on the appropriate date. In the meantime an editor looking for a filler found our entry, failed to take note of the embargo date, and published the story a couple of days early.

And then there was the occasion when Edward Fiske, education editor of *The New York Times,* got access to the SAT score data from someone who, Fiske stoutly maintains, had been made privy to the data without any restrictions on disclosure. Fiske published those scores as part of a front-page story in a Saturday edition, three days before our scheduled release date the following Tuesday. We were dismayed by his stealing our thunder but relieved that he had done so, when that following Tuesday turned out to be the day after President Reagan was shot in front of the Capitol Hilton. The SAT scores, with or without the name spelled properly, would never have made the front page that day.

But it was the controversy surrounding the release of state scores that proved to be the most troublesome over time; that was why I took advantage of the opportunity to deliver a paper on the subject at a meeting at Plymouth State College in Plymouth, New Hampshire, in 1986. That paper still manages to comprehend the situation pretty well, and I include most of it here as the only major hunk of my rhetoric in this book that has been published before. (Somehow it managed to make its way into a periodical called *Vital Speeches*.)

The following paper was delivered at the Eighth Northern New England Educational Tests, Measurement, and Evaluation Conference at Plymouth State College on March 26, 1986.

You have invited me to say something to you this morning about "The SAT and Statewide Assessment." It gives me some pause that only 15 years ago or so, that topic in all likelihood would not have occurred to any of us. The reason, of course, is that although the SAT had been in use for nearly 50 years as a common college entrance examination, by the early 1970s nobody had yet suggested that it might be used as some kind of national educational benchmark—an indicator, if you will, of the gross educational product, or GEP, stated in terms of the scores of college-bound high school seniors. I would like to begin by saying a little about that, because the notion that the SAT might be used in *statewide* educational assessment arises, as I see it, from its not-entirely-comfortable role in *national* educational assessment. Colleges using the SAT in admissions and secondary schools with substantial numbers of applicants had, for some time, been receiving summary statistics about, respectively, their applicant pools and test-taking cohorts. In the early 1970s a decision was made to formalize and enhance these reports in what would become known as the Summary Reporting Service. It had three elements that are salient for our purposes this morning.

First, beginning in 1971, students registering for the SAT were asked to tell, on a purely voluntary and confidential basis, a good deal more about themselves—their career interests, academic goals, extracurricular activities, family makeup and income, ethnicity, for example—than they had in the past. The assumption was that such demographic information, together with their scores on the SAT and the Achievement Tests, might yield valuable insights about them as groups—in school, in the applicant pool, and from year to year. The new form was called the Student Descriptive Questionnaire, and more than 90 percent of the students elected, and still do, to fill it out.

Second, whereas the earlier reports included scores for all test takers, whether sophomore, junior, or senior, the new reports dealt solely with the cohort of graduating seniors.

Third, the Summary Reporting Service generated mean scores for three "reference groups" to which the colleges and schools could relate their summary figures. These reference groups were the national population of seniors who had taken the SAT, as well as the comparable populations within each College Board region and within each state. State mean scores were available to colleges and schools within each state only with the consent of the chief state school officer.

The national college-bound senior population taking the SAT represented about a third of all high school graduates at the time and two-thirds of those who went on to college. It seemed to the College Board that the characteristics of this group—their activities, interests, ambitions, and, of course, their national mean scores (verbal and mathematical) might be of public interest. So, these newly available data on the national—not, let me note, the state—level, were released to the media for the first time in 1973. In publishing these new data, the Board was careful to warn that they were limited in meaning. They told nothing about the two-thirds of graduating seniors who did not take the test or about the 18-year-olds who did not graduate from high school.

In 1975, an alert education reporter noticed that the scores had dropped from the previous year—8 points on the verbal sections and 3 points on the mathematical sections. He asked for the figures for earlier years, and thus it was established that since 1963 there had been a gradual, steady decline involving at least 1 score point each year. The aggregate decline on the 200-to-800 scale was 41 points in verbal and 24 points in math at that time. Caveats notwithstanding, a change of that magnitude, displayed by such a large proportion of high school seniors on such a carefully constructed and equated test, clearly indicated that something was happening. To find out what, the College Board as the sponsor of the SAT, and Educational Testing Service as developer and administrator of the test under contract to the Board, jointly recruited a distinguished panel under the leadership of the Honorable Willard Wirtz.

That panel's report, delivered in 1977, had both good news and bad. The good news was that a large part of the decline—two-thirds to three-fourths of the 18 points in verbal and 4 points in math before 1970, and about a fourth of the 23-point decline in verbal and 20-point decline in math since—was because a larger and more diverse pool of students was taking the test. It was, in short, a reflection of the tremendous broadening of opportunities for postsecondary education which took place during those years. The bad news was that the remainder of the decline was caused by a variety of factors, the most salient of which might be summed up as a dilution of substance and a softening of standards in high school curricula. Thus we had the first signals of the perceived crisis in educational quality— the crisis that has occupied a large part of our national educational dialogue ever since.

As the decade turned, concern about educational quality produced a cascade of reports, which peaked around the issuance of *A Nation at Risk*. Meanwhile, following the first rush of public interest in the score decline and the Wirtz panel report, the scores continued to go down. Public interest waned. But when they did not decline in 1981, remaining instead at the levels of the preceding year, interest revived. Speculation abounded. Was the great decline over?

In the ensuing ferment of interest, the media asked for scores by states. Consistent with our longtime position that scores are the confidential property of the individual, school, or jurisdiction to which they refer, we declined. Nevertheless, one enterprising publication, invoking "sunshine" laws where necessary, managed to assemble a table of state scores—and got some wrong.

And so, in the interest of accuracy, and with the not-entirely-enthusiastic assent of chief state school officers, the College Board undertook to publish state-by-state score figures. At the same time we issued a further caveat, and I quote: "It is the College Board's position that comparison of states, districts, schools, or any other subgroups on the basis of SAT scores alone is invalid. The Board discourages any use of SAT scores as a measure of overall performance of teachers, schools, or state education systems. However, since comparisons have been made in the past—and not always with appropriate explanations—the Board issues state data both to ensure that the information is accurate and to place it in proper context."

We also explained the strong effect that participation rate has on state mean scores, as an example of one factor among many that could skew scores without telling anything about educational quality. That was in 1982, when the verbal went up 2 points, the mathematical 1 point—the first rise in SAT scores in 19 years. As each year since has brought a rise in at least 1 score point, interest both in the national scores and in the state scores has remained high.

In 1984 Secretary of Education Terrel Bell published for the first time his "wall chart" of comparative educational indices by state, including SAT and ACT scores. He took the occasion to make two major points: (1) The continued rise in SAT scores nationally indicated that the "educational reform movement," which he dated from the publication of *A Nation At Risk*, was indeed working. (2) The wall chart demonstrated that educational quality in the respective states, as measured by a variety of indices, was not necessarily dependent upon the resources applied, especially by the federal government.

Well, of course the secretary was using the state SAT scores in precisely the way that the Board cautioned they should not be: to compare the educational quality of diverse jurisdictions. So, through a progression of individually innocuous moves, a big shift had taken place from the SAT as one of a number of *national* indicators to the SAT as one of a number of measures of relative quality among *states*.

The absurdity of comparing a large industrial state like New Jersey—where most colleges and universities require the SAT, 65 percent of high school graduates take the SAT, and the means are 425 verbal, 489 mathematical—with a state like Iowa—where few institutions require the SAT, only 3 percent of high school graduates (most of them applying to competitive out-of-state colleges) take the test, and the means are 521 verbal, 576 mathematical—should be apparent at once.

Now in all fairness the secretary did show good judgment, as did his successor, William Bennett, in repeating the wall chart this year and in presenting along with the scores a number of other factors such as graduation rate, pupil-teacher ratio, expenditures per pupil, incidence of poverty, and minority enrollment. He also distinguished between states where the majority of students take the SAT and those in which the majority take the ACT Assessment. But the data provided are simply not enough to determine whether or not a state-to-state score difference signifies real educational difference between them.

Regrettably, the scores are attractive to the media—attractive because they are precise and easily comparable. As a result, even the scant context displayed on the wall chart was ignored, and the SAT and the ACT were given an exaggerated and wholly unwarranted prominence by the nation's press.

So the first thing I want to say about the potential use of the SAT in *statewide* assessment is that if its scores were to be used for purposes of comparing one state with another in contrast to comparing a state with itself over time—as an indicator of relative educational quality—that use would not be valid, that would be wrong. Am I then saying that the SAT is of no use in statewide educational assessment? Not at all. But if not, how should it be used?

Let me approach that question by reviewing the intended use of the SAT—that is, to help colleges make better decisions about their candidates for admission. It does that by helping to predict freshman-year academic performance. Used along with the high school record, it improves that prediction by about two-thirds of the difference between perfect prediction and the success rate in prediction that would result from pure chance. But the test does not measure factors like determination, energy, interest, or commitment. Thus it cannot be perfect in predicting what grades will actually be earned, and it can say nothing about the other kinds of success that a student may enjoy in college. And there *are* other kinds of success—for example, in leadership and contribution to the college community, or in outstanding athletic or extracurricular performance. So, we say that it should never be used in isolation to make decisions about candidates, that it should always be used in the context of other information, including but not confined to the high school record.

The SAT is also appropriately useful to the individual student in his or her decision making about what colleges to select—again, however, not in isolation but along with other information that is relevant. All of which is to say that as institutions compare one student with another, and as students compare themselves with their peers, the context is vitally important to the meaning of the scores.

Then how might a state use the scores in educational assessment? The key in the Board's view is in the distinction between *measurement* and *evaluation,* between what the SAT measures and what may be indicated by changes in SAT scores over time. That is, the simple set of two numbers that average the scores of students as a group is far too susceptible to influences other than the *quality* of education—the socioeconomic character of the community, the self-selection of the population that takes the test, the available resources for education, the mission of the school or system— too susceptible to these other influences to be of any legitimate use in measuring (that is to say, quantifying) educational quality for purposes of comparison between jurisdictions.

However, the *change* in those numbers over time within a single jurisdiction, other things being relatively equal, can be helpful in evaluating whether things are improving or not. If other indicators—for example, the graduation rate, the number of courses taken in academic subjects, the scores on other standardized tests—are also tending in the same direction, the evaluation is strengthened. And a careful examination of all the conditions impinging on the educational enterprise can provide some insight into the reasons for the tendency, whatever it may be.

Let me note here again the paradox that some positive developments in education may in fact have a negative effect on SAT scores. For example, the Wirtz panel found that broadening educational opportunity in the late 1960s, and to a lesser extent in the early 1970s, accounted for much of the national SAT score decline. Recently the Dallas Independent School District received a grant for a program, to be conducted with consultation by the College Board, to encourage more youngsters in that system to plan to go to college. At the announcement ceremony, I took the occasion to warn the media that if the program were successful, one outcome might very well be a dip in SAT scores, at least at the start, as the pool of test takers increased in size and diversity.

So the use of the SAT in *statewide* evaluation should not be in the comparison of one state with another, or of jurisdictions within the state, but in comparison within the state or within individual jurisdictions of the changes over time in the scores. Using the scores this way in conjunction with changes in other indicators is a legitimate form of evaluation.

But I should note that even used in this way, statewide scores can be misleading if there is a wide difference in conditions among districts within a state. For example, an improving trend in statewide scores may be created by a relatively small number of districts that have the resources to support improvement, while others stand still or even slide back. Even in a state as homogeneous as New Hampshire, there are, as you know better than I, large differences in the characteristics of the various school districts.

Now, I have been stressing caveats in the use of the SAT for educational assessment. In closing, let me turn to some of the positive reasons for using it in the way I have described. As we move ahead with our efforts to improve educational quality, it is becoming increasingy clear that some of the things we want to achieve—or that we want our students to achieve—may not be measurable directly. This is particularly true as we attempt to specify learning outcomes in the area of reasoning, or critical thinking, and in communication skills. They are relatively simple to state, and it is no great feat to determine if they have been achieved, but to measure them is something else again. I have in mind such objectives as "the ability to distinguish between fact and opinion" and "the ability to vary one's writing style, including vocabulary and sentence structure, for different readers and purposes" and "the ability to separate one's personal opinions and assumptions from a writer's."

Those particular statements are taken from the booklet *Academic Preparation for College: What Students Need to Know and Be Able to Do*, which is a product of the Board's own Educational EQuality Project and has been and is being adopted by a growing number of districts and states as the summary specification of their educational reform goals. At the request of those users, we have had a good deal of work done on the question of how to assess progress toward those goals, and to a large degree we have come to the conclusion that assessment will have to be in the form of evaluation rather than measurement.

Among the evaluation tools, we find, the SAT has a highly useful place that is supplementary to, but different from, its primary intended use as an admissions examination. Because the SAT does measure certain learned mental skills that cut across and are relatively independent of specific class-room subjects, we believe that it can be useful in evaluating the attainment of certain "higher-order" skills, or competencies, in reading, writing, math-ematics, and reasoning, which do not readily lend themselves to more direct measurement. At the minimum it is useful, in conjunction with other indi-cators, in evaluating whether students or groups of students have in fact improved their predicted performance in college.

And that, ladies and gentlemen, is the nub of my message: although the SAT was not originally intended as a tool for evaluation, wisely used it may be hepful. The numbers cannot be aggregated to measure directly the quality of education, or to compare quality across jurisdictions. But changes in group scores within jurisdictions can be used as part of, and one factor in, the evaluation process. And the test may become more useful in that sense as the progress—and process—we seek to evaluate places greater emphasis on competencies or performance outcomes that do cut across the curriculum and that do not lend themselves to quantification. But the numbers the SAT produces exude an aura of precision out of all proportion to their true significance—an aura of precision that in turn fosters an unsuitable reliance on them, to the exclusion or neglect of other indicators that are equally important and useful.

An important role for many of you is to make sure that policymakers in your state, or institution, do not use the scores from instruments like the SAT in inappropriate, if not incorrect, ways. Don't let them use scores in an absolute sense, but only in the sense of change over time. And only use change in scores in the context of change in other indicators. Above all else, be consistent in what you do, for nobody will believe you when you say declining scores are no indication of the health of the enterprise if you have been using rising scores to claim that it is thriving.

If SAT scores are used, wisely or otherwise, to evaluate the nation's or a state's or a district's schools, they are also misused to evaluate teachers, to assess their accountability. Early on in my years at the College Board I visited the high school in a small mill town in central Massachusetts. The principal was thinking about firing the English department because the students were getting much lower verbal than mathematical scores. Even at that early stage in my life with the SAT, I was able to point out the errors of his ways. First, for the general population, average SAT-mathematical scores are higher than SAT-verbal scores. Second, the town his school served was a manufacturing center that emphasized things mechanical and therefore mathematical. Third, a large proportion of the families in the town were Polish, and for a lot of their offspring English even then was something of a second language. The principal got my point.

If teachers or schools or districts are going to be compared and held accountable on the basis of test scores, they should, as I said at the Plymouth conference, be compared and held accountable on the basis of instruments designed to do that job. Such instruments today exist in an activity sponsored by the Department of Education and currently administered by Educational Testing Service—the National Assessment of Educational Progress (NAEP). The scores from it, not from the SAT, should be used to measure the gross educational product (GEP).

But for now, like it or not, the SAT is still in the political arena, and its entry into that arena has produced some interesting by-products. State legislatures, for instance, have seemed to play both sides of·the

fence. Some legislators want more tests as a basis for assuring accountability on the part of the educational establishment, while just down the
hall there are those who decry the influence of tests and call for what
has come to be known, misleadingly I believe, as truth-in-testing legislation. When I shared my thoughts on this schizophrenic attitude with
a professor of political science, he acknowledged the dilemma but added
to my frustration with the legislative process when he pointed out that
in at least two state legislatures, which he named, the instinctive response
in a roll-call vote is to vote Not Guilty!

Now while I found that to be an amusing story (and while I have
uncomplimentary things to say about some legislators in a moment), I
do have to point out that the state legislators I have met were serious-
minded and were interested in the welfare of young people. They were
at state hearings I attended because they had chosen to work on education committees. In thinking of their commitments, I couldn't help
being reminded of my college classmate who served in the United States
House of Representatives. Speaking informally at a class dinner, he
pointed out the complexity of the issues facing the Congress and the
resultant need for the members of the House to specialize. The individual
congressman simply doesn't have the time to become familiar with all
the aspects of a given issue or indeed a specific subject. That's why state
legislators, like the members of Congress, rely on the judgments of their
fellows who have chosen or been chosen to become expert on a topic.

Although I have great respect for the committee system, I have less
respect for the process by which it is conducted in Washington. I testified
several times before subcommittees of the House and the Senate. The
first was before a Senate subcommittee. In the instructions I received
ahead of time I was told I had exactly 10 minutes to make my presentation. That meant condensing about 20 pages of written testimony,
which I had prepared and was submitting, to four. Having carefully
honed my presentation almost to the exact second, I was startled to be
greeted by the presiding senator with, "Mr. Hanford, you see that green
light? When it goes on, you have five minutes. The yellow light? When
it goes on, you have one minute. And the red one? When it goes on,
you stop!" Not only was I dismayed by the unannounced and uncere-
monious halving of my time, I was outraged at being made to feel like
a naughty boy in the principal's office who had a misdemeanor to explain
and a limited time to do it in.

Witnesses at the kinds of hearings I attended are invited to come to
Washington at their own expense to testify. Then they get to sit uncom-
fortably in a well, with their elected public servants, at least those who

deign to attend, arrayed at a long, raised table peering down on them from on high. I was told of one lady who flew across the country to appear and was three minutes into the twenty-minute presentation she had been invited to give when there was a roll call on the floor. The presiding officer thanked her for her testimony and excused her; he didn't invite her to stick around and finish what she had to say. True, the legislators had access to her full written testimony, so they could know what she would have said. But if so, why the trip across the country and the aborting of her presentation?

Also, the hearings I attended weren't at all like the ones that get televised in prime time with all the members of the committee or sub-committee sitting there paying close attention to the witnesses; I was lucky if there were more than one or two subcommittee members in their seats and if those not chairing the hearing weren't reading the newspaper or talking to an aide. And there always seemed to be a lot of distracting movement up there behind the long, raised table, with members, aides, and messengers continually wandering in and out.

After one of my appearances I was so incensed that when I got back to the office, I composed a little essay titled "Who Works for Whom?" Colleagues who read the piece sympathized with my frustration, admired my analysis, applauded my rhetoric, and advised me to destroy the document. I did. I wish I hadn't so that I could have used it here.

But my biggest gripe in this regard isn't the hearing process; it is that some well-intentioned legislators, like some not-so-well-intentioned critics, occasionally take on an issue before they are fully informed about it. It's not necessarily that the basic idea they have in mind is flawed; it is that they start drafting legislation before they are aware of the complexities involved. Many of the battles we fought over the so-called truth-in-testing legislation when it was introduced in New York State had more to do with deficiencies in the bills' provisions than with the substance of what was being proposed.

Television and the SAT

In such instances the well-meaning but not fully informed legislators are something like some not-so-well-meaning and equally uninformed television talk-show hosts. Because the SAT was so much in the news, I was asked to appear on a number of television talk shows. I suppose one would say that the height of my TV career was marked by appearances on the "Today" and the "Phil Donahue" shows. My fellow guest on

"Today" was the president of Bowdoin College, which, as noted earlier, had received considerable publicity in 1969, 15 years before, by giving up its requirement that applicants for admission take the SAT. Neighboring Bates College, another excellent small liberal arts college in Maine, had just followed suit in 1984, and it was clear that NBC was hopeful of getting a good argument going between the president and me about the utility of the test. What NBC had failed to discover, and what I was careful to remind the Bowdoin president about before we went on the air, was that although Bowdoin had given up the SAT as a requirement for admission, it had retained it as a requirement for matriculation. In other words, a candidate who chose not to take the SAT, or not to submit scores from it if he or she took it for some other institution, had to take it before registering for classes. We had a nice, amicable discussion about the complexities of college admissions, the president and I, which I suspect didn't do much for the "Today" show's rating.

The "Phil Donahue" show was even more interesting for me in its aftermath than in the event, although I must say the experience was fascinating. The guests for the show that day in Chicago were the director of admissions at Harvard, the director of financial aid from Northwestern, and I. In the preshow warm-up we were told that although we were scheduled for a one-hour segment, if all went well we would be held over for another stint. All did go well and we were asked to do an encore. But it took several minutes to rearrange things—not the set, but the audience. It seems that in those days they bused in groups of women from all over the metropolitan area who had other exciting events on their day's itinerary. Because half the audience had to leave at what turned out to be halftime, the production crew had to rearrange the seating so that the theater still looked full. I saw a tape of the two shows some weeks later and could tell the diffrence, but I'm sure the regular viewing audience had no idea that the studio audience had been cut in half.

Not surprisingly, Phil Donahue took off after the SAT and consequently after me. I must say, however, as I found to be so often the case in such circumstances, my colleagues provided all the support the SAT needed. For just one example: I appeared on a live radio talk show in New York City, the "Sherry Henry" show, with David Owen, author of the then just published *None of the Above,* an attack on the SAT and ETS, and with Hal Doughty, then in charge of admissions at New York University. Like Phil Donahue, Sherry Henry had come to the show with a preconceived prejudice against the SAT, not to mention obvious sympathy for David Owen. But again, as did the representatives from Harvard and Northwestern in Chicago, New York University's representative provided a much more persuasive and credible defense than I could have mounted from my suspect and prejudiced perspective.

As I said, the aftermath of the "Phil Donahue" show was even more interesting for me than being on the show itself. It was clear that Donahue had a large viewing audience. I heard from people I hadn't thought of in years. Classmates of our daughters in high school and college wrote to ask if I was in fact their father. Many students and their parents wrote, asking for advice about how to do well on the SAT or how to get into the college of their choice. One letter was from our younger daughter. She was outraged at the treatment the three of us had received from our host. We had been seated on oversized hassocks, while Phil Donahue walked around posturing and delivering his barbed questions from on high, rather like a legislator at a hearing.

After that experience I was always very conscious of the physical surroundings in any media appearance. At one legislative hearing in Washington, the long, raised table was between the witnesses and a bank of windows that allowed light to shine directly in the eyes of the witnesses. Because of a tennis injury to my left eye, I have glasses with one dark and one clear lens. I pulled them out and put them on when I sat down to testify and, I believe, evoked a tiny bit of sympathetic response for my attempt to take the surroundings into account.

What bugged me about the Donahue and Henry shows, and others like them, wasn't just the misinformation about the SAT but the preconceived hostility toward the test that those hosts brought to their talk shows. Getting into college is serious business for young people and their parents, and I was dismayed by the misinformation that the media hosts so often promulgated and the frenzied hype that they frequently generated on purpose in their attempts to maintain their ratings by being controversial. Some of the misinformation, I am sure, was deliberately perpetrated. Other misinformation, I realized even before that 1984 "Today" show, was the result of the hosts' not having had their homework done for them. A couple of years after I joined the College Board staff, I was invited by a radio talk-show host to appear on a network program with him to discuss an article on education in the latest issue of a popular magazine. It was to be aired on the Mutual Network but taped ahead of time in a studio in New York City. I appeared at the appropriate address in midtown Manhattan. The exact location isn't important, but it could have been the corner of Madison Avenue and Fifty-fourth Street on, perhaps, the fifteenth floor. I was admitted to the studio, which very much resembled a plain business office, where my host and I warmed up. It turned out that while I had carefully studied the article we were to discuss, my interlocutor hadn't. I don't remember the main thesis of the piece, but I do recall that it made passing reference to education in the Soviet Union. As my host shuffled through the pages of the article at the last minute, his eye caught the reference and he asked me what I thought of the schools in Russia. I told him that I was not really informed enough on the subject to make any comment and expressed the hope that he would avoid it during the taping. (That's when I learned not to trust talk-show hosts. He asked me that very question just a few minutes after we had "gone on the air.")

After we had warmed up, I was ushered into the recording studio, which looked to me like a closet and had a window that looked south along whatever avenue it was. There I was introduced to the producer, whose only job at that moment was to run the tape recorder. It sat on an undersized desk with a blue and gold banner draped askew down the back of it and the legend Mutual Broadcasting Something-or-Other boldly emblazoned on it. And so to work! It happened to be the lowest-budget show I ever took part in. I say that because space for commercials to be dubbed in later was left blank on the tape we were using. On higher-budget shows they splice in the commercials.

So there we were, looking out over midtown Manhattan, when the producer turned a switch, pointed at the host, signaled "go," and the interview began with "Good afternoon, ladies and gentlemen. Here we are on the Boardwalk in Atlantic City, where our guest today is George Hanford, a member of the staff of the College Entrance Examination Board. We'll be talking with him about the article by . . . in the latest issue of *McCall's*. But first a word from our sponsors, the Atlantic City Convention Bureau and *McCall's* magazine." The session continued after silence for the commercial and went downhill through Russian education to the sign-off, when my host offered "thanks to our guest and a bottle of My Sin perfume to Mrs. Hanford." The perfume came in the mail some weeks later. It was without a doubt the show's most substantive payoff.

Other memorable appearances occurred in Houston and Los Angeles. In Houston I had been invited to take part in a television talk show where the College Board's EQuality project was to be discussed. I'd had a telephone conversation with the host, and because he seemed like a reasonable guy and because the show was on public television, I was rather looking forward to the occasion. As it turned out, the television studio was on the other side of Houston from the hotel where the College Board meeting I was attending was being held, and my colleagues who had arranged the event hadn't really left enough time for me to get to the other side of the city. Not that I could blame my provincial compatriots—like myself, from the compact, crowded East. Getting to the other side of Houston was like driving across the state of Rhode Island.

And so I was delivered to the studio with no minutes to spare, no time to warm up, no chance even to comb my hair. Instead, I was ushered immediately into the studio and onto the dais, where there was not one person but two persons, the host and a woman whose name I didn't quite catch in all the confusion of being seated and wired for sound. It emerged in the course of the show that she was the president of the local teachers' union, which was locked at that time in almost mortal combat with Houston's superintendent of schools. And if that wasn't sticky enough, the superintendent was to be the featured speaker at the College Board's meeting the next morning.

It was a recipe for disaster if I ever saw one. Caught in the middle of a local controversy on stage with a woman whose name I didn't know, talking about a topic of local concern with which I really wasn't familiar. However, it turned out to be the enjoyable occasion I had originally anticipated. The union president was not only engaging and articulate, she carefully avoided drawing me into her dispute with the superintendent of schools; and the host studiously avoided putting me on the spot by asking me questions that could be answered either in the abstract or with sweeping generalities, thus letting me play the role of interested but nonpartisan educational statesman. The lesson I learned in Houston was that not all television talk-show hosts were difficult to deal with.

As for Los Angeles, it too was for me the home of a congenial TV talk-show host. But it isn't so much the time on the air that I especially recall as a circumstance that immediately preceded it. I was sitting comfortably in the greenroom (apparently all television studios have greenrooms where performers and guests wait to go on) when a man approached me, introduced himself as an official of the station, and asked, "Would you mind being ascertained?" Now there's an invitation for you! At least it was for me, not knowing what being ascertained involved.

As the official explained it to me, each television station is required under its charter to take steps to find out, to "ascertain," from leading citizens what they consider to be the most pressing problems facing the community, the state, and the nation. When I understood what was expected of me, I said, "Youth unemployment." That observation came as the result of my involvement with the College Board's Educational EQuality Project. Through it we had discovered that employers want their new hires, right out of high school, to have the same academic competencies that colleges want their successful applicants to have: the abilities to read, write, speak, listen, and do math. Obviously young people don't have those competencies if they haven't graduated from high school, and there are far too many who haven't. One doesn't have to go more than 50 blocks north from the College Board's office in midtown Manhattan to observe the unemployment of young people in the black and Spanish Harlems of New York City, young men mostly, just "hanging out." There is a terrible waste of talent among them, a waste that is bound to become even more significant as both the number and the percentage of minority young men and women in the population grow—become worse, that is, unless we find the means to keep those high-school-age individuals in school longer and to offer them gainful employment when they graduate.

Television talk shows provide excellent opportunities for getting that message across to the public. The problem is that the message isn't really very controversial, and so the time is devoted not to dealing with it but to letting the critics take potshots at the SAT and inviting defenders like me to respond. I was never asked the Los Angeles television station official's question on the air—anytime, anywhere. So much for being ascertained!

Politicians, public servants, and the media. My SAT window on the world gave me an opportunity most people aren't privileged to have— the chance to observe from behind the footlights, so to speak, the kind of theater for which these players in the public eye are responsible. For those legislative hearings, televised or not, and those talk shows, as differentiated from serious panel discussions, are theater. That is why I chose to treat them together in this chapter along with the high drama of the SAT in the role of the GEP.

CHAPTER 8

The International Connection

A speech at the Harvard commencement in the late 1940s set the stage for my later appreciation of the perspective that the Scholastic Aptitude Test provided on the international scene. It was delivered by George C. Marshall, secretary of state in the first Truman administration. In the speech he left no doubt that America's price of victory in World War II was responsibility for the leadership of the free world. More specifically, he argued that the United States had an obligation not only to help rebuild the economies of the developed nations ravaged by war but also to assist new nations get established as the yokes of colonialism were beginning to be thrown off. His argument prevailed, and what soon came to be known as the Marshall Plan was put into operation.

We did help the nations of Western Europe and Japan rebuild and revitalize their economies, and the success of that effort is today particularly apparent in our onetime enemies, West Germany and Japan.

At the same time we poured dollars and technical assistance into the developing nations of the third world in Africa, Latin America, and Asia. Here the results are less clear. The economies of most third world countries, while loosely tied to those of their earlier colonial masters, still tend to be groping for stability. In virtually all of them, however, better education is perceived as essential not only to economic growth but to political enlightenment as well. Because the colleges and universities in most developing countries remain patterned after those of their onetime colonial masters, the opportunities for the United States to lend a hand have been limited. As a result, our most significant help has been not in restructuring educational practices abroad to take advantage of the United States model, but in providing opportunities in this country for students from new nations that simply don't have the necessary professors or facilities. Nevertheless, association with the SAT gave me the chance to observe the help being provided in both ways—limited technical assistance in connection with university admissions (particularly as it relates to testing) as well as practical assistance in bringing foreign students to the United States.

The College Board's formal participation in international education really developed as a result of the involvement of its first president (the title of the Board's chief executive officer was changed from "executive director" to "president" when the association became incorporated in 1957), Frank H. Bowles, in the conduct of an international study of university admissions on behalf of UNESCO during a two-year leave of absence in the early 1960s. Bowles's interest in the field, however, had its roots in the brief stint of the United States as a colonial power itself in the aftermath of the Spanish-American War.

Puerto Rico

During the decades when Puerto Rico was moving from colonial to commonwealth status under the United States flag, there were many who took a special interest in that process. One locus of that interest developed at Columbia University, where Bowles had been a student and where he was serving as university director of admissions when he was called to head the College Board in 1948. By the time I joined the staff in 1955, he had established close connections with the University of Puerto Rico and the island's broader educational community. Indeed, my first professional experience off the mainland came as a result of those connections. At Bowles's suggestion, Lawrence Springer, then headmaster of the Pingry School, and I were asked to advise FOMENTO, the island's economic development authority, on whether or not the Commonwealth government should subsidize schools where English was the language of instruction. Then as now, Puerto Rico was seeking to upgrade its economy by attracting industry to the island. Then as now, lower labor costs and tax incentives were the main attractions. Would that appeal be enhanced by the availability of English language instruction to the children of upwardly mobile young executives who might object to a couple of years of Spanish-based instruction for their children before moving back to the mainland? Were the schools that might receive assistance from FOMENTO any good? Were they worth the investment? Those were the questions Larry Springer and I were asked. Given the goals of the Commonwealth government and the quality of the schools we visited, our answers to those questions weren't hard to formulate. They were affirmative.

More troublesome for me were the legacies of that experience. For example, although I was sure that FOMENTO's goals would be best served by our recommendation, I came away uncertain about whether the long-term interests of those executives' children would be served. Isn't a second language a good thing to have? I came away, too, not only with a renewed appreciation for the ability to deal with more than one language but also with an explicit recognition of the importance of education to an economy, particularly a developing one, although for reasons much more fundamental than FOMENTO's in sponsoring our particular study. I also gained a better understanding of why Puerto Ricans move back and forth between the island and the mainland and some comprehension of the forces that differentially persuade Puerto Ricans to espouse commonwealth status, statehood, and independence for their island.

These forces are, of course, the same forces that have been in tension in many of the world's newly formed but economically underdeveloped nations, and their presence in Puerto Rico explains why I have chosen to discuss the SAT's relationship to the Commonwealth in this chapter on the test's international connections. The Puerto Rican experience provides a bridge for better understanding of developments at home and abroad.

By the time he returned from his UNESCO-sponsored study of university admissions, Frank Bowles had seen and heard enough to reach the tentative conclusion that there was a need for a Spanish version of the SAT, which could be used not only to serve the higher education institutions on the island but perhaps also the Spanish-speaking countries of Central and South America. To test that latter proposition, Bowles engaged the services of Adolfo Fortier, then head of the Department of Public Administration at the University of Puerto Rico and a former assistant in the admissions office at Columbia. Fortier was asked to make an intensive survey of the university admissions scene specifically in the Commonwealth and more generally in the rest of Latin America. I got involved in the project in 1962, when Bowles asked me to join Fortier during the middle of his swing around South America, to make sure that our emissary was not only asking the right questions but also giving the right answers to the questions being asked of him. He was!

As a result of Fortier's findings and recommendations, the decision was made to proceed with the development of a Spanish SAT. But it was not a decision simply to translate the SAT into Spanish. Instead, *La Prueba de Aptitud Académica* was developed from scratch in Spanish by a Puerto Rican staff in Puerto Rico, working with a team of consultants from Central and South America and using the specifications called for in the development of regular editions of the regular SAT in English. In that process, every attempt was made to keep the questions as culture-free as possible so that the test could be used broadly throughout the Spanish-speaking countries of the hemisphere.

The fact of differences in the vocabularies between the Old World and the New World, as well as among the Spanish-speaking peoples on this side of the Atlantic, was demonstrated early on in the experience of a Roman Catholic priest and member of the faculty of a prestigious church-related university in Colombia. Rather than being housed with the other members of the consulting team, Father Jaramillo was staying in the guest house of a convent in San Juan. At breakfast the first morning, the young postulant serving him inquired, "*Quiere usted chinita?*" His problem in responding was that *chinita* is a uniquely Puerto Rican word for orange, derived from the fact that the fruit was identified with the country of China and then given the usual Spanish diminutive ending *-ita*. Where the priest came from, however, a *chinita* was a prostitute. He always maintained that his response—in Spanish, of course—was, "What hospitality!"

Today the Prueba de Aptitud Académica (PAA) is used as the main admissions examination by the Commonwealth's colleges and universities. Its fortunes in the rest of Latin America, however, have varied over the years with differential effect on the finances of the operation. The College Board underwrote all the developmental work that went into the construction of the test, as well as the start-up administrative costs. But as the test's popularity in other countries grew, it was possible to begin to put the enterprise on a self-supporting basis. It was, that is, until the advent of the economic and financial crises that have overtaken our southern neighbors in recent years. They put such a heavy strain on the rates of exchange that the universities there could no longer afford to buy the PAA and its related services. Today the use of the test outside Puerto Rico has dwindled to the point where some subsidy from the parent College Board is occasionally necessary, a contribution, if you will, to efforts to provide equal access to higher education for one of the nation's largest and most impoverished minorities.

Those subsidies have, in my judgment, been warranted on other grounds as well. At their base is my perception (one not necessarily shared by all my predecessors) of the College Board as an educational enterprise that need not be conducted on an "each tub on its own bottom" theory but rather on an "all tubs in the same boat" philosophy—comparable to the situation in a university where the tuition income from large freshman survey courses helps underwrite the costs associated with senior seminars. On the international scene, the College Board's Puerto Rican operation provides a bridge to the developing countries of Central and South America. The PAA provides a mechanism that colleges and universities in the United States can use in importing Spanish-speaking applicants from that part of the third world, while the College Board office in Hato Rey serves as a base from which operational services and technical assistance can be exported. As already suggested, on the national scene the tests and other services sponsored by the College Board on the island constitute a significant part of the association's commitment to civil rights and equal educational opportunity for one of our country's major minorities.

I had frankly hoped at the outset that the PAA would also help in the identification and assessment of academically qualified Spanish-speaking students on the mainland and that its use would serve to identify academically able Hispanic young men and women who were presumably being discriminated against by the SAT. After all, I kept hearing about all those Mexican American and Puerto Rican young people whom the English-based SAT was keeping out of higher education. As it turned out, at the secondary school level (and I emphasize that qualification) the SAT was doing as good a job as the PAA and frequently even a better one. The reason was obvious; by the time these youngsters got to high school, the education they were receiving was in English. The sad fact is that many youngsters for whom Spanish is their first language do poorly on the SAT not simply because they don't know English, but because they aren't fluent in Spanish either.

Language Problems in the United States

That point was made in another way in a modest research study done on the streets of Boston back in the 1960s. The question being investigated was if the potential for college among street-smart young blacks using Black English might be more effectively assessed by testing them in the language of the streets. Many people believed then, and many still do, that there are lots of bright young people in the inner-city barrios and other ghettos of American cities who would do well in college if only they were given the chance—blacks, Puerto Ricans, and others who demonstrate their "smarts" in settings outside the schools. It is conventional wisdom today, for instance, that many young black males purposely fail in school because it is the "cool" thing to do.

To explore these beliefs, an oral test was developed in Black English and then administered on the street corners of Boston. The "candidates" were ranked according to their performance on the oral test. The same individuals were also asked to take a shortened version of the SAT. Again, they were ranked according to their scores. Although the scores earned on the short version of the SAT were low in comparison with those of the usual SAT population, the scores nevertheless ranked the "candidates" in the same order as the Black English oral test had positioned them. Any academic talent that was hidden in those young men and women was not obscured by the SAT but by their lack of training in the so-called standard English used in the classrooms of the nation's schools and colleges.

Philippines

The matter of testing in relation to the language of instruction was brought forcibly home to me in another former United States colonial setting, the Philippines. Ever since I had heard the issue of independence for the Philippines debated on the floor of the House of Representatives in Washington in 1933 (the act promising independence in 1946 was passed by Congress in 1934), I'd been intrigued by the possibility of getting a firsthand look at the Pacific's new republic. And so it was that in 1969, when the Rockefeller Foundation invited me to be half of a two-man team to provide technical assistance to the admissions office of the University of the Philippines, I quickly accepted.

In that assignment Richard Watkins, then a member of the staff of Educational Testing Service (ETS), and I were asked to take a look at the university's admissions and test-related activities. He provided the technical expertise in psychometrics and I the know-how in admissions generally. I'm not sure what Watkins's preconceptions were, but I know I undertook the assignment secure in the belief that the United States had the answer and that what was needed to put things in order was an instrument like the SAT.

In this last regard I have the feeling that I was like a good many United States experts, convinced that what had proved successful at home was easily exportable. It didn't take long for me to find out how misguided I had been. What's right for the United States isn't always right for some other nation, a lesson we still seem to be learning.

We worry a great deal about bilingualism in the United States and its effect on students whose first language isn't English. The Philippines make our problem seem very simple. There an applicant to the University of the Philippines from one of the outlying islands may have had to be able to communicate in as many as five languages: English (which was the university's language of instruction), Spanish (a legacy from the country's days as a colony of Spain), Pilipino (the then new national language), the local tongue (which, if the student was lucky enough to be from the region around Manila, was Tagalog, which formed the primary base for Pilipino), and in many cases a local patois. It wasn't an SAT-like instrument that was needed for admissions, but a reading comprehension test in English.

That experience in the Philippines, together with the College Board's involvement in Puerto Rico, convinced me that for most young people the high school years are just too late to focus on ensuring fluency in the language that will be used to deliver their higher education. Ability to deal with that language has to begin to be developed in the presecondary, or elementary and junior high, years.

Africa and Cultural Bias

Another useful lesson was learned not only in Puerto Rico but in Africa. It goes back to Father Jaramillo's *chinita*. As I have suggested earlier, one of the major contributions this country has made to the developing countries of the third world is the provision of opportunities for higher education. A number of special programs were introduced in the 1960s to help in this regard. One of the first was the African Scholarship Program for American Universities (ASPAU). Its founder was David Henry, a Harvard College classmate of mine who was the Harvard director of admissions at the time. Henry and his colleagues decided that one step in the process of selecting African students for admission to American colleges should be the administration of the Preliminary Scholastic Aptitude Test (PSAT)—that is, before it came to be used also with the National Merit Scholarship Qualifying Test (NMSQT). It turned out to be an experience that was valuable on several counts. Performance by the African students on the PSAT did assist in predicting how well they would do in American colleges and universities. That was the expected result. What was not anticipated at the outset was the contribution that the experience with the PSAT in Africa would make to testing in relation to the civil rights movement.

Early experimental administrations of the test in Africa made it clear that some of the questions were inappropriate for the African student. For instance, one item referred to blueberries and blueberry pies; but as one African pointed out, "Here we have no blueberries and no pies." Another question spoke of clothes hanging on a line to dry. As is the custom in many parts of the world, clothes are spread out to dry on bushes in Africa, not hung on clotheslines. As a result, versions of the PSAT, cleansed of United States cultural bias in the same way the PAA was cleansed of possible *chinitas,* were prepared for use by the ASPAU.

These experiences in dealing with cultural bias stood the College Board and ETS in good stead as attempts to ensure the SAT's fairness in assessing the academic potential of minority students were initiated. For many years items on the test have been subjected not only to pretesting but also to what is known as a sensitivity review. In that process, as pointed out in Chapter 5, persons of different ethnic, racial, and linguistic backgrounds take a careful look at each question that is headed for inclusion in an operational form of the SAT to make sure that it will not discriminate against minority candidates. The good old "oarsmen" and "regatta" item, an example in Chapter 5 of test words that elicited criticism, predated that practice. The point to be stressed yet again, however, is that the language and vocabulary of the SAT by and large reflect the language and vocabulary of the American college classroom and that, like it or not, familiarity with them is basic to academic success in higher education.

TOEFL

This lesson, learned in the international context in the 1960s, led to the joint development by the College Board and ETS of the Test of English as a Foreign Language (TOEFL). Evidence that a student was academically prepared for higher education in a country where English was not the language of instruction simply wasn't enough to assure United States admissions officers that this student could handle the language and vocabulary of the college classroom in this country; what those admissions officers needed to know was if a given foreign student could manage English. The TOEFL provides the needed evidence. In fact, it turned out to do the job at both the graduate and undergraduate levels, and because it does, sponsorship was delegated to ETS with College Board representation on the TOEFL governing board.

While TOEFL serves an important role in the import of foreign students, one of ETS's other major contributions to the field of international education has been the provision of technical assistance to developed and developing countries alike. As envisaged by its founders, ETS soon became the psychometric mecca of the United States. What they may not have foreseen was that it would become the world's fountain of testing expertise as well. The quality of its work, the reputation of its staff, and the currency of its research soon led scholars from around the globe who were interested in the field to beat a path to its doors. In response, ETS developed training programs in tests and measurement for them. Today one would probably find that many if not most of the world's leading psychometric authorities have studied at ETS at one time or another.

IAEA

The personal associations developed in this and other settings led to the emergence of an informal and then, in 1974, a formal network of institutions and agencies concerned with assessment. The latter, the brainchild of William Turnbull, president of ETS from 1970 to 1981, became known as the International Association for Educational Assessment (IAEA). This organization, affiliated with UNESCO and chartered in Brazil, serves primarily as a pivot point in the international exchange of ideas about tests and measurement. However, it does have one assessment instrument of its own. Called the International Test of Developed Abilities (ITDA), it was designed to deal with assessment at that point in the educational spectrum where there is the greatest transnational migration of students: college entrance. Patterned after the SAT, it produces scores in verbal and mathematical reasoning.

The process by which it was developed was a psychometric tour de force. Four versions, or forms, of the test were assembled according to a single, very demanding set of specifications in each of four languages: Arabic, Chinese, English, and Portuguese. With the help of test experts in Egypt, Hong Kong, the United States, and Brazil, enough questions for the four forms of the test were developed; each form was intended to pose exactly the same questions and elicit the same right answers in each of the four languages. Because of linguistic complications like the aforementioned "*chinita* and blueberry effect," it was assumed, correctly as it turned out, that only about one in four of the questions would prove to be psychometrically equivalent across all four languages. The four versions of the test were administered to students in their first language in each of the four settings, the results were analyzed to determine which questions worked properly in all four, and the surviving questions were assembled to produce a single operational form of the ITDA.

With a single form of the test available, the next question was and is: how does the ITDA relate to locally administered examinations? Two studies dealing with that issue have been conducted, and others are in the works. In the first, a group of students in the United States took both the ITDA and the SAT, and their performances on the two instruments were compared. Given the psychometric similarity of the two tests, it was not surprising that the correlation was high, suggesting that the results would be equally useful in predicting academic performance in college. The second study, conducted in England, was even more reassuring. It demonstrated that results on the multiple-choice ITDA were comparable with student performance on the more traditional university entrance examinations regularly used in that setting.

While reassuring, that finding was not too surprising. A 1967 study of "The College Board Scholastic Aptitude Test as a Predictor of Academic Achievement in Secondary Schools in England" concluded that "the results suggest that United States tests can work well in other countries but that certain items in any test might have to be changed to take into account cultural differences." That, of course, is just what the ITDA exercise was intended to do.

The hope is, of course, that through similar equating efforts, the ITDA can be used as a mechanism through which the verbal and mathematical reasoning abilities of college-bound students can be assessed regardless of their native language. For example, the College Board regularly studies the relationship between scores on the SAT in English and the PAA in Spanish. Although some psychometric purists have trouble with my crude methodology, I infer that if a score of W on the PAA is comparable with a score of X on the SAT and if a score of X on the SAT is comparable with a score of Y on the ITDA and if a score of Y on the ITDA is comparable with a score of Z on the English scale, then a score of W on the PAA is roughly comparable with the English Z. Thus, with the ITDA in place and equated to the examinations in a student's first language, the student will be able to demonstrate his or her potential for doing college-level work in that language—that is, present scores attesting to developed abilities in verbal and mathematical reasoning. The student may then take a separate test like the TOEFL to demonstrate the ability to operate in the "second language" of the foreign university he or she wants to attend. We've known for years that for most foreign students whose first language is not English, performance on the SAT is more likely to be a reflection of their knowledge of English than of the academic abilities they have developed. The availability of the means for assessing those abilities independent of the language in which secondary school instruction was received will greatly facilitate the international movement of college-bound young people.

Measurement of Other Qualities

But while the IAEA's International Test of Developed Abilities is designed to support that movement, the IAEA itself serves primarily as a mechanism for the international exchange of ideas about testing and assessment generally. For example, a continuing concern in many developed countries is the narrow range of abilities assessed by paper-and-pencil tests. It is the same concern expressed by many critics of the SAT. "But the test doesn't measure creativity or imagination, drive or motivation!" they complain. Recognizing that limitation, the College Board has, ever since I became associated with it and before, been exploring ways of expanding the bases of human assessment. And so, it turns out, have many other testing authorities in other countries. In IAEA meetings over the years, I have learned about the efforts to broaden those bases in Norway, Sweden, and England, for example.

Although I sense some disagreement over which country got into the act first, the Swedes and the Norwegians were among the early explorers of the concept. They sought to take into account what are known in the jargon of psychometrics as "nonintellective factors," personal characteristics that can be inferred from teachers' comments about students' attitudes and behavior, from the recommendations of others, and from students' activities outside the classroom. Although it's not clear to me who got in first, it is a matter of record that the Norwegians got out first. Apparently the results proved so unpopular as far as the public was concerned that the Norwegian Parliament put an end to the practice.

In hearing of this experience, I was reminded of my own in the field of admissions at the Harvard Business School. For a couple of years after World War II, I served as an assistant dean there, working mainly on the difficult task of selecting students. To catch up with the backlog that had built up during the war, we were admitting three classes a year instead of just one. For each class there were as many as seven applicants for each opening, and virtually all of them had not only strong undergraduate academic records but also valuable and often revealing wartime experiences with which to make their cases for admission. Our tough decisions were made on the basis of those records, those experiences, and the results of interviews with at least two members of the admissions team. As a result we were able to assemble some pretty interesting and successful classes. I became rather adept as an interviewer, adept enough, at least, for the school to ask me to do formal interviewing in the Chicago area after I left the staff. I was paid five dollars an interview.

While I was moonlighting for the Harvard Business School, however, a student at the Harvard Graduate School of Education undertook a research study of the interview process and put me out of business. Sam Kendrick, who, ironically, later joined the College Board staff at the same time I did in 1955, prevailed on the Harvard Business School for two years to admit half of each class by using interview results and half without using them. Kendrick then used the grades students earned, together with personal assessments made by their professors and fellow students, to rank them. The results were clear. In each instance, the half of the class admitted without using the interview results was superior. The lesson, too, was clear. Interview assessments tend to contaminate the written record of a student's achievements.

It is my understanding that the Norwegian Parliament was persuaded to act not on the basis of any such clear research evidence but on the basis of their concern that the academic side of schooling wasn't getting the proper attention. It has taken the Swedes somewhat longer to back off from the claims of success they were making for their system of broad-based, continuous assessment in the 1960s and 1970s. They made significant contributions to the field of measurement in their effort but are now tempering their enthusiasm and giving more weight to academic performance per se. Meanwhile, the examining authorities in England (and Scotland) have taken up the cause of broad-based assessment and are using "profiles" and "records of achievement" to assist in making decisions about who gets what kind of postsecondary education where. The motivations here are quite different. In Sweden a major impetus was a scientific one. The goal was to improve the science of measurement and share its success with the rest of the world. In England, by contrast, the motivations have less to do with scientific precision and are more concerned with social justice and economic development; England is seeking to deal with educational inequities as it upgrades the training of its labor force.

As I have suggested, the United States, too, is seeking to broaden the base on which educational decisions are made about young people. The work of Howard Gardner at Harvard and Robert Sternberg at Yale holds great promise of enlarging our understanding of the human intellect and how it might be assessed. In one area of his work, for example, Sternberg notes that most assessment requires students to answer questions posed to them. He believes that problem posing is also a very important ability and has some ideas about how to measure it. Also, the work of Warren Willingham at ETS, in the study of the role of personal qualities in the college admissions process, has provided new insights into factors that influence success in higher education. He has found, for instance, that persistence, or stick-to-itiveness, is a characteristic that can be identified and used to predict how well students will do in college.

But the critics of college admissions tests appear to want even more when they complain that the SAT doesn't measure such other traits as motivation and creativity. When it comes to motivation, I can't see how one can determine what a student's motivation will be in college. Circumstances change, and regardless of how a student may have done in secondary school, falling in love or losing a parent will motivate some students to excel and others to let things slide. As for creativity, it is a God-given talent that manifests itself in different ways and at different times for different persons. In my judgment, there are some things about human beings that can't and shouldn't be measured. In commenting on the admissions process, the president of a major university once said that he was more interested in the SQ than the IQ , in the soul quotient than the intelligence quotient. To which one of his less ardent admirers quipped, "Then he ought to move the admissions office to the Divinity School." Like the quipper, I believe there are some human characteristics that can't be measured, and those that can should remain the province of the admissions office. I take heart from my Scandinavian colleagues in this regard. School and college are for schooling, and assessments related to that process should concentrate on matters of the mind and the intellect and not on matters of the heart and the soul.

While the experiences in Norway, Sweden, and England serve to put the questions having to do with broad-based assessment in useful perspective, the Japanese search for technical assistance in university admissions has illuminated other aspects of the testing process. The SAT played an important and helpful role in that effort, an effort that stands in sharp contrast to an earlier, less successful one in the United Kingdom.

England

First, then, about the United Kingdom. In England there are several examining boards offering tests for admission to groups of universities. Most of their instruments are like the original College Boards, consisting primarily of essay or free-response questions and graded by individual examiners. Two considerations seem to have prompted the interest in the SAT that developed in England in the 1950s and 1960s. One was a recognition that the examinations offered by the several boards were different and that grades earned on them were not always precisely equivalent. It was thought that a test like the SAT might serve as a common currency among the examinations of the several authorities. The other motive was technical. By then a couple of the examining boards, particularly the Joint Matriculation Board serving five universities in the industrial Northwest, had become interested in the use of multiple-choice, objective tests and were eager to explore their wider use. As a result, an instrument like the SAT was developed and administered experimentally. But when it did no better than the existing examinations in predicting academic success in university, the whole idea was shelved.

Japan

The Japanese interest in the SAT concerned a much more critical issue, the familiar "hell of examinations" through which young men and women aspiring to higher education in Japan must go. In the 1960s Japanese educators began to explore the possibilities of what a test like the SAT might do to alleviate some of the tension, and for a dozen years or more, teams of Japanese educators and others visited the United States and the offices of the College Board. I remember two such occasions in particular. For the visit of the very first team of eight or ten individuals I was assigned the task of explaining the role of the College Board and the part played by the SAT in the college admissions process. Priding myself on my ability to speak very slowly and distinctly for the benefit of foreign visitors, I asked the assemblage clearly and precisely if they understood English. The visitors and their interpreter all politely nodded their heads in the affirmative. Whereupon I proceeded slowly and with impeccable diction to do my thing for 15 minutes or so. When I had finished, the interpreter picked up my monologue and proceeded to repeat in Japanese everything I had said in English. When it was all over,

I discovered that the initial affirmative nodding affirmed simply that they understood my question, not that they understood English.

As time went on, however, the familiarity of subsequent teams with our practices and our language increased, and I particularly recall a later visit that was conducted entirely in English. That fact didn't surprise me as much as did the presence on the team of a representative of the Japanese equivalent of our federal Treasury Department. What was he doing there? By this time the test development part of the process of introducing an SAT-like test into the university admissions system was pretty far along, and this team was exploring the administrative mechanisms that make the SAT work. The treasury official, it turned out, was interested in test security. Apparently the Japanese were going to use their counterpart to our FBI to ensure the security of their new test. Given our faith in the integrity of the individuals involved in our operation—the examiners who make up the tests; the employees of the companies that print them; the United States Postal Service, United Parcel Service, and the other private enterprises that deliver the test forms to the test centers; and the educators retained to administer the SAT in the schools and elsewhere—resort to the equivalent of the FBI may seem a bit extreme. But the Japanese approach appears almost benign compared with the steps taken in one third world country. There, the educators assembled to make up the examinations are sequestered until the examinations have been administered and returned to them for grading. Meanwhile the army takes on the responsibility for the distribution and on-site administration of the tests and for the return of the completed papers to the still-sequestered professors. The nefarious steps taken to beat the system that are implied by such security arrangements make the relatively few attempts at cheating in this country pale by comparison but do not excuse them.

In any event, at a time when many American observers perceive much that we might wish to emulate in Japanese educational practices, it is both intriguing and reassuring to observe that the Japanese now emulate the good old SAT. They use their version as an initial screening device in the university admissions testing process.

Reference to the FBI and the army in connection with college admissions calls attention to a general circumstance that needs to be kept in mind in any discussion of international education. The FBI and the army are creatures of the federal government, of centralized national authority. Their use in maintaining the security of the SAT or the ACT simply doesn't make sense in the United States. The SAT and the ACT are the products of private (albeit nonprofit) enterprises, and the students whose abilities they assess come from locally controlled school districts. In most other countries of the world, most students attend schools that are under the direct authority of centralized national government. In the Soviet Union, it was popular to observe that, if you knew what time it was, you could tell what was being taught in every Russian classroom. Even England has introduced a government-mandated "national curriculum."

Whereas England and Australia have several university entrance examining boards and the United States has its SAT and ACT, most nations have a single, centralized examining authority. That condition puts a different light on the role of university entrance examinations. Most other countries are testing what *is* being taught in the secondary schools by government decree. The College Board, through its Achievement Tests and its Advanced Placement Examinations, is attempting to test what, by consensus, school and college teachers *believe* is being taught in a majority of the nation's locally controlled secondary schools. In that circumstance the SAT plays a still different and very important role. Because not all schools have the same curriculum, the SAT is intended to assess the academic potential of college-bound students regardless of what they have been taught.

Global Problems of Education

The international scene provides many contrasts, and it also offers many similarities. The problems of dealing with educationally disadvantaged minority young people are not unique to the United States. Attention has been called to the linguistic hurdles faced by students in the Philippines. In his *Elitism and Meritocracy in Developing Countries,* published by Johns Hopkins Press in 1986, Robert Klitgaard uses the experience of the Philippines, together with the experiences of the People's Republic of China, Pakistan, and Indonesia, to illuminate the public policy dilemma of simultaneously accommodating the goals of selecting students for higher education according to academic merit and ensuring equality of opportunity reasonably to aspire to it. Provincial differences in the People's Republic of China, island differences in Indonesia (which, incidentally, I discovered is the fifth most populous nation on earth), linguistic differences in the Philippines, and religious differences in Pakistan present some of the same problems of racial and ethnic difference faced by black, Hispanic, and Asian American students in the United States. Aspiration to greater equality of educational opportunity has played a part in England's exploration of broad-based assessment. Issues of equity in testing for university admission have been raised on behalf of the aborigines in Australia and of the Maori in New Zealand.

The nations of the world have a great deal to learn from each other about the educational handling of minority and culturally diverse young men and women, and discussions about university entrance examinations like the SAT provide a useful avenue by which to approach the exchange of ideas. Indeed, the SAT plays a unique role in generating those discussions. It is, after all, the best-known test, undoubtedly the most researched test, and certainly one of the most highly respected tests in the world. Professionally, it has provided me with opportunities to gain insights that could be achieved only by seeing educational problems through the eyes of peoples from other lands. Personally, it has made it possible for me to associate with interesting people from other lands, people I would not have met were it not for the worldwide respect in which the SAT is held. Two examples from among many follow.

A minister of education from the People's Republic of China was visiting the United States in the mid-1980s with a team of his countrymen to learn about our American educational enterprise. I made the College Board and the SAT parts of his learning experience. He was fascinating, one of China's educated elite who had been degraded during the Cultural Revolution and only recently returned to a position of authority after the downfall of the Gang of Four. He knew the value and the importance of education; I knew he knew, not only because of what he was saying about education in the PRC but also because of the nature of the comments he made in correcting his much younger colleague, who was acting as his interpreter. His command of English was far superior to that of his professional translator. It was clear that he had observed and was deploring the damage that the abandonment of university entrance examinations had done to his country.

Anisio Teixeira was the Mr. Education of Brazil when I visited there with Adolfo Fortier in 1962. Frank Bowles had had Dr. Teixeira as a member of his UNESCO study team and arranged for him to be our mentor while we were in his country. Fortier and I made our courtesy call on the cultural attaché at the United States embassy in Rio de Janeiro. (There were then two United States embassies in Brazil, the old one in Rio, the former capital, and the new one in Brasilia, to which the capital had been moved in 1960.) I "naively" on purpose asked the attaché why he thought Frank Bowles had put us in Teixeira's hands instead of sending us through normal channels at the embassy. My question evoked no direct response, and the attaché changed the subject to something like the weather. When I later asked Anisio why, he replied, "They think I am a Communist."

"Are you?" I asked.

"No," he replied, "I am a believer in education. But the government is doing little to improve the educational lot of our people, and the Communists are promising to do more if they get the chance. Because I do want to get more done and make no bones about it, they classify me with the Communists."

"But," I interjected, "you say you don't believe in Communism. How do you square that with your support of Communist goals for education? If they get into power, won't they simply take over the schools and indoctrinate everyone with their special beliefs?"

"George," he said, "I believe so strongly in the power of education that I am perfectly willing to let the Communists supply it if nobody else will. In the end, the educated man will see the fallacies of Communism and reject it!" A few years later Anisio Teixeira was found under suspicious circumstances at the bottom of an elevator shaft. In my book, Anisio Teixeira was a true martyr in the cause of education.

There were personal moments overseas that were poignant in themselves. Never did I feel for my country more than at a meeting in Edinburgh, Scotland. The Scots, like the English in the 1950s and 1960s, were interested in the SAT, and I had been asked to talk about it to a Scottish audience. In introducing me, the presiding officer said that he knew I must be deeply saddened by the untoward event that had just taken place at home, the assassination of Martin Luther King, Jr. I was! At the other extreme, there was the joy of riding the Paris subways in search of the UNESCO offices with other members of the IAEA Executive Committee—the irrepressible Itai Zak, a Jew from Israel; astute and fun-loving Omar Hashim, a Muslim from Malaysia; and towering over the three of us, tall, black, and handsome Donton Mkandawire from Malawi. We were an unlikely quartet with hardly a word of French among us. I believe that just as national tragedies serve to bring peoples together, so, too, will the personal associations forged across national boundaries in pursuit of nonpolitical goals, like better testing, serve in the long run to do more than treaties and summits to create and preserve world peace.

Those poignant moments and those dedicated educators, those *chinitas* and blueberry pies, those Maori and rural Filipinos, those Norwegians and those Swedes, are all parts of the mosaic that the international scene came to represent for me. It's a mosaic that cries out for international cooperation based on education. I made that point in a convocation address I delivered in October 1984 at West Virginia Wesleyan College, Buckhannon, West Virginia. Here is what I said.

Usually audiences, particularly audiences with students in them, tend to greet me with something less than warm enthusiasm, associating me with the SAT and one of the more necessary but less enjoyable rites of educational passage and perceiving me as somehow being involved with keeping people out instead of helping them in. That's a perception that's hard to take, hard to take for someone who likes to think that what he's doing is more a help than a hindrance. That is why I am especially pleased at being asked to take on a role more often assigned to a practicing academic—pleased because I interpret that invitation as confirming your belief that the work of the College Board in education is an integral part of the academic whole and that it has played a part in recent decades in helping our colleges and universities open up, not close off, access to higher education.

With that assurance in mind, the message I want you to hear is a simple one—related to this year's theme at West Virginia Wesleyan as it approaches its one hundredth anniversary—one that asserts simply that education is man's best rational hope for peace and progress in the world. For me it is a familiar message that I have delivered often, but one that has taken on new meaning for me as a result of recent experience.

Last summer Mrs. Hanford and I had the once-in-a-lifetime privilege of spending two months in Asia and the South Pacific, visiting New Zealand, Australia, Singapore, Malaysia, Thailand, and Hong Kong. As a personal adventure, it was a mix of truly great experiences. As a professional experience, it was also rewarding and has provided a lot of food for thought, and in that context there are a few impressions that will help me make my point.

One impression is that many of the circumstances we face in the United States have either their counterparts or their mirror images elsewhere and that seeing familiar problems, or their obverse, in unfamiliar settings can frequently serve to shed light on problems we tend to see as peculiarly ours.

In Australia and New Zealand, for example, concern for the rights of the aborigines and the Maori, respectively, could be seen as mirroring our concern for our ethnic minorities. Yet the problems down under can be closely equated with ours only in the case of Native American Indians, who, like the aborigines and the Maori, were here (or there) before the white man arrived. The circumstances are different in the case of our Mexican Americans, who have colonial roots in both Mexico and the United States, and of the blacks, whom the white man imported. Or take Malaysia, where the problem of bilingualism for educators isn't the one we have of seeking to accommodate differently speaking youth in English-teaching schools but rather one of changing what were English-teaching schools into ones where Malay is the language of instruction.

A second impression was in the cities of Southeast Asia, where one quickly discovers that urbanization—the flight to the cities—is not a peculiarly American phenomenon. The crowds in Singapore and Kuala Lumpur, in Bangkok and Hong Kong, serve as a constant reminder of the population explosion that is fueling that flight—a topic addressed on this campus ten or a dozen years ago, I understand, by the late John D. Rockefeller III. At a meeting I attended in Bangkok this summer, one speaker observed that the world's annual rate of population growth has gone down from 2.9 percent to 1.7 percent over the last seven years. Applauding the reduction while lamenting the fact that the percentages are cumulative, he avoided speculation as to the cause. I would like to believe that it is due to a better understanding of the dangers of overpopulation resulting from better education. At the same time I would hope that the better education is not simply a better understanding of birth-control methods. I recall how well-intentioned efforts to export them to Latin America in the 1960s were perceived by many there as attempts by the United States to hold populations down in its neighbors to the south so that they wouldn't be in a position to recruit large armies to attack us.

Another impression had to do with the legacy of the West. Having visited Southeast Asia, I understand a little better the causes and the aftermath of what we know as the Vietnam War; there, it was just another episode in an ongoing conflict among the peoples of the region—a conflict complicated by the colonial intrusions of the British in Malaysia, of the French in Vietnam, and of the Dutch in Indonesia. Malaysia, for instance, isn't just on the Malay peninsula but includes about a third of the island of Borneo because that part of it was under British rather than Dutch colonial rule. And Malaysia is predominantly Muslim, not Buddhist like Thailand, because it was imported from another British colony, India. What became crystal clear to me in thinking about these circumstances is the wisdom of our schools in extending the social studies, beyond United States history and Western civilization, to include world history.

A fourth impression had to do with the interdependence of the nations of the world. The volume of automobile traffic in Sydney, Singapore, Kuala Lumpur, Bangkok, and Hong Kong—and particularly the last four—is a constant reminder of how dependent the world is on oil. Developments in the Middle East were obviously much on people's minds. But in the port at Fremantle in Western Australia I observed the obverse, a cargo ship being loaded with 25,000 live sheep for transport to the Persian Gulf. They were being shipped live so that they could be slaughtered in accordance with the religious customs of the residents of the oil-rich Middle East. And I found irony in the fact that Saudi Arabia is now importing camels from Australia, to which they were exported more than a century ago to help conquer the desert regions of the interior. Economically, as well as socially and politically, isolationism just doesn't make sense, and one of the real problems for the future will continue to be that of maintaining a balance between national and international interests that will ever so gradually move all three worlds toward becoming one.

Finally, by way of impressions, I have to say that while we were spared having to view the effects of the world's worst poverty and hunger in India and the results of nuclear war in Japan, we were not spared the reality that man is living not only in danger of a nuclear holocaust but also beyond his ecological and economic needs. Horrendous pollution attends those city traffic jams in the absence of mandatory controls. Cities are running out of drinking water. Bangkok, already below sea level, is sinking under its own weight at about an inch a year. And we were told at the conference there, 35,000 children die of starvation around the world every day. Shocking when you think of it but no more troublesome when you think of how the food problem would be magnified if they lived.

In my thinking about it, I was reminded of the young American physician who began his career in India some years ago. In the rural village to which he was first assigned, he discovered quickly that the reason many newborn children and their mothers died was that local religious traditions called for placing both ends of the umbilical cord in cow dung immediately after birth. He proposed an alternative approach, which was accepted. The infants survived, as did their mothers, who soon gave birth to other children. Within a couple of years, people of all ages, including the young children and the mothers saved only a short time before, died daily from starvation and malnutrition. There were too many mouths to feed.

The young doctor's next assignment was in a village whose contaminated water was the major cause of mortality. He knew how to solve the problem. But if he solved it, he knew, too, that the people he saved *this* year would be threatened with death by starvation next. What should he do?

If problems were simple, we would have solved them. There was no easy answer to the young doctor's dilemma.

In reflecting on all this—on the complex problems of national pride and global interdependence, of ecological suicide and nuclear war, of famine and overpopulation—I developed a syllogism. It has a preamble that goes like this:

The problems of the world are becoming more complex. Simple solutions won't work! Among nations, how can a proper balance be achieved between the demands of nationalism and the imperatives of global interdependence? Within nations, how can the interests of majority and minority, rich and poor, enfranchised and disenfranchised, indigenous and colonial, young and old, be accommodated? Neither patriotism nor tariffs nor more food nor birth control nor banning the bomb nor turning back the clock nor bilingualism alone is going to work. Achieving the right balance among these disparate factors and finding solutions to the other complex problems facing the world will require the best minds that men can produce.

And the syllogism goes like this. The problems of the world are becoming more complex. Finding solutions will require the best minds that men can produce. Minds are trained through education, and the best minds generally through higher education. Therefore, what you are engaged in here is pertinent to the solution of the world's problems.

That syllogism, of course, is the short-form justification for my opening assertion that education is man's best hope for peace and progress in the world. And there is a temptation to conclude with it. But if I were to do so, I would be being less than honest for, if you had listened carefully, you would have noticed a qualifier in that opening assertion—the adjective *rational*—education is man's best *rational* hope for peace and progress.

Education—knowledge and the ability to use it—education alone won't solve the world's problems.

It is necessary to their solution but not sufficient. There has to be another dimension, a dimension that is associated with what we know as religion; a dimension based on faith in man; a dimension that will ensure that education is used to solve problems that are economic and social, political and ecological, in ways that recognize the worth of all mankind, not of just a few; a dimension that leads to the definition of education so well articulated in the literature of West Virginia Wesleyan: of "intelligence seeking faith and faith seeking intelligence." Education so defined is man's best hope for peace and progress. The future is indeed in your hands, in the hands of those who give and those who receive education here. I am delighted to have had this brief opportunity to share in your effort, to suggest something of its broader significance, and to have become in some small way a part of it. Thank you for hearing me out.

CHAPTER 9

Life with an Association

Life with the Scholastic Aptitude Test meant life at "the College Board." I put those three words in quotation marks because they are used without differentiation, as I have used them throughout this book, to mean different things: the corporation that is still legally known as the College Entrance Examination Board, the association that comprises the institutions and other associations that are its members, and the bureaucracy that is responsible for the day-to-day operations of the enterprise. In all those capacities the College Board grew tremendously during the more than 31 years that I worked for it. As an association, the subject of this chapter, it increased from 188 members (166 higher education institutions, 22 education associations, and no secondary schools) to 2,588 members (1,162 colleges and universities, 20 higher education systems, 1,223 secondary schools, 93 large school systems, and 90 education associations). In doing so, the College Board became transformed from a homogeneous, closely knit group of participants with a single operational focus to a large, heterogeneous membership organization with a variety of agendas. Yet, despite the growth and the transformation, the member representatives never lost their hands-on concern for the conduct of their enterprise.

The Early Years

Claude M. Fuess's *The College Board: Its First Fifty Years,* which the College Board published in 1967, documents the growth of the College

Entrance Examination Board from an exclusive club to that 188-member organization I went to work for in 1955. In Chapter 2, I discuss the founding of Educational Testing Service (ETS), the "refounding" of the College Board, and the establishment of the College Scholarship Service (CSS). The decisions that led to those three developments, like the decisions noted earlier having to do with the release of scores to candidates and the introduction of the Student Descriptive Questionnaire (SDQ), were made by the members of the association on the advice of their elected governing body. In the early years of the century the membership *was* that body, but by the time I joined the staff, an elected Executive Committee had long since been necessary. In 1955 it was meeting in the Trustee's Room in Low Library at Columbia University, an elegant room that had once accommodated the entire membership.

Fuess's recounting of developments during the first 50 years suggests the clublike nature of the enterprise, vestiges of which lasted into the refounding era. As the number of members slowly increased from its original 12, it became clear that the membership could not continue to act as a committee of the whole in overseeing the operations of the CEEB. At first, oversight of the operation of the enterprise was handled by a group of leaders who got together informally the evening before the semiannual membership meetings to go over the actions to be proposed the next day. In time this group became known as the Ferry-Farrand Cabinet, named after two of the association's early leaders. When the need for a more formal arrangement was recognized and the Executive Committee chosen by the members was established, the cabinet continued to meet and to provide informal advice to the Executive Committee and the members.

Gradually, however, by the time of the refounding, the role of the Ferry-Farrand Cabinet had become less influential in CEEB affairs, and its meetings were devoted to sociability and the discussion of a single current CEEB-related issue. I was fortunate enough to be asked to join the cabinet and reveled in the opportunity to share ideas with College Board statesmen like Richard M. Gummere of Harvard and Edward S. Noyes of Yale; with then College Board leaders like Frank Bowles and Henry Chauncey, the founding president of Educational Testing Service; with Frank D. Ashburn of the Brooks School, Archie MacIntosh of Haverford College, B. Alden Thresher of MIT, and Eugene S. Wilson of Amherst; and with contemporaries like Richard Pearson and Harold Howe II, who found time in his busy schedule as United States commissioner of education to come to cabinet meetings. It was a unique and intimate organization with a single officer, a symposiarch whose responsibility was to choose a time and place for our annual get-together (usually in conjunction with the, by then, Annual Meetings of the members) decide what we'd have to eat, and determine what the topic of after-dinner conversation would be. A throwback to the CEEB's days as an exclusive club, the cabinet ultimately fell victim to the weight of the bureaucracy as the membership became ever more diverse, the locus of leadership more diffuse, and the time for fellowship around Annual Meetings of the College Board more limited. Its demise coincided with the end of an era at the College Board, an era that, though marked by the dominance of the original written College Boards, ultimately set the stage for the founding of ETS, the refounding of the College Board, and the rise to prominence of the SAT. For my part I am glad to have had that brief chance as a member of the cabinet to get a sense of what the good old days in the earlier years of the century must have been like at the College Entrance Examination Board. It provided a perspective that helped me better understand life with the latter-day SAT.

The rapid growth in membership that followed the refounding reflected the increased college attendance as colleges and universities looked to the College Board, with its proven record of service, for help in what has been called "the great sorting." The only qualification for membership in those days was the use of the College Boards—the SAT and the Achievement Tests. To pick up one of the loose membership threads in those refounding years, a survey was conducted to make sure that the then current members did indeed require either or both. One prestigious selective university that used the tests wasn't about to be told that it had to; institutions could and still can use the College Board's tests and other services without being a member. I don't recall the exact sequence of events (if that particular institution dropped out of membership for a while it's "in" now), but it wasn't too long before the absolute membership requirement of the use of the tests for admission was modified, and the phrase "regular and substantial use" was introduced. And not much later the meaning of "tests" was expanded to include the examinations of the Advanced Placement Program and the College-Level Examination Program.

Those specific relaxations reflected a more general stance adopted by the association in the late 1950s and early 1960s. Initially, the increasing size of the membership prompted the Executive Committee to recommend that because the informal associational arrangement then in place was no longer appropriate, the College Entrance Examination Board should be incorporated. In 1957 it was granted a charter as a membership corporation under the laws of the State of New York. By the early 1960s, applications for membership were increasing at such a rapid rate that the Board of Trustees of the new corporation, the replacement for the old Executive Committee, faced squarely up to the question of whether the organization should undertake to restrict the size of the membership in the interests of maintaining something of its original exclusive character (which, not so incidentally, served to attract new members who wanted to rub shoulders with the Ivy League in the councils of the College Board). The alternative was to encourage membership growth in the interests of ensuring that the association's constituency would be more representative of the diversity that is the hallmark of higher education in the United States. That issue was most hotly debated in the Committee on Organization and Functions, appointed by the trustees to study the situation and make recommendations for the next steps. The substance of that debate was shared with the members, and in the end the committee, the trustees, and the members chose the expansion route.

The deliberations leading to those decisions to incorporate and not to limit membership triggered the consideration of a specific matter of fundamental importance to the governance of the association. Before incorporation, all policy decisions made by the Executive Committee were subject to review and ratification by the members at their then semiannual meetings. In 1957 the question was whether that protocol should be written into the charter of the new corporation. The reason for raising the issue had to do with the rights and privileges of elected corporate officers (directors, trustees, governors, and the like). In the business world, for instance, authority for the conduct of a corporation is vested in the directors elected by the stockholders. If the stockholders don't like the way the corporation is being "directed," they can vote the rascals out; otherwise, the stockholders' ability to influence the administration of the corporation is severely limited. In short, directors on boards in the business world know that if their boards decide that certain actions should be taken, they will be taken. Should that same authority be vested in the trustees elected by the members of the College Board? As the scope of the association's operations and other activities grew, that question was revisited twice: first by the Committee on Organization and Functions in the early 1960s and again by the Bylaw Revision Advisory Committee a decade later.

Each time it was raised, Herbert Wechsler, the wise legal counsel of the College Board, asked, "Have the members ever taken an unwise or inappropriate action?" Each time the answer was no. True, on occasion the members either had questioned an action taken by the trustees or had acted contrary to the trustees' advice, but their actions could not be considered unwise or inappropriate. Four examples will make the point.

Membership Initiative

At an annual membership meeting in the late 1950s, the members called into question the trustees' decision (described in Chapter 2) to assist ETS in meeting its plant expansion requirements. The arrangement appeared to put an unduly heavy strain on the College Board's financial resources, and why did ETS need the money anyway? The members didn't overturn the trustees' decision, but they did demand a fuller explanation for it. To supply it, the staff organized a series of meetings in different parts of the country, to which the members' representatives were invited. These sessions proved useful in two ways. For the short run, they provided a medium for making the point that the "capital grants" to ETS were in the College Board's self-interest. For the long run, they served to call attention to the need to provide opportunities for the members to "associate" with each other at times and places other than at annual membership meetings in New York City. That call from the members for an accounting by the trustees led directly to the establishment of the College Board's six regional offices and paved the way for the regionalization of the membership as called for by the Bylaw Revision Advisory Committee in the early 1970s.

This committee was appointed in the aftermath of the flap over the introduction of the Student Descriptive Questionnaire, and my second example of membership reaction pertains to that controversy. The question whether the College Board should add such an instrument to the services it provided in connection with the Admissions Testing Program was raised early in Arland Christ-Janer's presidency. There were many in the constituency who opposed the idea on the grounds that it would violate students' privacy or cost too much or simply wasn't needed. Staff opinion, like the advice we had received from the field, was divided. When it finally came time, after a long period of deliberation, to fish or cut bait, Christ-Janer asked me as his number two man if I thought we should go ahead. Conscious of the competition from the American College Testing Program—from whom we had adapted the idea—I didn't hesitate and said we should go ahead. And so the recommendation to introduce the SDQ was made to the trustees and, with their approval, to the membership. The problem was that while we policymakers were debating the "larger" issues of privacy, cost, and need, the technicians had gone too far in building into the proposal provisions for using the data supplied by students on the SDQ to produce a "predictive index" of probable academic performance in college as well as a counterpart financial aid derivative. The opponents of the idea latched on to these two intended outputs and called the whole proposition into question on the floor of the annual membership meeting in 1970. In fact, much more than the specific proposal itself was at stake.

Using the trustees' recommendations as his point of departure, David Dudley, then in charge of admissions at Illinois Institute of Technology, without actually doing so, called the de facto self-perpetuation of the Board of Trustees into question. In a masterful display of political acumen, relying on his distinguished gray hair, emphasizing the quaver in his voice, and calling now and then for a glass of water, he used the trustees' support of the idea of a predictive index to suggest that the leadership might be losing touch with its constituency. As some of his supporters put it, "If admissions officers are going to use a predictive index, they want to use one for their own individual institutions, derived from their own validity studies, not some 'canned,' centrally computed figure that would also confuse applicants more than help them." As it turned out, the proposal to introduce the SDQ was approved but stripped of the predictive index and its financial aid counterpart—approved, that is, in a form different from the one recommended by the trustees because the members refused to act as rubber stamps.

In the aftermath of that contretemps, the Bylaw Revision Advisory Committee was appointed to look into the broader, governance-related issue. Under the wise and statesmanlike leadership of its chairman, Norman C. Francis, president of Xavier University of Louisiana in New Orleans, the committee met, consulted with the members at regional gatherings, and concluded that the right both to nominate and to elect trustees of the College Board ought to be, at least in part, regionalized. The result was the establishment of formal subgroups of members aligned with the six regional offices that had been founded as the result of the earlier findings of the Committee on Organization and Functions.

The six regional offices were not put in place all at once. The first was set up on the West Coast, where an informal West Coast Committee, consisting of all the members of the College Board west of the Rockies, had been meeting since the early 1950s because getting to meetings on the East Coast was so time-consuming and expensive. The Western Regional Office, then in Palo Alto, and now in San Jose, California, was soon joined by two others: the Midwestern Regional Office, outside

Chicago, serves the Midwest; the Southern Regional Office, described in Chapter 5, now in Atlanta, serves the South. Then—to avoid the appearance of overlooking the interests of the College Board's more traditional membership—a Northeast Regional Office staff operating out of the national headquarters in New York City was assembled. But the press of numbers and the practicalities of geography suggested that four field offices weren't enough. As a consequence the northeast region was split in two with an office outside Boston (New England Regional Office) to service the six New England states and another, at first still in New York City and later moved to Bethlehem, Pennsylvania, to take care of what are known in education circles as the Middle Atlantic States. This Middle States Regional Office is now located in Philadelphia. Also, a four-state Southwestern Regional Office was carved out of the Southern Regional Office's original domain. The members in the states served by these now six regional offices became the formal regional constituencies established in the wake of the controversy over the SDQ. In pairs, each regional membership elects one trustee every three years so that each region is represented on the Board of Trustees at all times. And each year, each regional membership elects an individual to serve on the 12-person National Nominating Committee, which is responsible for nominating the other, at-large trustees. And all because the members of the College Board had twice chosen not to act like rubber stamps.

My other two examples of membership initiative come out of quite different contexts. There was the occasion in the early 1960s when the College Board had tests but no authorized dates on which to administer them. In those days it was the practice to have the members vote to set the times at which the SAT and the Achievement Tests would be given the following year. At one annual membership meeting, the articulate and persuasive guidance counselor from our daughters' high school objected to one of the dates on the schedule being proposed and persuaded a majority of the member representatives to vote against the trustees' recommendation. When they did so, everyone assumed that the schedule would revert to an earlier formula for setting the dates, which would avoid the distasteful date. The assemblage then went on to deal with the other matters on its agenda. Fortunately, somebody suddenly realized before the business meeting adjourned that the members had not only rejected the unwanted test date, they had left the College Board without any dates on which to administer the tests the next year. A revised set of times was prepared and adopted. That, I would say, was the closest the membership ever came to an irresponsible action. However, it did have the advantage of communicating to the membership the realization that too close involvement in the operation of its enterprise could be disastrous, and as a result, procedures were adopted that ensure prior consultation in regional and other settings on important corporate issues before the trustees. Test dates, for example, are such an issue.

My fourth example of the no-rubber-stamp attitude of the members involved the Writing Sample. The absence of written exercises in the College Board's admissions tests generated a certain amount of protest by both college English professors and admissions officers. The controversy seemed to die down after a 20-minute essay was included in the English Composition Test (one of the Achievement Tests) in the 1970s. Before that, however, there had been a number of attempts to "rectify" the situation. One resulted in the introduction of the Writing Sample in December 1960. Led by Bill Wilson of Amherst, a number of admissions officers had called on the College Board to provide an opportunity for students to present evidence of their abilities to write. They didn't ask that it be graded, simply that provision be made among the College Board's regular test offerings for a sample of a student's writing to be composed under normal, secure testing conditions, duplicated at ETS, and forwarded for evaluation to the colleges to which the student was applying. The trustees took the proposal under advisement, sought the advice of the appropriate committees, and then recommended against it. However, a majority of the members took issue with the trustees on the matter and voted for the introduction of the Writing Sample. It lasted until the introduction of the essay in the English Composition Test, which replaced the Writing Sample as an incentive for schools to teach writing.

The occasions on which the members have either rejected the trustees' recommendations or taken issue with their actions have been few, and some will observe that they took place in the 1960s and 1970s. In response, I would note that the mechanisms put in place as a result of those examples and other episodes like them to inform the trustees of membership reaction to matters of important moment to the association, which are on the agendas of meetings of the Board of Trustees, have served their purpose. Today there is far less likelihood that the trustees will take an action with which the members disagree. But the opportunity for doing so remains under the bylaws of the association. And I know that there are dedicated and concerned individuals in the constituency—like Emery Walker, who led the effort to eliminate misleading precision in SAT score reporting; Dave Dudley with the SDQ; and Bill Wilson on behalf of the Writing Sample—who can make a case for disputing the trustees if ever a case should again need to be made, and they would win. The wisdom of Herbert Wechsler's legal advice still obtains.

CSSA

Back at the Bylaw Revision Advisory Committee in the aftermath of the SDQ affair, the committee was also recommending that the College Scholarship Service Assembly (CSSA) be allowed, like the regional assemblies, to participate in the trustee election process by having one trustee of its own choosing on the Board of Trustees at all times. That there was such a body as the CSSA in place within the governance structure was evidence of other dimensions or kinds of growth that took place in the 1960s and 1970s. For example, the Committee on Organization and Functions considered student financial aid an integral part of the College Board's mission to help bridge the gap between secondary and higher education and had recommended that the stake of the financial aid community in that transition be recognized within the governance structure of the College Board. Accordingly, the College Scholarship Service Assembly, a formal association of institutions using the programs of the College Scholarship Service, was established.

Its authority, however, was limited to electing the members of its oversight body, the College Scholarship Service Committee (CSSC), and to advising the CSSC on what actions it should take. In turn, although the CSSC acted in reality as the de facto governing body for the operational and associational activities of the College Scholarship Service, it was then, and still was in 1990, a standing advisory committee to the trustees of the College Board. In effect, just as the College Board members have veto power over the actions of the trustees, so, in this case, the trustees, not the CSSA, have veto power over the actions of the CSSC.

I can recall only one instance (it was in the early years of the CSSC, before the establishment of the CSSA, and was strictly a political, not an operational, matter) when the trustees acted to override a position taken by the CSSC. This arrangement, not surprisingly, sticks in the craw of the financial aid officers who represent their institutions in the CSSA. More about that later. For the discussion of membership growth, it can be said that while the interests of the student financial aid community were recognized by two membership and governance studies as legitimate concerns of the College Board and relevant to its mission of assisting students in the transition from school to college, a satisfactory accommodation of that financial aid subconstituency within the governance structure of the parent association had not been found when I left the staff in January 1987.

Secondary School Membership

Another subconstituency achieved a satisfactory settlement of its claims to representation within the parent association during my presidency. But it was reached only after a long and laborious evolutionary process that began with the founding of the College Board in 1900. The careful reader will have noted that, until the time of the refounding, institutional membership was reserved for higher education. At the first founding, however, the leaders of the new enterprise realized that college and university deliberations about college entrance and college entrance examinations would be aided by input from secondary school educators. Therefore, an elite group of them were elected to serve as representatives-at-large. Fifty-seven years later the need to institutionalize the participation of the secondary sector was recognized, and provision was built into the charter and bylaws of the new corporation for 50 member secondary schools, about a quarter of the collegiate membership. Over the years the ratio was further relaxed, first to a third of the entire membership, then to no less than half, and finally in 1984 to parity—a complex, formula-driven parity but parity nonetheless. Because the last was achieved while I was president, much of the credit seemed to rub off on me, but the action was in truth the culmination of long and arduous effort to effect recognition of the equal stake that schools have with colleges in the college admissions process.

Institutional Representation

Although membership in the College Board (and in the College Scholarship Service Assembly) is institutionally based, the privileges of membership are exercised by individuals appointed by their chief executive officers to represent their institutions in the deliberations of the association. The character of that representation has changed over the years. In the beginning, college and university presidents attended meetings and spoke for their institutions. But as their campus administrative duties became more complex, responsibility for many of those chores was

assigned to subordinates specializing in a particular aspect of an institution's operation. Admissions officers and financial aid administrators
are cases in point. As these changes were made, admissions officers began
to represent their colleges or universities at meetings of the College
Board. And later the same thing happened in secondary schools, but not
in the student financial aid area. Those early representatives-at-large
were usually independent school headmasters or public high school
principals. Today, a guidance counselor is more likely to cast his or her
school's vote. In the case of the College Scholarship Service, however, it
was the financial aid officers who initially took part in the activities of
the College Scholarship Service Assembly, and they still do.

The existence of these separate subconstituencies of individuals
within the overall institutional membership has been responsible for
some of the more interesting and perplexing challenges faced by the
bureaucracy servicing the association. One of the outcomes of Frank
Bowles's refounding was the establishment of college admissions as a
profession distinct from the broader constituency served by the American
Association of Collegiate Registrars and Admissions Officers (AA-
CRAO). An association of individuals rather than institutions, its focus
was and is on the functions performed by the registrar, who in earlier
days often acted as the admissions officer on the side. The 10 collo-
quiums on college admissions sponsored by the College Board in the
late 1950s and early 1960s served to focus the professional interests of
those in charge of "the great sorting," and the publications deriving from
the papers delivered at them served to create the beginnings of a literature
for the newly recognized profession. In this way, even though the individuals involved were technically representing their institutions, the College Board came to serve in a very real sense as their professional
association.

The emergence of the student financial aid profession followed the
same course with the founding of the College Scholarship Service in
1954. The history of the growth of that operation within the College
Board, from a central duplicating service to a complex computational
enterprise whose costs now account for approximately a third of its
parent's entire budget, and of the contributions to the success story by
the leaders of the CSS constituency deserves a volume in its own right.
But while the admissions professionals remained content with the opportunities to associate with their peers provided by the College Board,
the American Association of Collegiate Registrars and Admissions Officers, and the National Association of College Admissions Counselors

(like the College Board, despite its name, then an institution-based association), the financial aid practitioners soon founded their own professional organization, the National Association of Student Financial Aid Administrators (NASFAA).

These different histories have in a way been at the heart of many of the difficulties impeding a satisfactory accommodation of the CSSA participants within the governance structure at the College Board. As did the secondary school representatives, the student financial aid officers want "equality of power." Other college and university administrators are skeptical of the need. They point out that giving voting power to the financial aid folk, and thus in effect giving two votes to a higher institution member, would be inconsistent with the "one institution-one vote" principle on which membership in the College Board has been based from the outset. Further, a split vote by representatives from the same institution wouldn't make sense. Although the CSSC has been left pretty much alone to direct the operations of the CSS, the financial aid officers still want recognition in the governance structure equivalent to that enjoyed by those admissions officers who actually are the voting representatives of their institutions. I will watch the working through of this dilemma with interest, but I will do so firm in my conviction that the College Board is not the arena in which to settle on-campus rivalries between individuals from the two professions it helped spawn.

This summary (and incomplete) recital of associational developments at the College Board properly suggests that life on the membership front was never static and that the challenges to the staff bureaucracy responsible for serving the association were perplexing: accommodating the sheer numbers; helping to establish two new professions and then having to deal with the rivalry between them; adapting to the natural tensions between headquarter and field office staffs, exacerbated by the instincts for self-determination on the part of regional offices responsible for constituencies that are not only geographically diverse but have different needs and expectations of the College Board; and accommodating a membership that knows its own mind.

Although such challenges might be perceived as getting in the way of the bureaucracy's other responsibilities, including sponsorship of the SAT, they have in my judgment been evidence of a vitality and a concern on the part of the persons involved. They care about the organization and the young people that it and their institutions serve. Their participation in meetings of the association, their willingness to serve on its committees and on its other councils, their attendance at its workshops and training sessions, and their attention to its publications and other forms of communication ensure that in the final analysis, the policies of the College Board are sound and in the best interests of young people. Like the founding of ETS and the emergence of competition from ACT, the involvement of the members has helped to preserve the integrity of the entire enterprise.

CHAPTER 10

Life in a Bureaucracy

Life with the SAT meant life at the College Board as it was transformed from a small secretariat into an educational bureaucracy. In financial terms during my more than 31 years with the organization, it grew from an enterprise with an annual budget of $1,750,000 to one with an annual outlay of nearly $130,000,000, almost a 75-fold increase. You have to develop a bureaucracy of sorts to deal with that great a growth and that large an enterprise. Bureaucracies, in turn, need housing, spawn meetings, generate travel, and require their executives to do a lot of public speaking. This chapter is about housing, meeting, traveling, and speaking at the College Board.

Housing

There is an old saying to the effect that "you are what you eat." (One young lady is reported to have said when she heard it, "Then let's order something rich!") There has to be a counterpart having to do with buildings. It would go something like this: "Where you live reflects how you live." I believe that to have been true about the homes of the sponsor of the SAT. The progression of the Board's headquarters in New York City, from a shabbily genteel brownstone on Dean's Row on the Columbia University campus to the modern but modest appurtenances of the Interchurch Center on Riverside Drive adjoining Barnard College to the glass and chrome commercial office building at 888 Seventh Avenue to its permanent landmark home at 45 Columbus Avenue, had to have had something to do with the Board's gradual transformation from an exclusive club to a business enterprise, from a small educational association to a large bureaucracy, and then back to something in between.

When I joined the College Board staff in 1955, the offices were in an old five-story brownstone building on West 117 Street. My first desk was in the hall on the second floor. It reminded me of the location that the famous Deerfield Academy headmaster, Frank Boyden, chose for his—the landing between the first and second floors of the academy's main building, where he could see the boys as they moved from class to class. I, too, used to get to see everybody who ventured above the first floor. But the staff grew, and the College Board took possession of the brownstone next door. I was then duly promoted to the room off the hall I had been occupying. I'm not sure what purpose it had served in the abode's decanal residency days, but brownstones are long, narrow buildings just one room wide. The anteroom to my office had the look of a pantry about it and housed the College Board's ancient safe. It also served as the anteroom to the bathroom. It looked like an ancient bathroom and was used as such, which meant that there was almost as much pedestrian traffic in my "private office" as there had been in the hall.

The office itself was shelf-lined and full of books. One set was the *Oxford English Dictionary,* which I must say provided unparalleled temptation for just plain browsing. One book that I especially remember had a title something on the order of *An Illustrated Guide to the Habits of the Orders.* Referring to dress rather than behavior, it described and displayed the "uniforms" worn by nuns. The book proved useful and made me seem more knowledgeable than I really was about the sisters' religious orders. The College Board was and is blessed with membership on the part of a number of Roman Catholic women's colleges and with representatives from them from a variety of religious orders. The most memorable for me was Mother Eleanor O'Byrne, president of Manhattanville College. An active participant in any meeting she attended, Mother O'Byrne always sat in the front row, knitting away steadily like Madame LaFarge, but ever alert. She had the uncanny faculty of being able to put the right question or make the right comment necessary to rescue an audience from confusion, boredom, or mayhem.

Mother O'Byrne's order wore a very confining habit, with a headpiece that must have acted like blinders for a horse and served, I am sure, to focus the nuns' attention. Some years later the trustees of the

College Board held a meeting in conjunction with our office in Puerto Rico. (Mother O'Byrne had been a trustee herself at one time but had long since retired.) At one of the open sessions I observed a familiar face in the front row but couldn't place it. The owner was a nun dressed not in black but in white with an off-the-face headpiece. When the session was over, she came up and greeted me with the unforgettable voice of Mother O'Byrne. She'd been called out of retirement to act as president of one of her order's colleges in Puerto Rico and was wearing its concession to the local climate. The color of her habit and the shape of her headpiece may have changed, but she'd lost neither the sparkle in her eye nor the sharpness of her mind.

Mother O'Byrne wasn't the only "religious" to reveal herself or himself in a new light in Puerto Rico. At an earlier trustees' meeting there, Monsignor Geohegan, then the diocesan superintendent of schools in Providence, Rhode Island, went down to the beach to recover from a traumatic experience that had befallen him just after he had checked into the hotel. He was unpacking when his roommate was ushered in, the attractive woman then serving as associate secretary of the College Board. They agreed that under other circumstances it might have been a congenial arrangement but decided in the light of existing ones to part. Monsignor finished unpacking, put on his bathing suit, and went down to the beach to recover.

Sitting on the beach and enjoying the sun, I was surprised to see one of my college roommates coming down for a swim. But as he came closer, it dawned on me that it was Monsignor Geohegan. He'd always looked vaguely familiar to me but I never could make the connection until that day on the beach in San Juan. Without his priest's habit and without his glasses, he was the spitting image of roommate Al Hunt. Clothes do make the man, or the woman.

Another trustee of the cloth also made his mark on my memory in Puerto Rico. He was Brother Gregory, then president of Manhattan College. We'd just sat down for dinner in one of the more distinguished hotels in San Juan and had been given our menus when Brother Gregory burst out with the closest he could come to a blasphemy and added, "But I want fish!" That was back in the days when American Roman Catholics observed Friday as a fast day and weren't supposed to eat meat. It was a Friday and Brother's comment didn't make sense to me until he explained. Centuries ago, after the Spaniards had finally beaten off the Moors, the Pope freed Hispanics from the requirement of fasting on Fridays. Apparently this concession was interpreted to mean that anyone in a Spanish-speaking country could eat meat on Friday and Brother Gregory had been looking forward to doing so. But the temptation of the local fish dishes was just too much.

As for clothes making the man, the nature of the man doesn't hurt. The man I most enjoyed going into restaurants with was Father Bill Ryan, president of Seton Hill College in Greensburg, Pennsylvania. Father Ryan was an imposing gentleman, well over six feet tall, with a military carriage and an air about him that demanded attention. Maîtres d's would fall all over themselves seeing that we got a good table and received attentive service. He was unique in other ways, too. He had a Ph.D. in philosophy, earned, as I understood it, in Italy. He was a gourmet cook of the first order; I can personally attest to that. And he had been a parish priest when he was called by the sisters there to become president of Seton Hill. I'm sure there must have been others, but a male president of a Roman Catholic women's college was pretty unusual in those days. Whatever the reasons, restaurateurs recognized him as the man of distinction that he indeed was.

As for clothes making the woman, Father Ryan had an admissions officer at Seton Hill who was a demon of a Ping-Pong player. Her order's habit in those days was of the long, flowing variety, and one of the extracurricular sights around the edges of College Board meetings was sister swooping around the Ping-Pong table demolishing everyone in sight.

But the swooping didn't last, and my *Illustrated Guide to the Habits of the Orders* lost its utility when the era of relaxation in the religious orders' dress code set in. Many greeted the new freedom gladly, but there were those who longed for the good old days. In those days, when you could tell a nun was a nun by what she was wearing, it not infrequently happened that when a group of nuns went into a restaurant, some good Roman Catholic patron would pick up their bill. That fringe benefit is much less available as the sisters have come to look more like businesswomen.

The chain of reminiscences set off by that guidebook on my office shelf hints at both the atmosphere that prevailed and the changes that were taking place at the College Board when I arrived. It was still an intimate and comfortable place to work, but the traditional members of the association were being joined by new constituencies that were, as in the example of the Roman Catholic colleges, providing the appealing brand of leadership represented by Mother O'Byrne, Monsignor Geohegan, Brother Gregory, and Father Ryan. Times were indeed changing.

That single brownstone was the first of four locations for the College

Board's headquarters during my life with the SAT. In 1955 four of us joined the professional staff and nearly doubled the complement in the process. But even then we could hold staff meetings around a regular luncheon table at the Columbia Men's Faculty Club across West 117 Street. Even before the Men's Faculty Club and the Women's Faculty Club were merged in the 1960s, however, the numbers taking the SAT and the Achievement Tests and participating in the College Scholarship Service had continued to burgeon. We poked holes in one of the brownstone's walls and occupied the building next door. But Columbia was growing, too, and when we needed more space a couple of years later, the university couldn't supply it. In fact, it wanted to get its hands on what we had. It was at that point that possibilities outside the Borough of Manhattan first began to be explored. Frank Bowles and I, as the association's chief financial officer, spent hours looking at possible sites in Westchester (New York), Bergen (northern New Jersey), and Mercer (mid-New Jersey) counties, which are today occupied by innumerable corporate headquarters. We were especially attracted to a large house near the Tappan Zee Bridge, a few miles up the Hudson River; the thought was that the headquarters could be there, supported by a small satellite office for meetings in New York City. But the trustees thought otherwise and decided that the College Board's headquarters should remain in Manhattan, near a college or a university if possible.

A solution presented itself in the form of the Interchurch Center then being built on Riverside Drive adjacent to the Barnard College campus. The owner of the building, the National Council of Churches, needed other nonprofit organizations to fill up its new building, and the College Board took advantage of the situation by renting part of the second floor. But the bureaucracy kept growing to keep pace with the increasing demands for its services, and we were soon forced to rent additional space in an apartment house that Columbia had recently acquired about five blocks away. The only advantage to that schizophrenic existence was the exercise that accrued from walking between the two locations. The 10 years in the Interchurch Center, however, provided a transition from an educational to a commercial setting. The staff was housed in an office building, not a campus one, and gradually came to think of itself as made up as much of office workers as of educators.

By 1969, however, we were on the move again, this time to an airtight skyscraper in midtown Manhattan. Getting there was something of a fluke. Again, the possibility of moving out of the city was explored, but again, the trustees, an entirely new lineup of them by that time, decided that the headquarters should remain in New York City, near a college or a university if possible. One of the possibilities we seriously considered (in my opinion it was the ideal solution even though it wasn't near an educational institution) was the Andrew Carnegie mansion and Blair House compound across from Central Park on Fifth Avenue at East Ninety-first Street. It was then owned by Columbia University and used to house its School of Social Work. Because the school was removed from the main campus, the university wanted to relocate it closer to home. John Mullins, later to become the College Board's vice president and treasurer, and I invested considerable time and effort in working up a comprehensive financial offer for the two buildings. Our offer was refused, and Columbia "donated" the property to the Smithsonian Institution for their National Museum of Design, using our offering price as the valuation. We were disappointed but took some consolation from the fact that our having been "used" helped to enrich the supply of national treasures.

With that possibility foreclosed and nothing available on Morningside Heights, we set our sights on a new building going up on Columbus Circle some 60 blocks to the south, near Fordham University's Manhattan campus. The problem was that the landlord was insistent that we take a 20-year lease and absorb the risk of subletting the expansion space we thought we needed. As a bargaining chip, the College Board's real estate advisers began negotiations with the owners of a building nearing completion at 888 Seventh Avenue, "at the corner of Seventh and Fifty-seventh," as we used to tell people. Those directions, incidentally, were misleading; 888 Seventh Avenue is L-shaped, and the arms of the L surround an older building that is actually on the southwest corner of the intersection. Not only that, the entrances to the building proper are on Fifty-sixth Street and Fifty-seventh Street. The only Seventh Avenue entrance to our erstwhile glass ivory tower, as I used to call it, is the door to an offtrack betting parlor. As the reader will now have realized, the Columbus Circle landlord stuck to his guns and the College Board's headquarters ended up in an impersonal New York City office building blocks from any college or university campus. We did get a more favorable long-term arrangement whereby we could lease back to the owner for a short term the expansion space we didn't need immediately, but we paid what were at the time premium rental rates for four floors of very desirable space of its kind—which never seemed to me to be quite the College Board's kind. But while the rates were high to begin with, and escalation clauses were built into the agreement, 15 years later we were paying what was by then a very reasonable rental.

It was when we began to ponder the much higher costs we would have to pay when those 15 years were up that we began seriously to think about the College Board's owning its own building.

In reality, 888 wasn't all that bad. It was much closer to the city's hotel and entertainment districts than Morningside Heights was. The fact of the former saved substantially on taxi fares from the hotels to the office, and the availability of the latter added to the appeal of serving on a College Board committee. Those of us who had offices that faced north had a spectacular view of Central Park, one that always mightily impressed visitors. Parking for those of us who commuted by car was available in the basement, as it had been at the Interchurch Center. (It is not available in the College Board's new home at 45 Columbus Avenue. All new office buildings in midtown Manhattan have to provide underground or other parking space; the new headquarters building, however, isn't new.) Except for the fact that a few windows blew out soon after we took occupancy, the building at 888 was clean, well maintained, and well managed. But if we'd really wanted to renew our lease, the rent would have gone through the ceiling.

In addition to those pros and cons, the 45-story building at 888 Seventh Avenue was obviously a commercial one in which the College Board was only a minor tenant. It looked like a business building and it felt like one. You ran into all kinds of strange types in the elevators, and even though the College Board's offices consisted of a three- and later four-story compound accessible only through the lobby on the twenty-second floor, we had to have locks on the ladies' rest room doors. Handbags were known to disappear, and at least once a year some weird character would be discovered wandering not so aimlessly through our quarters.

We moved to 888 soon after Arland Christ-Janer became president in 1970. Among other things, he brought with him a vocabulary new to the College Board. "Sales" and "marketing" came into common usage, given credibility, in a way, by the setting in which our offices were then housed. As I suggested earlier, the College Board's attention in those years was focused on the admissions and financial aid processes and in responding to the competition for services related to them. In such circumstances, marketing and sales became not only acceptable but necessary, and the 888 setting proved hospitable to such efforts. I'm not suggesting that the College Board became business-oriented because it moved to a commercial office building, but the move did help in the "becoming."

In any event, despite the "pros" and because the potential costs of staying put seemed so high, we began the third search for an alternative headquarters site. Again, the possibility of moving out of New York City was explored. The big air transportation hubs dominated the early thinking. The College Board does operate in a world of committees and has to have its central office conveniently located for people coming in from all over the country. For a variety of reasons Atlanta, Chicago, Dallas, Denver, Houston, and St Louis fell by the wayside, leaving New York City and Washington, D.C., as the finalists. There was considerably more opportunity for staff input this time around, and it was interesting to observe the sharp differences of opinion that developed over the choice to be made. There is a commonly held belief that the chief executive has the decisive say in such cases. That hadn't been true in the late 1950s when the trustees decided the College Board should stay in New York City, but I have to believe it was true in the early 1980s when I recommended to the trustees that we look for property to buy in Manhattan. Just as Frank Bowles and Dick Pearson were reluctant at an earlier time to accept the ETS invitation to locate on its campus in Princeton for fear the staff would become preoccupied with technical, psychometric issues, so I was later reluctant to have the staff become infected with "Potomac fever" and preoccupied with political rather than educational matters in the Washington area. The trustees agreed with me. (It's not that the College Board does not have a presence in the nation's capital. Then, as now, it had two: a Washington office, which has now become a center of respected expertise and analysis on public policy issues in education, with responsibility for coordinating the Board's government liaison activities in both Washington and the state capitals; the other is an International Education office, from which the Board's overseas activities are conducted.)

Finding suitable property in New York City wasn't easy. We looked at schools, apartment houses, lofts, and a warehouse. The warehouse proved to be the most promising. Called the Sofia Building after the name of the moving company that was using it as a furniture storage facility, it had been built in the early 1930s for long-term automobile storage. My theory is that when the Great Depression took its toll of those who wanted to store their Rolls Royces while they traveled in Europe, the tall, narrow building was converted to the moving company warehouse that it remained until 1983. At that point some innovative speculators, recognizing the appeal of the Sofia Building's art deco style, decided to take a chance on converting it to a condominium with offices on the lower floors and luxury apartments on the upper ones. This effort involved getting permission from the New York City Landmarks Preservation Commission to alter the structure slightly, primarily by putting in windows; as a storage garage and a warehouse, it had needed very few. What was important to the developers and, I must admit, to the College Board, was that the building is distinctive, as its landmark status properly suggests.

If locating an appropriate property in which to invest was difficult, the complexities were nothing compared with the problems involved in financing the purchase. In the end, however, it was accomplished primarily through the medium of low-interest bonds issued through the New York State Dormitory Authority and approved by the state legislature in Albany. (That arrangement isn't quite as unusual as it sounds. The Dormitory Authority's original scope had much earlier been expanded to include assistance to nonprofit enterprises generally, and the College Board as a New York State not-for-profit corporation qualified for help.)

Finding the property, negotiating the lease, arranging the financing, and overseeing the conversion of our particular space in the condominium were matters I wisely left to trusted right hands: Merritt Ludwig, senior vice president for administration; Anthony Kearney, vice president and treasurer; and Norman Parsons, vice president for administrative services. Having acted aloof and presidential during the whole process, I finally became directly involved in building-related matters after we had moved in. The problem that needed a decision at the highest level was what to put in the niche at the end of the lobby near the elevators. (The College Board entrance is on Columbus Avenue. The entrance to the apartments on the upper floors is on West Sixty-first Street.) The choice provided a challenge in that the setting called for something vertical and, of course, art deco. As I was to discover, most art deco objects are horizontal. About the only pieces tall and narrow in that style are replicas of the Empire State Building, and my colleagues had wisely decided that wouldn't do. The aficionados of the late 1920s and early 1930s did, however, go in for what I gather is called neoclassical statuary, and a tentative decision had been made to purchase a wet-draped female statue in that style. That is when I got into the act. The question was, "Would women on the staff be offended by what could be perceived as a male chauvinist choice?" And who better to ask it than the president?

Before making my decision, I went over to the art store district on the other side of Manhattan to take a look at the statue myself. She looked more classical than suggestive to me. It was a handsome piece of sculpture, but the drapery did cling. When I asked the advice of a number of women on the staff, I tried to describe the statue in neutral, nonpejorative terms. Virtually without exception, each said she wouldn't mind having the statue in the lobby but feared that some of her female colleagues would. Armed with that advice, I went back to Third Avenue to look for an alternative. He appeared in the form of a neoclassical fighting man dressed in a loin cloth and striding forward, with one arm stretched out and down behind him holding a sword and the other stretched out and up in front with his hand, like a policeman's, stopping traffic. About the only complaint I heard was to the effect that he seemed uninviting, but then staff members aren't prone to complain to presidents. I liked best the observation that, with his outstretched palm facing the elevators, he was telling people, "Back upstairs with the lot of you. It's not time to go home yet!" But whether one likes the statue or not, the important thing to me is that it is in the College Board's own lobby, in its own house, and subject to its own and not somebody else's whims. And for me, the College Board's having its own "home" again, as it did in those Columbia brownstones and did not in the Interchurch Center or at 888 Seventh Avenue, was a positive and important development in the life of the SAT.

True, 45 Columbus Avenue smacks of being an office building, but the distinctive art style takes the edge off that drawback. Across the street from Fordham University's midtown campus, just down Columbus Avenue from Lincoln Center, on the edge and not in the middle of commercial midtown Manhattan, the location lends itself to a comfortable accommodation of the College Board's educational and commercial interests. It's self-contained, the rest rooms don't have to be locked, and you can open the windows.

Meetings: An Essential Part of Life at the College Board

An added attraction was the availability on the second floor of the Sofia building of space for a reasonably large-sized meeting room, a facility that had been sorely lacking at 888 Seventh Avenue. Meetings are an essential part of life with the SAT. Scarcely a day goes by without a meeting of one or more committees, task forces, panels, councils, or working groups in the home office in New York City. And that's only at the headquarters. The regional offices sponsor meetings galore throughout the year on behalf of the parent organization. My last *Annual Report,* for 1985–86, notes that "regional staff attended 820 conferences, gave 624 presentations, and made 892 visits for a total of 2,336 training events reaching 89,000 people." As suggested by that excerpt, staff members are invited to take part not only in sessions sponsored by other associations but in internal staff meetings as well. Living in this kind of world, staff members get to meet in a great variety of places. I certainly did.

One of the sites I will always remember is the Fontainebleau Hotel on Miami Beach. The ownership has since changed, but it used to be the most presumptuous hotel I have ever encountered. Signs in the hallways, for instance, directed guests to the "North Ocean" in one direction and to the "South Ocean" (not beaches, mind you, but oceans) in the other. The senior officers of the College Board once met in the Boom Boom Room to discuss matters of important moment with their counterparts from ETS. That setting wasn't quite as strange as one might imagine. The American Council on Education (ACE) has, to my recollection, held at least two annual membership meetings at the Fontainebleau. The session in the Boom Boom Room was held on short notice at a time when we were all attending one of those ACE conferences and all the regular meeting rooms had long since been booked. That was the occasion, too, when my wife, Elaine, encountered a large number of college and university presidents cavorting in one of the "oceans" while I was conscientiously attending one of the enlightening "breakout" sessions in the hotel. As she reported it, one of the presidents looked around and, seeing so many of his colleagues in the water, yelled out, "It looks as if we have a quorum. Let's take a vote!"

The Fontainebleau conjures up other memories as well. For example, there was the time several years later when I was attending a session at which the inevitable distinguished panel, this one including soon-to-be Under Secretary of Education Checker Finn, was holding forth. Finn finished his presentation and was settling back comfortably in his chair behind the head table when suddenly one of his shoes appeared from under the skirt that hides head-table sitters' legs and feet from the audience. The loafer slipped quietly down the two feet or so to the floor of the auditorium and sat there unobtrusively.

For sessions of that kind I had developed two approaches. One was to sit quietly in the back of the room so that I could escape in case things got too dull, a not uncommon practice that explains why so few people sit up front at education meetings, or other kinds as well. My other, unorthodox approach, the one I was using on the occasion of the fallen shoe, was to show my regard for the speakers—and not infrequently earn brownie points with them—by sitting in the front row and practicing my "squinting," the technique described in Chapter 4 when academic competencies were under not-so-serious discussion. And so it was that I was able to catch Finn's eye as the errant shoe slipped down and to give him a reassuring nod. While the next speaker was winding up his remarks, I quickly dashed off a note, and as the second panelist was sitting down and the third was approaching the lectern, conveyed the note to Finn, dropping the note by the shoe, picking up both note and shoe in a single swoop, and delivering the shoe under the skirt and the note into Finn's hand. It read, "This is a cover note." Afterward, Finn agreed that he owed me one. I never cashed it in, but it was always reassuring to know that I had "one" to cash in with the Department of Education.

Another pleasant memory of Miami Beach is a conversation with the author James Michener. He was doing research for his book *Sports in America* (New York: Random House, 1976), and I was in the midst of my sabbatical leave. In the book his commentary on that encounter goes as follows: "The second man on whom I relied for guidance came to my attention by accident, and a most fortunate one it was. I had spoken on cultural matters to a gathering of college presidents, and afterward they asked me if there was anything they might do to reciprocate, and I surprised them by saying that I'd like to talk with some of them about athletic programs at their schools. So they convened an informal breakfast . . . [and] . . . brought with them a man I did not know, either in fact or in reputation, and he turned out to be the gem of the morning. He was a tall, well-groomed scholar with a deceptive Irish brogue that could have been a New England heritage, an obvious lover of sports and a genial approach to the follies of the world." All of which was very satisfying for my ego, but my friends were never sure it was really I whom he was talking about. No one had ever described me as well-groomed or a fashion plate.

Other interesting settings for education meetings I attended include Mountain Shadows, a YMCA camp, the Plenium Club, and Airlie House, among others. Mountain Shadows is an upscale resort in Scottsdale, Arizona, just outside Phoenix. The College Board once sponsored a meeting there, which I remember for two reasons. The first was a practical concern. We'd been led to believe that it never rains in Arizona. But it did rain while we were there, in buckets, and Elaine had to buy a raincoat, which has stood her in good stead for a number of years in less hospitable climes. The other reason I remember it is that, because the subject was the sorry plight of minority youngsters in higher education, we received more than one complaint about holding a meeting on that subject in such a plush setting. But Stephen J. Wright, a distinguished black educational statesman who was there, soon relieved my mind on that score. He observed, "Effective thinking about complex issues is never hampered by comfortable surroundings."

That credo is one I came to appreciate more fully when budgetary considerations prompted us to hold an officers' retreat at a YMCA camp. The rooms were spartan, the food wholesome but dull. That was OK. The chairs were the problem. They were of the metal folding variety, and after we had been attached to them for a few hours, I fear our powers of concentration started to wane.

At another end of the spectrum (please note I don't say "*the* other end"), there was the Plenium Club, the new conference facility on Long Island that we helped inaugurate. Unlike the YMCA camp, which was out in the country, the Long Island facility was in the middle of a parking lot at the intersection of two of the heavily traveled parkways that crisscross the Island. At one point I declared my intention of going for a walk, and Steve Wright, who had since become a vice president of the College Board, asked me to buy him a pack of cigarettes. I wandered down to the local downtown to make the purchase. It wasn't a big, impersonal shopping mall but more of a small-town Main Street for one of the neighborhoods in the Borough of Queens. I went into a drugstore and asked for a couple of packs of cigarettes. After I'd paid for them, the druggist, in typical small-town style, said he'd seen me arriving on foot and asked where I was staying in the neighborhood. I named the facility and he said, "Oh, the whorehouse." I could do nothing but confirm his surmise. When we had arrived the day before, we'd immediately been taken on a tour of the place. There was an exercise room in the basement and the dining room looked like a nightclub. But the bedrooms were the giveaway and mine was the prize. It had two mirrors in the ceiling and no closet. It turned out that the place had indeed been built as a bordello where men from the many office complexes in the vicinity could sneak off for "lunch" with the ladies of the house. Apparently, though, the men in that vicinity didn't have that kind of appetite, and so the facility underwent a metamorphosis of sorts and became a "health club," which explained all the equipment in the basement. The attraction was supposed to be that it provided a spot where men could take their secretaries out for lunch and health. But that didn't work either, and the owners were trying to turn the place into a legitimate conference center. As with the YMCA facility, we were trying to save money. (We got a price break to serve as a come-on to potential corporate users.) But again we paid the price, this time of untested (for our purposes) facilities. The YMCA facility and the Plenium Club served to confirm Steve Wright's observations about Mountain Shadows.

Finally by way of example, there was Airlie House. It's near War-renton, Virginia, an hour or so outside Washington, D.C. I remember it not so much because of the setting but because of what had happened there. It is a very gracious and well-appointed conference facility, and because I'd heard such good things said about it but had never been there, I was looking forward to taking full advantge of the opportunity to experience its ambience. My advantage, however, wasn't full. I don't recall the subject of the meeting to which I was invited, but I do recall that it had been called by a high official of what was then the United States Office of Education and that the participants included a number of distinguished and busy educators. We were attended by a couple of very minor functionaries from the OE who didn't themselves appear to be too sure why they, or for that matter we, were there. The meeting was scheduled to last two and a half days; at the end of the first day and a half, when the high official had failed to show up or to show any interest in what he'd gotten us there to discuss, one of the university presidents took the bull by the horns and declared that he thought we may as well go home. We did. A good many more meetings I attended over the years should also have ended that way. For me, the Airlie House lesson was an important one. If there isn't a need for a meeting, don't meet. And if you do meet, make the experience worthwhile for the participants. By and large, my colleagues at the College Board did just that.

Traveling

Getting to meetings involved travel, and I was fortunate enough to be able to travel to all fifty states and halfway around the world in four directions on College Board business. Those trips qualify me, in the manner of all frequent fliers, to top anybody else's horror story about getting from here to there. I will resist the temptation to recite my full repertoire, however, and resort to only one story. It happened on the return leg of my first transcontinental round-trip by jet aircraft. After the plane was loaded, we were delayed for about an hour in the Los Angeles airport while something "mechanical" got fixed. It was a beastly hot summer day and the heat inside the aircraft became almost unbear-able. But finally we were "up, up, and away" on TWA. Except for the noise from some pleasantly stewed folks in the rear seats, the flight was uneventful until the pilot came on about 45 minutes before our scheduled landing in New York. What he had to say went very much like this:

"Ladies and gentlemen, this is your captain speaking. We are currently over Harrisburg, Pennsylvania, and about to begin our descent into the New York area. From here on we're going to be pretty busy on the flight deck and this is the last chance I'll have to speak to you before we land. I do want to apologize for the delay in Los Angeles but we had to install a new Freon pack." (No wonder we had been so hot. Freon is what generates air conditioners' coolness.) "And oh, yes, one other thing. I do want you to know that Mr. Robinson, one of our TWA vice presidents, is flying with us today." (A collective sigh of approval went up from the passengers. Mr. Robinson had had to endure the heat like the rest of us.) "Mr. Robinson is a great guy, folks, and, Mr. Robinson, I want you to know that we're all behind you!"

Whereupon one of the rear-seat rowdies yelled out, "Well, for crissake, get back up front and drive!" I liked that line and told the story frequently in those early days of my life with the SAT. The reason it stuck with me, though, wasn't that it is such a great story; it isn't. But the reference to Harrisburg, Pennsylvania, made a lasting impression on me. Harrisburg is a good four- or five-hour drive from New York City, and we were going to cover that distance in less than three-quarters of an hour and while slowing down to land in the process.

It was then that the implications of the speed of jet travel first really struck home. It did indeed make the world and the nation smaller, another manifestation of the technological revolution of which the SAT was a part. Hand scoring was like the horse and buggy; the optical scoring machine is like a jet. We even briefly considered not establishing regional offices on the grounds that staff could conveniently get to any school and college in the country from one of the New York area's three airports. But that would have inhibited any feeling of proximate ownership on the part of the College Board's membership, a feeling that was so evident in those early meetings held to discuss the capital grants to ETS. As it was, modern air travel made it possible to visit more schools and colleges and to get to meetings faster. And going to meetings often meant giving or hearing speeches, for life with the SAT involved life at, or in front of, the podium.

Speaking

Early on in my career at the College Board, I delivered the opening remarks at a gathering of Advanced Placement chemistry schoolteachers and college professors at my father's undergraduate alma mater, the University of Illinois at Urbana-Champaign. To make the point that I didn't want to appear to be with them under false pretenses and that I was there as a bureaucrat and not as a chemist, I began my presentation by noting that I had not studied chemistry since my freshman year in college. "Nevertheless," I said, "I do know a good story about gunpowder, which I understand is a chemical compound." That turned out to be one of the funniest punch lines I ever delivered. It brought down the house! I had no idea why. Had I misspoken? Was my fly open? Was somebody making gestures, obscene or otherwise, behind my back? In any event, I plunged ahead with the story of the indigent actor and the Provincetown theater manager. Thank goodness, it's a good story and got a hearty response from the chemists. When I sat down, the man sitting next to me passed over a note that read, "Gunpowder is a mixture, not a compound." Later, when all the other presentations had been made, he asked, "Did you know what you were doing?" I gave what I meant to be an enigmatic smile and what I hoped was a knowing nod, and said, "I never give away professional secrets."

One of the other unexpected responses occurred near the end of my time with the College Board. The Board's National Forum was being held in San Francisco. (Annual membership meetings had long since been folded into much more broadly based yearly conferences called National Forums.) Sally K. Ride, the nation's first woman in space, was to be the featured speaker at one of the luncheons. I was presiding. My assignment was to introduce Fred Hargadon, our senior vice president, who had admitted Ride to Stanford when he was dean of admissions there. He in turn was to introduce Astronaut Ride. But as the luncheon was getting under way, Hargadon was at the San Francisco airport waiting for our speaker to arrive from Houston. As I explained to the audience, "We seem to have no trouble getting men on the moon, but we don't seem to be able to get an astronaut off the ground in the Houston fog." As Hargadon was gathering intelligence on her estimated time of arrival, I was attempting to fill in the time at the podium. In the process I was using up all my better jokes and stories between courses to keep the assemblage from getting too restless about Dr. Ride's obvious absence. (In fact, one of the reasons I soon thereafter made my decision to retire was that I'd used up all my good stand-up material at that San Francisco luncheon.) As the dessert plates were beginning to be removed, it was clear from the lateness of the hour that we'd have to do without Sally Ride at lunch. As I rose to address the audience yet again, I was intending to say, "I have no intelligence as to when our speaker will arrive, and so we are postponing her appearance until later this afternoon." For once the fates were really with me. As soon as I had gotten the first four words out of my mouth, the audience broke into peals of laughter. Of course, what I'd said, and had the good sense to stop when I'd said it, was simply, "I have no intelligence!" As I had done at the University of Illinois so many years before, I smiled knowingly and adjourned the luncheon meeting.

Dr. Ride did finally arrive and she did make her presentation late that afternoon. Her theme was the need to attract more women into the fields of science. Her arguments were persuasive, her own example compelling. But what impressed me most was that unlike so many other activists, she didn't bemoan the fact that society was discriminating against somebody. Instead, she was making the point that women have the capacity to succeed in the sciences and ought to go about doing so.

Normally, meal-connected speeches follow the food, as Ride's was intended to do. After observing this phenomenon for quite a few years, Elaine developed the theory that speeches would be more effective if they preceded the food. Only once, however, did the two of us together witness her theory in practice. Ernest Boyer, president of the Carnegie Foundation for the Advancement of Teaching, had John Gardner, founder of Common Cause and educational statesman par excellence, speak on leadership—before dinner. The content and the timing were just right. I disagreed with Boyer on a number of issues over the years, but I take my hat off to him for accomplishing with his enterprise what I was never able to with the College Board. But then the president of the Carnegie Foundation for the Advancement of Teaching, unlike the president of the College Board, isn't answerable to a constituency. Try as I might, I was never able to convince the committees in charge of our meetings that before-meal speeches are better than after-meal ones.

The Association of Alumnae Secretaries of Independent Schools for Girls was more enlightened and once invited me to make a before-luncheon speech at its annual meeting. At the time, I was a trustee of the Dwight School in nearby Englewood, New Jersey, and it was through that connection and because of my association with the College Board that I was asked by the head of the school, on behalf of the association, to be the wrap-up speaker just before the final luncheon. I took my assignment seriously and attended all the sessions for two days, continually adapting my remarks to the issues that were on the alumnae secretaries' minds. All the sessions were held at Dwight, which was acting as host for the event—all, that is, except the final session, which was held at the local country club. The association's officers, who had apparently become embarrassed over the years by the tendency of some alumnae secretaries to drift away during the final after-luncheon speech, decided that I should speak to them over sherry at their luncheon tables before the meal was served. However, they forgot to advise the country club to close the bar. Most of the women, seeking relief after two days of intensive discussion, got a belt or two under their belts before they came into the dining room for sherry. Never before were my remarks received with such enthusiasm, nor have they been since. The alumnae secretaries laughed not only at my jokes but at just about everything else I had to say. I sat down to thunderous applause and proceeded to enjoy my lunch.

That opportunity to have an after-speech meal nailed down for me the validity of Elaine's theory. I'd earlier learned that if I ate a full meal before giving a speech, I neither spoke nor digested well, but until the alumnae secretaries' luncheon, I'd never known whether I could enjoy an after-speech meal. I did! In retrospect, I realize that my failure to convince the College Board committees of the wisdom of before-meal speeches was just another example of the conservatism of the educational establishment when it comes to the conduct of its own business. Properly perceived by the public as politically liberal, educators on the whole are arch conservatives when it comes to education. I have made the point, for instance, that although the nation's schools and colleges take pride in their efforts to achieve racial integration, they undertook those efforts not on their own initiatives but in response to mandates from the courts. But the alumnae secretaries, coming primarily from what had to be upper-class, politically conservative backgrounds, didn't feel themselves bound by traditional educational protocols and therefore put my luncheon speech where it belonged.

All the other luncheon, and dinner, talks I gave were after-meal affairs, and I tended to confuse head-table waiters and waitresses by refusing food or taking my portion and then only toying with it. It sometimes bothered other head-table associates, too. A businessman sitting next to me at a midday meal at Texas A&M University saw me pushing my food around but not eating anything and asked, "What's the matter? Are you nervous or something?" I said yes, and then gave him the line about neither digesting nor speaking well if I spoke after eating. He looked dubious until the retired bank president and onetime college president on my other side leaned across me and declared, "If a man's not his own doctor by the time he's 40, he's in deep trouble!" After that remark, I never worried about my idiosyncrasy. Others have it, too, I find. But observing many mealtime speakers firsthand over the years, I discovered that most of them managed to put away a healthy repast before going to the podium.

That Texas A&M luncheon was memorable for another reason. I wanted to make the point that people often shoot from the hip in criticizing something without taking the time to find out what they are talking about, the point made in Chapter 7 in my discussion of talk show hosts. At Texas A&M I was talking about critics of the SAT. I used the experience of one of our sons-in-law as an analogy. Our older daughter and her family had gone to visit her sister and her family in Fort Collins, Colorado. Number One's husband is a doctor, and he was interested in visiting the School of Veterinary Medicine at Colorado State University to compare notes in his field, hematology. At CSU he happened to meet one of the nation's leading experts on hibernation, a man who had earlier been the target of one of former Senator William Proxmire's Golden Fleece awards for his "study of the hibernation habits of Kodiak bears." What the senator had failed to take into account was the connection, then just beginning to be scientifically established, between veterinary science and human medicine. In this case, as our son-in-law put it, "How is it that bears don't have to go to the bathroom for months on end? Specialists in kidney diseases in humans have a lot to learn from the hibernation habits of those Kodiak bears!"

When I told that story in Texas, it evoked a vociferous and sympathetic reaction. I learned that Senator Proxmire had once given his award to the agency that sponsored a Texas study of "the sex life of the screwworm fly." On the surface, it sounds as ridiculous as the exploration of the hibernation habits of Kodiak bears, but it, too, has equally serious implications. I learned two things on the spot there in College Station, Texas. First, the screwworm fly gets into the ears of cattle, screws itself into the tender skin, and creates an open sore in which fatal infections can find a hospitable home. Second, the most effective way to control insect growth is to make the males infertile. The study of the sex life of the screwworm fly was a serious attempt to find a solution to a serious problem—how to sterilize the male screwworm flies in order to prevent the spread of serious and sometimes fatal diseases among cattle. Those experiences kept coming back to me again and again over the years when I was faced with uninformed criticism of the good old SAT.

One of my other attempts to use humor in a presentation to make a serious point produced not just one fallout but several fallouts. On the way to a meeting in San Diego, the strap on Elaine's leather purse broke, and we visited a fix-it-while-you-wait shoe store to get it repaired. To pass the waiting time, we read the signs that plastered the walls from floor to ceiling. As one of them observed about its companions, "Many

of these signs are fit to print but not fit to be shared in polite company."
Among those that could be shared were three that said something about
the nature of the establishment itself:

- People who believe the dead don't come back to life should be
  here at quitting time.
- Notice to all employees: New incentive plan. Work or get fired!
- The management of this establishment is not responsible.

I used those three to set the stage for presenting to the San Diego meeting
what I came to call my "shoe store wisdom," or "the cobbler's pre-
cepts"—three sayings that seemed to me to be particularly appropriate
to the tasks in which my colleagues and I were engaged in the bureaucracy:

- Why is there never enough time to do it right but always enough
  time to do it over?
- Stupid questions make better sense than stupid answers.
- When all else fails, follow directions.

After recording these at the shoe emporium, I came across another saying
in a store window, one that made me feel better about the condition of
things on the top of my desk:

- A creative mess is better than tidy idleness.

That reminded me of an old standby:

- A turtle gets ahead only by sticking its neck out.

Having delivered myself of these gems at the meeting, I found it wasn't
long before one of my fellow meeting-goers reported that she'd seen the
following as the title for a sermon in one of those glass-encased bulletin
boards outside a church on Madison Avenue in uptown Manhattan:

- Life is like tennis. You can't win without serving.

A few weeks later I mentioned this evolutionary progression at an informal luncheon that followed a meeting of the Executive Committee of
the Education Commission of the States at which I had spoken. Then
Governor Charles Robb, later to become Senator Robb, of Virginia, was

the host. He politely heard me out and then observed, "George, you're wrong. In my business you have to win to serve!"

Whatever the truth about winning and serving, the shoe store wisdom stood me in almost as good stead as "Rollo-isms," which I learned about from Henry Winkler, then president of the University of Cincinnati and chairman of the College Board. Dr. Rollo was a hospital administrator who was leaving the university to administer a hospital in Rhode Island. His colleagues took the occasion to reminisce about his ability to turn a neat if unconventional phrase. Among the Rollo-isms published for that occasion are the following favorites of mine, which I used frequently (including the occasion of Sally Ride's delayed arrival in San Francisco):

- Ignorance of the law is bliss.
- I've got to get my momentum moving.
- Pussyfooting around the bush.
- The cast has been dyed.
- Up a tree without a paddle.
- Even an old horse can learn to drink.
- Don't fall over your laurels.

The last was particularly appropriate to a number of occasions. We'd taken great pride, for instance, in arranging for Sally Ride to speak at that San Francisco luncheon and proceeded to fall over our laurels in being unable to deliver her on time. As I said at the time, "It's like being up a tree without a paddle."

One takes a kind of pride from association with public figures like Sally Ride and Chuck Robb. (Please note the familiarity implied by my use of their first names.) When I became president of the College Board in 1979, I'd never met a sitting governor face-to-face. By the time I retired seven years later, I'd met a slew of them, mostly those young Southern governors who had recognized the economic stakes of their states in the education of their future labor forces—men like Robb of Virginia, Alexander of Tennessee, Clinton of Arkansas, Graham of Florida, Riley of South Carolina, and White of Texas, as well as DuPont of Delaware and Ashcroft of Missouri, both of whose states straddle the Mason-Dixon line. I was particularly proud of my home-state governor, Thomas Kean. His commitment to education has been unparalled and was responsible for great improvements in education on behalf of New Jersey's young people during his two terms in office.

A different governor was responsible for another dose of prideful name-dropping, Michael Dukakis of Massachusetts. Through our EQuality project I'd become involved with the business community and its efforts to improve academic standards in the schools. One such project was the Boston Compact. The sponsors took advantage of the presence of the Prince of Wales, who was in the area for the celebration of Harvard's three hundred and fiftieth anniversary in 1986, to convene a special meeting of interested parties. Knowing of Prince Charles's interest in youth unemployment, they invited him to participate. He accepted and made helpful contributions to the deliberations. After the session, Governor Dukakis invited the participants to join the prince at a stand-up buffet luncheon in the Massachusetts State House. As a result, I was able to tell people that I'd had lunch with the Prince of Wales. What was of particular interest to me on that occasion, and later to friends whom I told about the affair, was his ability to meet and greet people while juggling his plate, knife, fork, and beverage. Always gracious and never seeming to turn anyone aside, he was able to keep circulating and meeting new people. When Elaine heard my observation on this score, she remarked, "Of course he did. That was one of the many things he was brought up to do—properly!"

The prince's participation took the form of a panel discussion rather than a formal presentation. Panel discussions are standard fare at education meetings. I took part in a good many myself. Unlike the prince's, most of them are tedious affairs; each panelist tries to get his or her preconceived point across without reference to what has previously been said. I learned that the first year I was at the College Board. It was an evening affair in Westchester County, outside New York City. There were, as I recall, seven of us ranged along a table set up on the local high school auditorium stage, six panelists and a moderator. After about an hour or so of heavy going, I looked down along the table from my position at right end and caught the eye of the man playing left end just as he was raising his eyebrows in a gesture of boredom and frustration. We'd hardly met, but some kind of mental telepathy was operating. We immediately picked a verbal fight with each other and managed to liven up the last half of what was otherwise a pretty dull evening.

We made a point of getting to know each other afterward. He was John Hafer, then director of admissions at Syracuse University in New York State and later president of Curry College in Milton, Massachusetts. He was one of the very few admissions officers I know who went on to become college presidents. The University of Pittsburgh produced two: Bernie Adams, who moved up the administrative ladder to lead Ripon College in Ripon, Wisconsin, and Jack Critchfield, who became president of Rollins College in Winter Park, Florida, before going into private business as a chief executive. Neale Berte, who served in our Western Regional Office for a time, became president of New College at the University of Alabama and later of Birmingham-Southern College. By and large, but with many notable exceptions, college and university presidents come out of the ranks of teaching faculty and not up through the administrative hierarchies. A number of college admissions officers, however, particularly from the prestigious private colleges, have gone on to serve as independent secondary school headmasters. They, too, have to serve on panels.

Perhaps the most frustrating panel I encountered was part of an annual convention of school administrators in Long Beach, California. It was early in my career at the College Board, and not yet knowing any better, I put a good bit of time and effort into preparing my presentation—"not," according to the instructions I had received, "to exceed 10 minutes." Because short presentations always take longer than long ones to prepare, it was a time-consuming task. Then I traveled across the United States to take part in this monster education rally. The time for my appearance was drawing near and I proceeded to the assigned room. There I found the head table set for nine: five panelists, two reactors, a ringmaster, and a recorder. When the time for starting the session arrived, there were eight people in the audience and no one came late. So much for panels. I tried to avoid them whenever I could.

There were times, however, when I had to play the game. One of them was at a meeting of the New England membership in New Haven, Connecticut. At dinner the head table had 11 people—some of them, like me, there to perform and others to receive recognition. Head-table sitters, of course, have to be introduced, often a tedious process. To do the honors that evening, Janette Hersey, the director of admissions at Connecticut College and regional chairperson, approached the lectern and said, "It is now my pleasure to present the people at the head table. On my left, your right . . ." Whereupon the five individuals to her left rose as one, took a bow, and sat down to loud applause. Thank goodness it lasted a while. It gave the five of us playing on the other side of the line time to get our act together; when Hersey was finally able to say, "And on my right," we sat there coolly and simply waved our hands in acknowledgment. Life in the bureaucracy has its rewarding moments.

Head-table sitting was another questionable benefit of being a senior officer at the College Board. When I was senior and executive vice president, I always got to play end, a position I sometimes identified with football's "lonesome end" made famous by the United States Military Academy in midcentury. Protocol assures that an end at a head table has to spend half the meal talking to thin air on his or her exposed side. I came to envy those folks in the middle of the line and looked forward to the day when I might get into the conversational thick of things. Except that when I became president and moved to middle guard, I realized too late that I was sitting next to the podium, behind which, when conversation was in order, there was also thin air. So much for the privileges of leadership!

Indeed, I often commented only half facetiously that I had thought when I became president, I would be my own boss, only to find that I was constantly being told what to do, where to go, whom to see, what to say, and when to say it. In a way it was like living the "Yes, Minister" life as portrayed in the public television series—similar in the sense that even a bureaucracy as small as the College Board's has a built-in momentum, if that's not redundant, that makes it very difficult to effect important change. I came to rely on the "tugboat" theory of management. In its application, the bureaucracy equates to a huge ocean liner: it's very difficult to get it to change course quickly on its own without stripping the gears. What is needed is a tugboat or two. My two biggest tugboats were the EQuality project and the Commission on Precollege Guidance and Counseling.

In other regards, my administrative style could only have been described as loose. My belief was that the bureaucracy I inherited was manned and womanned by competent persons who knew what they were doing and needed a minimum of administrative interference. I did make a few assignment changes when I took over to let people know I was in charge, and I attempted to fill the top managerial positions that opened up with the best talent I could find. Then I devoted my time to policy issues and tugboat management. It worked and what success I enjoyed during my seven years as president was due in large measure to the men and women who served on the staff. And I like to think that there was considerable success. When we took over, the College Board was facing a substantial deficit, experiencing the difficult fallout from the overhasty passage of so-called truth-in-testing legislation in New York State, and treading water in response to the challenge of the Advisory Panel on the Scholastic Aptitude Test Score Decline. Together we managed to turn the financial circumstances around with six years of better than break-even operations, to adapt to the legislative challenges, and to put the Educational EQuality Project and the Commission on Precollege Guidance and Counseling in place.

The support provided in these efforts by the members of the staff and by the people who served the College Board as trustees and as members of the myriad committees, councils, panels, task forces, and working groups gave the lie to what I always claimed to be my administrative credo: "Always behave like a duck. Calm and unruffled on the surface but paddle like hell underneath." The Board staff and constituency made my work in the bureaucracy, and therefore my life with the SAT, enjoyable, rewarding, and generally unruffled both above and below water.

Afterword

Most of my professional staff colleagues "consult" for the College Board
after they retire. I didn't. My predecessors, Dick Pearson, Arland Christ-
Janer, Sid Marland, and Bob Kingston, left me alone to do my thing as
president. I figured my successor, Don Stewart, deserved no less. But
even so, my life with the SAT didn't end in January 1987. I kept busy
in a number of public service assignments for my home state of New
Jersey and in a variety of other activities. Three among the latter kept
my association with the SAT alive: serving as a member of the National
Commission on Testing and Public Policy, maintaining my membership
in the International Association for Educational Assessment, and keeping
up with the critical thinking movement on the National Council for
Excellence in Critical Thinking Instruction.

Service on the National Commission on Testing and Public Policy
permitted me to see the SAT in a broader perspective both psychometrically and socially. Testing at the College Board is concerned with
education. The commission was concerned with testing for both education and employment. Consideration of the problems related to assessment for and in the workplace served to put testing in schools and
colleges in a somewhat different perspective for me. I was particularly
intrigued, for instance, by the criterion issue. In education, grades constitute the criterion by which academic success is measured. Thus, the
usefulness of SAT scores is validated by comparing them with the grades
given by a team of college professors. In employment, on the other hand,
the criterion for success on the job is not as precisely defined, differs

with the specific demands of the job itself, more often than not requires a variety of abilities and skills that are frequently not in the least academic, and is often in the form of a rating by a single supervisor. Despite these differences, there is what I consider to be an employment counterpart to the SAT, a broadly based set of ability tests called the General Abilities Test Battery (GATB). It is the test over which the difference of opinion about affirmative action between the Justice Department and the Labor Department developed. Its task of predicting quality of job performance is, it seems to me, inherently much more difficult than the SAT's of predicting academic success in college.

My experience with the commission also confirmed for me the wisdom of the College Board's insistence that its tests should not be used alone in making high-stakes decisions about individuals. I was surprised to learn about the many educational and employment tests that are being used alone in this way. Just as admitting students to college without taking more than their test scores into account is wrong, so classifying youngsters in the schools on the basis of test scores alone is wrong. And equally wrong, I am now convinced, is using test scores alone to do the highly complex task of predicting performance on the job.

The commission's deliberations also served to corroborate, as far as its particular domain was concerned, the general observation that ours is a litigious society, with suits and countersuits dotting the testing landscape. The commission heard a lot about them. Fortunately, the world of the SAT has been relatively free of litigation, although it has been the direct target of litigation's partner, legislation. By contrast, testing for employment has been the subject of many actions in the courts. What has been reassuring to me is the tendency of the courts to act as cautious watchdogs, particularly in relation to testing in the schools. Enlightened judges, in my opinion, are those who see educational testing as the province of educators and believe that the courts should interfere only when there is gross violation of society's wishes as written into law. I hope that enlightened legislators will take the same approach.

And finally, the discussions that attended the commission's work reaffirmed the preeminence of the SAT as an assessment tool. It's not just the psychometric qualities of the test but also the College Board's prescription for its proper use that serve as benchmarks in the assessment of tests. It provides the standard against which other tests are judged. Witness to its standing is given not only by psychometricians but also by its detractors, who singled it out as the object of so-called truth-in-testing legislation on the grounds that if you can emasculate the leader, you can more easily pick off the followers.

At the same time the SAT, as the leader, has had to carry a lot of the negative baggage created by other kinds of tests—by tests that are unreliable and invalid and by tests not purged of biased items—and by the misuse of multiple-choice, objective test scores to admit children to kindergarten, of test scores alone to determine who is ready for upper-division study in college or who is competent to teach, of standardized test scores to show that all schools are above average, of tests to discriminate, and of tests for purposes for which they are not intended. The litany could go on. The commission, with my full agreement, determined that there is too much testing and too much misuse of tests. Its remedy, though, did not call for throwing out the SAT baby with the bathwater that is, to mix some metaphors, muddied by the fallout from the negative baggage. Rather, it recognized the limited utility of tests and called for their proper use, a use most clearly evident in the SAT.

But if service on the commission heightened my appreciation of the SAT as a testing instrument, my participation in the International Association for Educational Assessment and in the critical thinking movement only strengthened my belief in the centrality of what it measures.

Preparing papers for delivery in both settings had the salutary effect of focusing my thinking in this regard. Annotated excerpts from two of those papers follow.

In both I reviewed the evolution, described in Chapter 4, of the reasoning competency from its beginnings as John Monro's "drawing conclusions from data" to its recognition as a focal point of academic learning in the "grandchildren of the Green Book," its recognition as "a Basic Academic Competency in its own right as well as one that is essential to learning the Basic Academic Subjects . . . as central, not only as an integrating competency cutting across the first four—reading, writing, speaking and listening, and doing mathematics—but also as a separate, definable competency, like the others, necessary for adequate access to the content of the six basic academic subjects." In such circumstances, "it becomes clear that reasoning, or critical thinking, is and always has been at the heart of academic learning.

"While the facts of history to be taught may vary from time to time and from place to place, the ability to interpret their meaning remains the same. While the elements of science to be taught may vary from time to time, the ability to reason about them remains the same. While the books to be studied as literature may vary from place to place and from time to time, the ability to think critically about them remains the same.

And, while the mix of subjects that constitute the college preparatory curriculum may vary, the ability to reason about them is transferable among the many configurations. . . .

"The ability to reason with words and numbers is, I repeat, at the heart of learning and just happens to be what the Scholastic Aptitude Test is intended to assess, and while the SAT does not purport to measure all the facets of reasoning or critical thinking, it remains one of the best surrogates we have. . . .

"As far as college entrance examinations are concerned in all this, I would note that the College Board offers Achievement Tests to help determine what students have learned in the academic subject areas and the SAT to assess their abilities to reason with words and numbers. The great strength of the latter is its freedom from curricular restraints of any kind, whether the student today learns his or her United States history in Minnesota, Massachusetts, or California. And it provides the same measure of these abilities now, after World War II, the atomic bomb, and men on the moon, as it did when I was in secondary school over a half a century ago.

"Now take what I have had to say about the complications within the United States in determining curricular content and examination coverage, setting aside those caused by the absence of a centralized [educational] authority, and cast those problems into an international context. For the problems encountered by a small percentage of the United States, substitute those faced by hundreds of countries, add the differences in language, and then take account of national sovereignty. When you do, it becomes clear that it is unreasonable to think of common subject-matter examinations that would have worldwide currency. But if I am right that reasoning is at the heart of learning and that a measure of an individual's ability to reason is a satisfactory indication of that individual's ability to succeed in academic work at the university level, then a test of verbal and mathematical reasoning like the SAT, equated across languages, would facilitate the international movement of students that is so vital to man's struggle to transform today's three worlds into tomorrow's one."

As noted in Chapter 8, the International Association for Educational Assessment has succeeded in developing such an instrument in each of four languages. Now the challenge is to realize the full potential of that International Test of Developed Abilities.

In the meantime, back on the domestic front, "I get fed up with those who argue that the SAT is irrelevant or old-fashioned or that it discriminates. Reasoning is no more outdated or irrelevant or discriminatory than the other three R's—reading, writing, and arithmetic. For the life of me, I can't figure out why some otherwise intelligent people won't accept the fact that a product of the twentieth century can have a timeless quality to it!

"Please understand, I applaud the work being done by Howard Gardner and Bob Sternberg in expanding man's knowledge of the nature of intelligence. And I am fascinated by the ever-widening exploration of the right brain–left brain phenomenon and acknowledge that man's and woman's intelligence is not confined to the logical, sequential thinking required by the SAT. But the promise of these new developments should not be used to deny the basic premise of the SAT, when in fact what they will do will be to supplement it.

"Reasoning is at the heart of critical thinking, and the SAT gets at some—certainly not all but an important 'some'—of what reasoning is all about. After all, words and numbers as used in the verbal and mathematical sections of the SAT are the basic tools with which students learn. Just because the SAT was developed in this century doesn't mean that what it measures didn't exist before. And by the same token, just because promising new developments in understanding the nature of intelligence are in the works doesn't mean that what the SAT measures will soon be out of date.

"It is my contention and firm belief that the SAT deals with what might be called an 'eternal verity'—a truth that is at the heart of the learning process now and always will be. Words and numbers are the tools with which students in school learn, and learn to think."

That belief gave important meaning to my life with the SAT.

Index